The Discerning Clear Gaze of Yoga

The Discerning Clear Gaze of Yoga

Gidi Ifergan

equinox

SHEFFIELD UK BRISTOL CT

Published by Equinox Publishing Ltd.

UK Office 415, The Workstation, 15 Paternoster Row, Sheffield,
South Yorkshire S1 2BX
USA ISD, 70 Enterprise Drive, Bristol, CT 06010

www.equinoxpub.com

First published in Hebrew in Israel in 2022 by Resling Publishing, Tel-Aviv.

This English edition published in 2024 by Equinox Publishing Ltd.

British Library Cataloguing-in-Publication Data

A catalogue record for this book is available from the British Library.

ISBN-13 978 1 80050 484 4 (hardback)
978 1 80050 485 1 (paperback)
978 1 80050 486 8 (ePDF)
978 1 80050 588 9 (ePub)

Library of Congress Cataloging-in-Publication Data

Names: Ifergan, Gidi, author.
Title: The discerning clear gaze of yoga / Dr. Gidi Ifergan.
Description: English edition. | Sheffield, South Yorkshire ; Bristol, CT : Equinox Publishing Ltd, [2024] | Includes bibliographical references and index. | Summary: "Inspired by the psychology of yoga, the author offers a meditation focused on the sense of self and the cultivation of a discerning clear gaze"-- Provided by publisher.
Identifiers: LCCN 2024013399 (print) | LCCN 2024013400 (ebook) | ISBN 9781800504844 (hardback) | ISBN 9781800504851 (paperback) | ISBN 9781800504868 (epdf) | ISBN 9781800505889 (epub)
Subjects: LCSH: Mindfulness (Psychology) | Self-consciousness (Awareness) | Yoga--Psychological aspects.
Classification: LCC BF637.M56 I74 2024 (print) | LCC BF637.M56 (ebook) | DDC 204/.36--dc23/eng/20240412
LC record available at https://lccn.loc.gov/2024013399
LC ebook record available at https://lccn.loc.gov/2024013400

Typeset by Sparks – www.sparkspublishing.com

Contents

Preface vii
About the Author ix

1 Introduction: Metamorphosis of a Gaze 1
2 The Sense of I-am-ness *Asmitā* 33
3 The True Self *Puruṣa* 64
4 The Discerning Clear Gaze *Viveka-Khyāti* 85
5 Meditation on the Sense of I-am-ness 112
6 Concluding Observations 142
Appendix: *Yogasūtra*: Authors, Texts and Readers 149

Glossary 155
Bibliography 164
Index 169

Preface

In April 1996, I went to Varanasi in India to study Patañjali's *Yogasūtra*, and especially the *viveka-khyāti* (discerning wisdom or insight). This insight discerns between the sense of I-am-ness, the phenomenal 'I' which is part of the world of phenomena, and the true Self.

Studying alongside Śri Śiv-Śankar Tripathi, was both a theoretical and a profoundly experiential journey. The experience left a deep and unforgettable impression on me that later became a great source of inspiration, for which I am deeply grateful.

Unfortunately, over the years, my notes of those encounters have now been lost. This book is the fruit of the memory of those sessions and is based on theoretical–academic study and many years of Yoga and Dzogchen practice.

About the Author

Dr. Gidi Ifergan is an author, a teacher and a researcher of Indian philosophy and Tibetan Buddhism at The Monash Centre for Consciousness and Contemplative Studies, Monash University in Melbourne, Australia. He is the author of *The Man from Samyé: Longchenpa on Praxis, Its Negation and Liberation* (2014), *Negation and Liberation in Longchenpa's Teachings* (2015, in Hebrew), *Self-discovery in the Psychology of Yoga* (2018, in Hebrew) and *The Psychology of the Yogas* (2021) and *The Light and the Mirror: The Discerning Gaze of Yoga* (2022, in Hebrew).

Ifergan teaches philosophy, meditation and yoga in different frameworks, from academic ones to yoga teachers' training programs, home studio classes and workshops.

He has undertaken extensive studies of Dzogchen teachings in Tibetan Buddhism; participated in retreats with Dzogchen master Chögyal Namkhai Norbu from 1992 to 2018; and has been studying classic forms of Indian yoga with Master Śri Brahma Gopal Bhaduri and his senior disciple Śri Śiv-Śankar Tripathi, which included travels to Varanasi, India since 1994.

Ifergan is an accomplished classical guitarist and he has released two albums with Cala Records (UK): *Vast Expanse* (2016) and *Down Celestial Avenue* (2018). Recently he has composed *kaivalya*, that was commissioned by The Monash Centre for Consciousness and Contemplative Studies as part of their official launch as a centre at Monash University, Australia.

1 Introduction: Metamorphosis of a Gaze

In the middle of the first millennium BCE, a significant historical–cultural trend began to take shape in India. Some people began to leave their homes and villages, and abandoned the society that had been governed up until then by Vedic principles – principles that outlined the social order of the castes, family life, and religious world of rituals – and embarked on a journey of solitude in the forest.[1] There, in the woods, they practiced celibacy, yoga, meditation, and contemplation. Adopting such a lifestyle, they gave up – or even negated – the prevalent culture, and produced an alternative culture, one of the *forest*. In this journey, they abandoned the deities identified with particular control domains such as climate, fire, water, or art. They ceased to perform the meticulous rituals that served those deities, replacing desires to control certain phenomenon and events through religious rituals with the desire to be completely liberated from what binds one to the world of phenomena.

What generated this move to the forest? There are several hypotheses, all of which are equally plausible: one of them centres on the religious–political conflict of interest of the priesthood, the Brahmins. This situation arose because of the co-dependence between the Brahmins, who performed rituals of sacrifice, and those who paid them who would benefit from the rituals. The Brahmins were thereby supposed to take upon themselves the residues of the violence inherent to the sacrifice ritual, such that while drawing their livelihood from performing such rituals, they had to deal with substances contaminated with death (the dead scarified animal) that were considered impure and embedded with negative karma. The term *karman* was originally applied to properly performed ritual action. Later, it was ethicised to include any kind of right action within an impersonal system of causality, where one's present circumstances are the consequences of one's past deeds, and one's present actions will cause one's future circumstance. In that sense, negative karma would entail negative future circumstances.[2]

The dilemma stemming from this dependence and frequent contact with residues of violence meant that the Brahmins, at times, failed to achieve the goals for which they performed the rituals; thus, many of the despairing left their villages and turned to the forest. Another hypothesis contends that the knowledge and ideas that merchants carried with them on their journeys ignited the imagination of the common people and stimulated their curiosity about life in the forest. A further hypothesis revolves around a severe epidemic, whereby the shelter of the forest offered a possible existential alternative. In any case, the term forest does not appear here in its ordinary sense – a jungle or a remote village in the heart of lush vegetation, let alone a barren wilderness. It is essentially a complex ecosystem, which combines aridity, water, vegetation, and animals, and all of these together create an ideal living environment for humans. Moreover, metaphorically the forest is a place that symbolises an empty yet clear mind, which serves as a space for the dawn of Self-knowledge.[3]

The Upaniṣads, a body of works composed from the middle of the first millennium BCE, documented and described the process of this journey into the forest,[4] and the life that was possible there. The authors of the Upaniṣads emphasised the wisdom and experience required for such a complex journey, which involved turning one's back on Vedic day-to-day existence, and navigating the friction between the mode of family man or person in the world, and the life of renunciate or yogi.[5]

A story from the *Bṛhadāraṇyaka Upaniṣad* may help us to gain an understanding of the nature of this friction. The story takes place in the socio-cultural context of the prevailing caste system in the eighth century BCE. In this story, the sage Yājñavalkya informs Maitreyī, his childless wife, that he is leaving for the forest in the pursuit of Self-realisation. Before he leaves, Maitreyī asks him to teach her about the true Self. An intimate dialogue develops between them about the true Self.[6] Many commentators and scholars see it as a story of spirituality and deep intimacy. But beneath the surface, the story seems to be saturated with conflict. Given that it is a situation of crisis, Maitreyī, more than likely is angry and confused. She feels abandoned and suffers the pain of being childless, which will mean that she receives no inheritance according to the customs of the time. The inheritance will be passed on to Yājñavalkya's other wife, the mother of his children, and Maitreyī will be considered a miserable widow who is physically alive but socially almost dead. In that moment of crisis, Maitreyī turns to her husband Yājñavalkya with a bitter, silent anger and asks him to guide her toward the immortal knowledge of the Self.[7]

The forest, therefore, is a metaphor for a physical and mental space that is not bounded by a constricted system, a place where a person is 'out of themselves', out of a restrictive framework. This is a space where self-knowledge may spontaneously occur. On this journey to the forest, as illustrated by the story of the sage Yājñavalkya, the yogi must first extricate himself from Vedic society, turn his back on it and seek to leave behind his day-to-day self, including his values, family and social relationships, and material and intellectual property.[8]

In this way, the renunciate yogi also seeks to leave behind the ordinary phenomenal gaze, the gaze that turns everything into an object, including the other. The phenomenal gaze is shaped according to how objects are recorded in the mind – image, information, content, and label – which is driven by the tendency to objectify. This tendency precedes the phenomenal gaze itself, and is continually present. The phenomenal gaze is the exclusive gaze through which a person has become accustomed to seeing themself and the other, a gaze determined by the requirements of daily existence, and imbued with the culture, conduct, behaviour, and non-verbal communication a person has learned from his parents and teachers. It is a collection of identifications, mental imprints, behavioural patterns, and causes of affliction – all of the sedimentary substances which are the components that underlie the process of gazing.

Having sketched the outlines of the Vedic world and the ascetic–yogic movement in relation to the Upaniṣadic turn to the forest, and the tensions that arose between those living 'within the Vedic frame' and those who have 'left it behind', I would like to return now to the historico–philosophical background of the *Yogasūtra*. This text, which will be at the focus of this book, was composed by the sage Patañjali, most likely in the third century CE, after the end of the Upaniṣadic period (which ran from about the first half of the first millennium BCE to the second half of the second century CE). Raveh labels this historical phase the Sūtra period. *Sūtra*, literally, means the 'thread' that binds the pages on which the verses are written, the thread that binds a bundle of verses or, more metaphorically speaking, a thread 'stitching together' a variety of ideas, themes, and knowledge.[9]

This literary tendency, which prevailed during the beginning of the Common Era, entailed an effort to collate and systematise philosophical tenets and trends which had existed when the sūtras were composed, for example Upaniṣadic philosophical trends. Other works of the same literary genre are:

- the *Brahmasūtra*, which revolves around the inquiry into the non-duality of *Brahman*, the ground of being, which is beyond the phenomenal world, and the individual Self, the *Ātman*;
- the *Nyāyasūtra*, notable for a focus on knowledge and logic, and the absence of any discussion of the Vedic rituals;
- the *Vaiśeṣikasūtra*, which deals with themes which are simultaneously epistemological and metaphysical;
- the *Mīmāṃsāsūtra*, which is mostly dedicated to the notion of dharma as religion, including ritual obligations to be performed as prescribed in the Veda;
- the *Kāmasūtra*, the verses which deal with passion, dedicated to the erotic dimension of existence, which attempt to reorient the human person from mundane existence by pointing to what they should be striving for in their existence;
- and of course the *Yogasūtra*, the text that will be at the centre of this study.

Along with the *Yogasūtra*, I will also delve into the seminal text of the Sāṃkhya School, the *Sāṃkhyakārikā*, which itself also belongs to the same literary genre of *sūtra*.[10] This text, which was written by Īśvarakṛṣṇa (350–450 CE), constitutes the classical summary of the philosophy originally formulated by the sage Kapila (sixth century BCE), and forms the metaphysical basis for the philosophy of yoga, which I will elaborate upon later. At this point, it will suffice to say that Sāṃkhya philosophy might be characterised as a 'discernment philosophy'. It is a reflective discrimination conducted by means of inferential reasoning, shifting between the peculiar dualism of the world of phenomena (*prakṛti*), either in its potential or manifested state, which includes the mind in its many permutations, and one's inherent and contentless pure awareness, the real Self (*puruṣa*).[11] Such discernment leads to liberation.

The *Yogasūtra* is written in Sanskrit and is composed of 195 precise and concise verses. Almost every term in this text is a key concept, requiring decipherment, interpretation, and comparison both to its previous appearances in the text and to other classical Indian texts. Currently, many who read this text rely on a range of classical, modern, traditional, and academic commentators, some of whom I, too, will discuss in this work. One might ask why I have chosen to revisit the text today, despite the view expressed by David Gordon White[12], who has observed that the *Yogasūtra* today is unjustifiably extolled by the yoga subculture as a perennial classic and a guide to yoga practice. Why revisit and study a text forgotten in India for hundreds of years and maligned when it was discovered in the West, gaining recognition only in the last 40 years through a massive wave of translation into more than forty languages? Enormous amounts of texts have been written on the *Yogasūtra*, within the classic Indian tradition, contemporary academic institutions and studies, and New Age yoga subculture. In these circumstances, one may well wonder about the possibility of saying anything new about Patañjali's iconic text.

Philipp A. Maas has emphasised the continuing importance of research and study of Yoga by completing a critical edition of Patañjali's *Yogaśāstra*, together with its classical commentaries, arguing that this will assist in refining our knowledge of classical Yoga and the mutual influences between it and other philosophical and religious schools of thought. Such efforts will help us to develop an understanding that the philosophy of Yoga is much more than Sāṃkhya theory combined with soteriological practice. According to Maas, the text – together with its classical commentaries – reflects debates, polemics and mutual influences between Sāṃkhya, Yoga and Buddhist schools of thought that could improve our understanding of the complex interrelation between Hinduism and Buddhism in India. Furthermore, it also reflects polemical discussions with the philosophical school of the grammarians, with Mīmāṃsā, Nyāya and Vaiśeṣika. Such studies of the Pātañjala *Yogaśāstra* will also be fruitful for our understanding of the general history of Indian philosophy.[13]

However, here, I have chosen an approach that is similar to that of other contemporary researchers, such as Christopher Chapple, Mikel Burley, Ana Laura Funes Maderey, Stephen Phillips, Arindam Chakrabarti,

Stephanie Corigliano, and the contemporary commentators mentioned earlier. Like them, I approach the *Yogasūtra* in a thematic way, exploring notions of body, imagination, death, idealism, realism, and the science of meditation, themes that have not yet been explored in the academic literature on the *Yogasūtra*.[14] It is in this context that I seek to approach the *Yogasūtra* as a philosophical work, and as a guide for instruction of the yoga practitioner; for, despite being concise, it offers a great wealth of material for contemporary thought. In my view, it remains a relevant teaching aid for contemporary practice not just a text for philosophical interpretation and contemplation. Returning to the original text of the *Yogasūtra* allows us to find new meanings hidden between its lines. I am interested in thinking along with the concepts in the *Yogasūtra*, delving into the discerning insight as a specific subject in the context of the psychology of yoga, and proposing a possible model of meditation related to it. This model makes the sense of I-am-ness the object of a meditation that we can begin cultivating today, with the intention of achieving immense psychological benefit.

One of the stand-out metaphors that Patañjali employs to characterise the true Self and distinguish it from the ordinary mind, including the phenomenal world that it grasps, is vision and, hence, the gaze. The true Self is the seer, the mind is the action of sight, and the object is the seen. Vision is the power in action that discerns and identifies objects through the eyes, a mental discernment, judgment, observation, or inquiry; the outcome is seeing the cause, or the main point. The connection between sight and insight has long been known, manifesting itself in a variety of common expressions in our language such as: 'justice must not only be done, but must also be seen to be done'; 'I cannot understand what he sees in her'; 'seeing eye to eye'; 'sees fit'; 'we must see what is required to be done'.

It is surprising to find that the word 'theory', borrowed from the Greek, also means 'looking at, viewing, beholding'.[15] Sight is the most dominant expression of thought and of how a rational person perceives the world. Simultaneously, the dominance of the gaze – so to speak – is transparent and, hence, it is hidden and almost invisible. That is to say, clear vision is expected to underlie thought and what is self-evident, even though it is not itself discernible or recognisable. This elusive nature of the phenomenal gaze is precisely the reason why yoga's philosophy and practice teaches the urgency of freeing oneself from the dominance of the phenomenal gaze that veils the seer, the true Self. The phenomenal gaze, the exclusive gaze through which one has become accustomed to seeing oneself and the other, affects others as well. When directed at the other, it may cause stress, anxiety, and emotional arousal. In some encounters, a mutual gaze may arouse interest, attraction, attention, or sexual intention.[16]

The gaze is determined by the way the object is reflected in the mind that is looking at it. It is what the object in focus – a person or a thing – evokes in the viewer, whether these are feelings, memories, thoughts, desires, or rejections, everything that emerges from a given image and captures the viewer's attention. The viewer then identifies with a particular detail of the image and becomes fixated with it. So, too, the viewer fixating on some particular details of the image can become an object of viewing, for the other or for themself, just as a lecturer delivering a lesson can also be 'observing' themself from an external viewpoint during the lecture.

The renunciate yogi seeks to leave the phenomenal gaze behind and get free of its exclusive binding and its distorted perception of reality. How will the one who is fixed in the phenomenal gaze manage to get free of its confines, and from everything that it may generate or bring about? Is it at all possible to develop a free gaze 'staying in the forest', a gaze that is not absorbed with the mundane and is not laden with identifications or mental imprints, patterns of behaviour, and causes of pain? What would such a gaze without the occlusion of these sedimentary materials be like? What is the 'gaze in itself'?

The text's essence is stated immediately in the first verse – that what follows is a set of instructions (*anuśāsana*) for those who seek to free themselves from the chains of the everyday reality occupied with suffering. Patañjali outlines a profound psychological framework that provides a key for understanding the human psyche which will be at the centre of my study in this book. The framework can explain how a person thinks and conducts themself, and why they do so. According to Patañjali, anger and jealousy are concrete manifestations of causes of affliction (the five *kleśas*). The causes of suffering are the tangible expressions of mental patterns (*vāsanās*), which are one's inclinations and patterns of thinking and behaviour. Their roots lie in hidden and dormant mental imprints (*samskāras*) etched in one's mind as a result of reacting to previous experiences. Raveh provides an accurate analogy that clarifies the connection between mental imprints and behavioural tendencies: the *saṃskāras* (the mental imprints) are like atoms, he notes, while the *vāsanās* (the behavioural tendencies) are like molecules. A *kleśa* is similar to a molecular unit. Like a mould, it dictates the shape, volume, intensity, expression, and manifestation of any given tangible *vāsanā*.[17] All of these together constitute the conscious and unconscious materials that underlie the phenomenal gaze. These materials envelope and conceal the true Self, the pure awareness, and from the moment that pure awareness dawns and the yogi abides and settles in it, these sedimentary materials are absent from the mind.

Later in this book I will expand on these concepts. For the time being, we can come to understand the psychological themes embedded in the complex and intricate relationship of *saṃskāras*, *vāsanās*, and *kleśas* through the character of Ebenezer Scrooge, the protagonist of Charles Dickens's 1843 novel *A Christmas Carol*. The psychological profile of this character allows us to shed light on the psychology of yoga without getting caught up in the complex problems that arise when attempting to apply contemporary Western theories of psychoanalysis on the *Yogasūtra* of Patañjali. Scrooge (a surname derived from a slang word meaning 'stingy') is a tough, tight-fisted, greedy, and very rich businessperson. A brief description of Scrooge's psychological makeup can show us how the mental imprints etched into his mind relate to states of feeling or identity. If we articulate all of these imprints, we will expose states of identity such as 'I am not loved', 'I am unimportant', 'I am not wanted', or 'I am helpless'. Mental imprints are the totality of Scrooge's inner attitudes and beliefs about himself and others. His emotions and identity as an adult have been shaped by memory-dependent feelings which are consequences of his early childhood experiences of acute poverty, rejection, loneliness, abandonment, mistrust, and lack of physical safety. Like the atoms in Raveh's analogy that was discussed earlier, the patterns of thought and behaviour are crystallised into a molecule, which is Scrooge's habitual tendency – a *vāsanā* – acute stinginess. This tendency is reflected in the expressions of the *kleśas*, the causes of affliction: Scrooge's deep aversion (*dveṣa*) toward waste, his resentment at parting from his money, his reluctance to share his coal supply with his clerk; his greed and strong attraction (*rāga*) to situations that allow him to amass a fortune; his identity as a rich, arrogant businessman who knows the ways of the world (*asmitā*), despite his ignorance and lack of awareness of his own stinginess and its implications;

and, finally, a strong sense of survival and self-preservation which is also a means of resisting the fear of death (*Abhiniveśa*).

According to Patañjali the cause of suffering lies in the misidentification of the world of phenomena with the principle of consciousness (as pure awareness). The world of phenomena (*prakṛti*) is composed of both the outer world and the inner-mental world of a person. It is the 'I' (the sense of I-am-ness, *asmitā*), in the existential and everyday sense. The principle of awareness lies beyond the body and thoughts: it is the 'true Self', as pure awareness (*puruṣa*). Suffering stems from the confusion between these two principles and their mixing with each other. According to Patañjali: "'I-sense' (*asmitā*) comes into being when the power of the seer (*dṛkśakti*) and the power of seeing (*darśana-śakti*) appear to be one and the same.'[18] The sense of I-am-ness means a phenomenal, earthly, and existential everyday 'I', the centre of internal processes such as thinking, wanting, imagining, and bodily actions. It is at the base of every one of our thoughts or actions and is ingrained in our language. An expression of this, for example, is when the phenomenal self utters the phrase, 'I breathe', and unwittingly imposes this attribute on the true Self. However, the true Self is 'transcendent', that is metaphysically distinct to all psycho-physical phenomena constituting *prakṛti* or nature and therefore does not breathe at all. However, we still superimpose the breath upon the true Self as if the action of breathing belonged to or was generated by it. In fact, the one who breathes is the phenomenal self of a psycho-physical entity that is a fundamental component of the world of phenomena (*prakṛti*).

This misconception is similar to the saying 'the Sun goes down'. It is now known that the Sun does not do the moving at all; it is the Earth that moves around it, rotating on its own axis. We confuse the Sun's stillness with the Earth's motion, and this confusion is embedded in our language and conceptual processes. The 'seer' is a synonym for the 'true Self' – *puruṣa* – the primary presence, pure awareness, the still and eternal otherness that is not involved in the world. 'Seeing' is the exercise of the power of the seer that relates to the mind as a centre of thinking, willing, and perceiving. The principle of pure awareness or the true Self arises in the human mind, and enables in it the power of perception as a power realised in the world. At the same time, the sense of I-am-ness arises, an integral part of the mind. The mind 'is sure' that it is not only an instrument of dynamic perception but also the source of primordial awareness, of the seer, *puruṣa*. Identifying the two as one, as an indistinguishable unit, produces *asmitā*, the sense of I-am-ness. Suffering stems from the confusion between these two principles and their misidentification with each other.

From a Buddhist psychological point of view, based on the four truths formulated by the Buddha (Sanskrit: 'Awakened One', 5th century BCE), the founder of Buddhism who is the *vaidyarāja* (king of healers), the cause of the *duḥkha* (suffering, dissatisfaction, frustration) is *tṛṣṇā*, the craving or thirst for certainty, safety, pleasure, and the eternal. These cravings are an inseparable part of the mental processes that generate a subjective sense of being, a solid, continuous, real ego that is nothing more than a collection of habitual tendencies and impressions.[19] Thus, one acts out of identification with one's belief system, feelings, emotions, and becomes attached to all of the events, situations, and phenomena experienced in everyday life. Moreover, this ego projects itself on both the conscious and subconscious levels, thereby solidifying and sustaining the craving for safety, certainty, and pleasure, and the tendency to avoid situations of sorrow and pain. However, from a yogic perspective, once the discerning and clear gaze has reached the peak of maturity, the confusing misidentification between the true Self and the sense of I-am-ness can be resolved by the arising insight that distinguishes between them, and this profound understanding may lead to liberation.[20]

The fictitious identification between the sense of I-am-ness, a fundamental component of the world of phenomena, and the true Self as the principle of pure awareness significantly implies that 'I am not who I think I am'. Such insight goes against our most basic intuition concerning ourselves. Moreover, when the sense of I-am-ness is put into question, this can generate a new flood of further discursive thoughts: how will I reveal the pure awareness or the true Self inherent in me, which precedes everything?; how am I supposed to achieve something that has always been inherently within me (pure awareness)?; how can I become what I already am?; how can I unravel the confusing entanglement between the sense of I-am-ness and who I really am?; how do I stop the sequence of identities that my sense of I-am-ness takes on, which is fixated on them and which bind me to everyday existence?

Perfecting the yogic gaze into a discerning clear gaze, requires the direction of the phenomenal everyday gaze to be shifted inwardly, away from the world of external objects towards the interiority of the mind, which in itself is external to the true Self and fundamentally different from it. Patañjali labels this shift of the phenomenal gaze *Pratiprasava*. To achieve this a person is required to gradually develop a composed attentiveness, and as the practice of meditation progresses, it becomes seasoned and stabilised. In Patañjali's words: 'In their subtle form, they (the *kleśas*) can be overcome by involution (*pratiprasava*).'[21] The central meaning of involution in this context is an inverse process of evolution in the sense of a return to origins. Changing the direction of the phenomenal gaze is the first step towards diluting and resolving the causes of affliction and restraining mental processes. It entails relinquishing the habitual tendency of the mind to objectify, and to instead converge towards its source and become still. Within the movement of awareness towards our innermost interiority, even the positive attitudes and beliefs necessary for the realisation of yoga – such as the perception that the body is not the true Self – need to be relinquished as these are attachments of the ego that must be abandoned.

In order to establish this shift in the direction of the phenomenal gaze we need to understand how the habitual tendency to objectify arises. When someone encounters a particular object that captures their attention, it will arouse in them some level of attraction or aversion and generate a series of mental processes in relation to that object. In the case of Scrooge from Dickens's story, money is one of the most intense objects of his attention. His greed stems from a hunger or thirst for things that goes far beyond what he actually needs to live and, no matter how much he acquires, he will never feel fulfilled or content. Drawing on psychoanalytic thought, greed can be seen as a product of a destructive power directed towards the very core of I-am-ness, resulting from a primary and inexhaustible sense of deprivation. When the feeling of shortage is so deep and strong, it can fixate a person entirely on the missing object to compensate for the feeling. In the case of Scrooge, the lack of money was experienced as childhood poverty. Compensating for this, his life becomes a journey aimed at the acquisition and storage of the missing childhood object (money).[22]

In *pratiprasava*, one is required to shift the focus of attention away from objects and establish an inner mental gaze that will assist in reducing distractions. Such a gaze will reduce the chance that the mind will be overwhelmed and flooded with mental processes in the encounter with some object, whether external or internal. These processes may spontaneously be triggered by memories of previous similar encounters. Any such encounters may lead to the generation and perpetuation of pain and suffering, and so quietening such distracting mental processes is the meaning of clearing the gaze! The method may be driven by the intellect to identify the factors that motivate one to perpetuate one's conditioned existence, the patterns of thought and behaviour resulting from such existence,[23] and thereby expose the 'blind spots' that obscure mental clarity. The culmination of *pratiprasava* is in the dissolution of the phenomenal ordinary mind into the source, the base or root of the world of phenomena (*prakṛti*), of which it is an integral part.

Patañjali emphasises that the gaze can also become clearer even when the phenomenal gaze is turned outwards. To do this it must adopt '… friendliness (*maitrī*), compassion (*karuṇā*), joy (*muditā*), and equanimity (*upekṣā*) toward the happy, the suffering, the virtuous, and the unvirtuous (respectively)…'[24] This means that cultivating moral rules of conduct towards oneself and others can also promote the clarification of one's gaze. Given these rules of moral conduct, in the forest context mentioned earlier, we can understand that, for Patañjali, yoga students are not expected to immediately retire to the *forest*. Instead this process happens gradually, during which time they may be involved in normal social interactions. The gap between the active person 'involved in the world' and the renunciate yogi, who turns 'away from involvement in the world', is not so clearly delineated. What is required is a moderation of the gap between the two modes of existence, such that the passage from one to the other is emptied of friction. One then abides in stillness or becomes ultimately detached from the phenomenal world.

Cultivating and assimilating rules of moral conduct – such as non-possessiveness (*aparigraha*), cleansing (*śauca*), contentment (*saṃtoṣa*), self-study (*svādhyāya*) – requires mental attitudes that are mostly inconsistent with the way yoga is cultivated in the West. The practice of yoga in the West is mostly identified with its physical aspect. It emphasises the individual's responsibility to invest in themself and shape their character to maximise their personal productivity, health, happiness, and intelligence.[25] Seen in this way, physical yoga may be an example of what Foucault called 'technologies of the self'. These are essentially a collection of practices that allow a person to act and influence their body, psyche, thoughts, and behaviour in order to create profound change in themself.

The view is that this change will also manifest in one's ability to create and produce, to be healthy, happy, and sane. Such an understanding of yoga – which is an 'investment of the individual in themself' that produces an inevitable 'return' – is well reflected in public discourse, particularly in yoga magazines, websites, and advertisements. What this amounts to is an individual self-care strategy that has the potential to become a self-empowerment, a form of 'human capital' that reduces mental stress, promotes good health, and allows someone to draw closer to other 'self-invested' individuals.[26]

In a related line of criticism, a modern yoga practitioner who does not take into account the textual, philosophical, psychological and ethical foundations of yoga could also be seen to adhere to a form of 'spiritual materialism', a concept coined by Tibetan teacher and scholar Chögyam Trungpa (1939–1987):

> It is important to see that the main point of any spiritual practice is to step out of the bureaucracy of ego. This means stepping out of ego's constant desire for a higher, more spiritual, more transcendental version of knowledge, religion, virtue, judgment, comfort or whatever it is that a particular ego is seeking. One must step out of spiritual materialism. If we do not step out of spiritual materialism, if we in fact practice it, then we may eventually find ourselves possessed of a huge collection of spiritual paths. We may feel these spiritual collections to be very precious … We believe that we have accumulated a hoard of knowledge ... But we have simply created a shop, an antique shop.[27]

Consequently, a spiritual practice whose whole essence seeks only to attain a higher and improved version of the everyday phenomenal ordinary self, an 'I' who is committed to the pursuit of the efficacy and improvement of personal well-being, as a smart investment in oneself, only serves to further bolster the ego. Such an 'I' perceives reality in a distorted manner, as the knowledge and experiences gained can cause pain and sorrow. For example, having the perception that the poor, those who are overweight, or those who are unemployed can only blame themselves can cause suffering by ignoring one's own social responsibility for ensuring the efficiency and availability of social services such as education, health, and welfare that are available for those who are in distress and require assistance. In this way, the cultivation of friendliness (*maitrī*), compassion (*karuṇā*), joy (*muditā*), and equanimity (*upekṣā*) toward the happy, the suffering, the virtuous, and the unvirtuous (respectively), has the capacity to clarify the mind and its phenomenal gaze.[28]

Along with ethical rules of conduct that encourage cultivating *pratiprasava*, an inner gaze that honestly contemplates how one shapes one's priorities, desires, and self-image exposes one's motives, hence enabling their examination. First and foremost, implementing ethical yogic rules of conduct clarifies the mind, by allowing mental distractions to recede and fade. Such cultivation opens up a mental space suitable for one-pointed meditation,[29] a long focus on one object, whether it be tangible or subtle. One-pointed meditation creates a mental field between the yogi, the meditating subject, and the object. No discursive thoughts or stimuli can intrude that mental field and distract the meditating subject. In that manner, it further enhances clarity.

Moreover, in adopting ethical yogic rules of conduct as mental attitudes, yoga practitioners create a defensive line between themselves and any negative thoughts, feelings, and behaviours that may arise. Such a desire to follow ethical yogic rules of conduct may divert one's phenomenal gaze from its tendency to focus outwardly on objects that evoke attraction and aversion, and thereby one can avoid causing oneself and others sorrow and pain. A tendency to violate mental, social, and ethical norms indicates habitual anger, jealousy, and confusion, feelings that to one degree or another compel a person to actions that may lead to endless cycles of suffering and ignorance.[30]

The poles of the axis that stands for inner convergence, *pratiprasava*, are the phenomenal ordinary gaze on one side and the discerning clear gaze on the other. As inner convergence is purified from its tendency for objectification, and its consequences, it creates a mental space for the rise of insight that discerns between the sense of I-am-ness and the true Self. Here, *vairāgya* – as an uninvolved, desireless, or indifferent gaze – supports and participates in that process of purification that leads to the pole of a discerning clear gaze.

Vairāgya should simultaneously accompany the repetitive practice of yoga (*abhyāsa*), both the practice of yogic meditation (*samādhi*) that appears in the first chapter of the *Yogasūtra*, the *Samādhi-Pāda*, and also of the eight limbs appearing in the second chapter, the *Sadhana-Pāda*. Bryant argues that *vairāgya* is an absence of desire, a lack of thirst for sensory objects, and it stems from the ability to identify and recognise the flaws that exist in the satisfaction of lust.[31] According to Patañjali, *vairāgya* is the awareness of the power inherent in cultivating dispassion towards objects. Vyāsa, who was the first commentator on the *Yogasūtra* in the fifth century CE, gives examples of such objects – drinking (alcohol), sex, food, and power – and believes that demonstrating dispassion towards them means the absence of attraction or aversion toward these objects, a lack of interest in them.[32] Such dispassion stems from an understanding that these objects of desire are temporary and that trying to avoid or satisfy them will cause frustration. The feeling of frustration can motivate the desiring subject to act out and hence accumulate karma.

Patañjali provides another explanation for *vairāgya*, as dispassion for the *guṇa*s, the three forces operating in the world of phenomena (*prakṛti*) that stands for the ultimate *vairāgya*. Āraṇya[33] refers to this form of ultimate *vairāgya* as *para vairāgya* (ultimate *vairāgya*). In ultimate *vairāgya*, awareness of the power obtained from dispassion arises spontaneously with the knowledge of the true Self, which is discerned and isolated from the world of phenomena. The essence of this form of *vairāgya* is that it also requires the relinquishment of the discerning insight, because the three *guṇa*s are still active within it.

According to Vyāsa, and to Bryant who follows in his footsteps, ordinary *vairāgya* as dispassion for sensory objects is an uninvolved or indifferent gaze, which is almost devoid of any effort. Such *vairāgya* is (almost) a perfect condition. Perfection here means that it must occur by itself without any preceding intentionality. I enclosed the word 'almost' in parentheses for the simple reason that even indifference to action or inaction is still a thought process, and as such indicates that the sense of I-am-ness and the mind are still somewhat active. The *guṇa*s are still in some sense active even when the *sattva* quality is the most dominant. The *guṇa*s describe the dynamics of existence and the array of forces operating in the world of phenomena, which includes the sense of I-am-ness. The three *guṇa*s (or qualities) are: *sattva*, which is purity, clarity, serenity, and neutrality; *raja*s, which is activity and passion; and *tama*s, which is staticness, heaviness, and lethargy. These three qualities imply that 'the mode of being' or 'the way of functioning' and 'manifesting' of *prakṛti* are in constant interaction with each other. Hence, at any particular moment, one will be more dominant than the others.This can be visualised as a triangle whose sides frequently change in length: as one side grows longer, the others contract, and the angles where the larger side meets the other sides become more acute. The desired and dominant *guṇa* in yoga is, of course, *sattva*. Therefore, it is desirable to strive to reach its purest state, and this state is established in the *buddhi*, the seat of the intellect, discernment, intuitive wisdom, and intelligence. When the *buddhi* is wholly purified and emptied, even of the insights that have long been accumulated within it, this is supreme *vairāgya* and it entails a state of dispassion in which the *guṇa*s are not active.

Raveh[34] believes that *vairāgya* occurs on its own, arising from the repeated discipline of yoga practice. According to Raveh, in the early stages of practice, or even in advanced ones, *vairāgya* will not yet arise, and so the uninvolved gaze in these stages will be rare. For example, imagine a practitioner is attending a yoga class, either at the beginning of their journey or even as a practitioner in the advanced stages of their practice, and while performing their exercises looks at a neighbour and compares themself to that other practitioner. In that case, the practitioner's gaze may be mixed with the desire to 'be like the neighbour' or even better. Another example is a practitioner who participates in a meditation class, and their neighbour breathes loudly and moves around restlessly. If the practitioner experiences thoughts of aversion, such as irritability and judgment about their neighbour, then their gaze would also be involved entirely in judgment. If the practitioner wants to train and cultivate this detached view during yoga's repeated practice, this would still be involved from the beginning with the aspiration to cultivate, enable, and develop an uninvolved gaze, and perhaps even impose it on the yoga practice. Unlike Raveh, however, I do believe that the practitioner is required to cultivate an uninvolved gaze as an ordinary *vairāgya* already in the early stages of practice. Such cultivation is acquired by adopting the ethical yogic rules of conduct to the point where a mental space is created through the effort of practice, and this serves as a space for the spontaneous arising of the supreme *vairāgya*.

The yoga practitioner is required to continue and establish this uninvolved gaze, stabilise it, and settle into it. Until then, they will continue in the movement between involvement and non-involvement in mundane day-to-day existence. Cultivating an uninvolved gaze through discernment that identifies and recognises the flaws in satisfying cravings helps to discern one's sense of I-am-ness from the tangible or subject objects which it tends to possessively associate with itself. This supports the development of a discerning and clear gaze. Its culmination is the steadfast discerning wisdom that continually distinguishes between the sense of I-am-ness and the true Self, which ends up dissolving into the source of mind. In this book, the discerning and clear gaze and the discerning insight, *viveka-khyāti*, will be closely examined. What is the clear and discerning gaze? What is its place on the roadmap of yoga Patañjali outlines on the way to realising the true Self, the pursuit of liberation? Moreover, and more specifically, what is its place in the stages of yogic meditation that Patañjali sketches? How does it develop? What is its purpose, and what is its meaning?

Already at this stage, it is clear that if the (artificial and confusing) weave between the world of phenomena and the true Self is the cause of suffering, then dismantling and undoing of the weave means the undoing of suffering, which is what occurs with the rise of discerning insight. The discerning gaze is assimilated into the mind and leads to its transparent revelation of the true Self. The motive for undoing the weave is not only intellectual curiosity but also an existential need. The discerning insight, which unravels the (artificial and confusing) weave between the world of phenomena and the true Self must be more than a collection of explanations of reality. Such explanations, however profound, are nothing but ink on paper. Nevertheless, they are essential to the process, as they attest to a real attempt, even if only a mental one, to divert the gaze from the world of objects to the inner world, to the interiority of mind; this is an initial step to turning the gaze to the discerning insight which is also accompanied by various kinds of practice.

The notion of *viveka-khyāti* has been pivotal to the Sāmkhya, one of the earliest schools of philosophy in India, which provides yoga with a metaphysical framework. Essentially, it is the systematic enumeration and rational examination of each of the elements and components of the world of phenomena. Such an inquiry is carried out through philosophical reasoning into the essence of the world of phenomena (*prakṛti*), leading to the profound insight that it is radically different from pure awareness. The purpose of this activity is to lead one to an understanding of the truth underlying reality, which is the unsurpassed truth. This rational exploration of the various components in the world of phenomena encompasses the five elements, ten sense organs (the five of perception – *buddhīndriya* and five of action – *karmendriya*), the mind, the sense of self (*ahaṃkāra*) and the intellect (*buddhi*). It seeks to describe the dynamics of existence and the array of forces that operate within the world of phenomena that influence human beings. These forces are examined according to the way they manifest in the three *guṇa*s, or qualities, which as I explained earlier in this chapter are *sattva*, *raja*s, and *tama*s. These three qualities constantly interact with one another. At any given time, one quality will dominate over the others, like a triangle whose shape is constantly changing, as I also explained earlier.

Sāṃkhyan inquiry culminates in focusing on the intellect, the organ of inquiry. Once all those components, including the intellect, become known, the Sāmkhya philosopher realises that the true Self is not an integral part of the world of phenomena. Discriminative discernment, that is the discriminative wisdom (*viveka khyāti*) of the manifest, the unmanifest (*vyakta* + *avyakta*) and the knower (*kṣetrajña*) is fully realised with the release of the true Self from its entanglement with the world of phenomena, a release in the sense of a detachment. Release through detachment arises as an involuntary and spontaneous realisation. However, according to Patañjali the ground for such release stems from the deliberate and voluntary restraint of mental processes, both conscious and unconscious. At their core these are a psychological network that can explain the way a person thinks and behaves. Underlying this network are the causes of affliction (the five *kleśa*s), which are the concrete expression of mental patterns (the *vāsanā*s), which are the inclinations of a person's character, and the patterns of their thought and behaviour. These causes of affliction and inclinations are rooted in the dormant latent mental imprints (*saṃskāra*s) which have been etched into the mind through the impact of prior experiences.

Patañjali[35] distinguishes between two types of *saṃskāra*s: the *vyutthāna* and the *nirodha saṃskāra*s. *Vyutthāna saṃskāra*s force the mind to direct its gaze outwardly at sensory objects, in the same way a magnet is attracted by metal objects, an attraction which in turn generates various mental processes and activities. Thus, these mental processes thereby perpetuate a distorted perception of objects and the sense of I-am-ness, the perceiver.

Such *saṃskāra*s cause the pain and suffering that perpetuates conditioned existence. *Nirodha saṃskāra*s, on the other hand, intensify the control of mental processes by employing the eight limbs of yoga, and still these processes. They enable the birth of an insight that discerns between the world of phenomena, the sense of the ego, and the true Self.

As the practice of yoga intensifies, the *nirodha* type of *saṃskāra*s block and still the *vyutthāna saṃskāra*s, and the mind becomes more peaceful. The more that yoga is practiced, the more the layer of *nirodha saṃskāra*s will grow and solidify as they resonate and merge with similar mental imprints that have previously been imprinted in mind with sufficient intensity. Hence, as the layer of *nirodha saṃskāra*s are thickened, mental processes grow quieter, and the mind becomes peaceful for more extended periods of time. A practitioner of yoga who persistently and systematically fosters the *nirodha* type of *saṃskāra*s achieves not only the mind's release from the grip of the *vyutthāna* type, but also the emergence of the discerning insight and total concentration, and with this the dawn of Self-knowledge abiding in it. Over time, however, the practitioner will also have to relinquish the *nirodha saṃskāra*s, however positive and sublime, and empty their mind of them.

In sūtra 1.17, Patañjali clearly states that it is possible to overcome the mental processes – including the layers of *kleśa*s, *vāsanā*s, and *saṃskāra*s – and neutralise them to the point of completely emptying the mind of them. Restraint is achieved through *dhyāna*[36] (meditation), that is, a uniform, stable, and continuous concentration on a particular object, such as the *samādhi* practice, characterised by thought, contemplation, a sense of bliss, and a sense of I-am-ness. In sūtras 1.42–47, Patañjali mentions again the category of cognitive *samādhi*, which is directed towards an object. In these sūtras he elaborates on the notion of cognitive *samādhi* and its four classifications within the context of the *samāpatti*, which is the meditative process of integrating with an object of meditation. This is a process that is established through concentration on an object, for example, by aid of inquiry or visualisation, and then proceeds into an enduring or sustained form of concentration in which the object is the only thing that occupies the mind, without such perception being affected by mental and psychological process.

In the first stage, *savitarka*, a cognitive *samādhi* is accompanied with thought processes that depend on an object for its instigation. This must be a tangible object upon which the yogi chooses to focus, over time, with the intention of integrating with it. To begin with, the object is entangled within the mind with various conceptualising processes, concerning the object's label, the object itself, and ideas that are associated with it. When these automatic or conditioned connections between the object itself, the label for the object, and the knowledge associated with it disintegrates, the yogi advances to the next stage, *nirvitarka*.

At this point in this type of *samādhi*, the yogi merges with the tangible object into a state of integration that is devoid of thought and the conceptualising activity that characterised the previous stage. In such a process, the memory is purified of content relating to the tangible object, including the time in which it was first encountered, the place, the circumstances, and the impression it left on the yogi in the past. The mind continues to be emptied of mental processes, reflecting the object more purely; and the object as it actually is becomes the only thing that occupies the mind, as if the yogi is seeing it for the first time without any conceptualisation, attraction, rejection, or identification.

In the next stage, the yogi continues to advance in the practice of *samādhi* by intensely concentrating on the visualisation of a subtle object: for example, by visualising a mystical diagram such as a *maṇḍala* or a component of the subtle body such as a *cakra*. The yogi contemplates the components of this subtle object, the parts through which the mental visualisation are constructed, and beholds it as a mental image until it simply merges within his or her mind. The mind then reflects the object, for example, a mystical diagram, as it actually is. This process is termed *savicāra samādhi*, a contemplative observation of the object's details.

The yogi then progresses to another level of integration, in which mental activity is even more reduced than those involving visualisation – the *nirvicāra samādhi*. At this level of practice, there is no contemplative observation taking place at all. Instead, the object appears in the mind as it actually is, devoid of language, conceptualisation, or contemplative activity, without the processes that characterised the previous three stages described above. *Samādhi* without such mental processes is evident in the yogi's capability to 'hold' the mystical diagram that was mentally 'constructed' in the preceding *samādhi* in their mind. In the yogi's mind, a complete picture of the object is reflected instantly, at once. *Samādhi* here is refined and reduced to seeing only, a gaze that 'rests' on the object without discursive activity. The mental 'activity' is *sattvic*, consisting solely of transparent reflection, because the *sattvic* quality is dominant in the mind and occupies it. The establishment of such transparency still requires a tangible or subtle object, and depends upon it. This need is also a mental process that accompanies the cognitive *samādhi* in all of its stages, which means that despite reaching for those sublime states of mind, the yogi is not entirely free from deliberate or compulsive mental processes.

The climax of the integration between the subject and the object and the process of perception in the *nirvicāra samādhi* can be visualised as being like a reflection of an object in a polished, clear, and limpid mirror. The mirror and the reflection have become identical – they are inseparable, and they are made of one 'mirror' material. Time and space no longer exist between the reflection of the object and the mirror itself. Like a mirror cleared of all dust and oil stains, so too the mind is empty of mental processes, and only the object is reflected in it. Just as the reflection and the mirror cannot be separated, so the integration of the object with the mind is not affected by the imprints associated with particular times and places.

As mentioned earlier, in sūtras 1.42–47 Patañjali invokes the category of cognitive *samādhi* directed towards an object, either tangible or subtle, and details its various stages. Surprisingly, however, unlike in sūtra 1.17 he does not mention the two other types that belong to this category of *samādhi* – an object-oriented cognitive *samādhi*, one involved with a sense of happiness (*ānanda*) and the other involved with a sense of I-amness (*asmitā*). Kenneth Rose states that the *samādhi*, which is characterised by thought and absence of thought, contemplation, and absence of contemplation on a tangible or subtle object – is very different from the type involved with a sense of happiness (*ānanda*) and a sense of I-am-ness (*asmitā*). In his view, a sense of happiness and a sense of I-amness are fundamentally different from objects for meditation since they are two subtle types of objectless transcendental consciousness.[37] On the one hand, Rose assigns them to the category of object-oriented cognitive *samādhi*, the *saṃprajñāta samādhi*, and on the other hand he sees them as a state of objectless awareness that constitutes a higher form of *samādhi*, one that does not depend on an object for its establishment, which is *asaṃprajñāta samādhi* and culminates in liberation. I believe that had this been the case, the yogic process would have reached its perfection at the height of the *samādhi* involved with the sense of I-am-ness (*asmitā*). I, therefore, disagree with Rose's statement. The sense of bliss as a passive state and sense of I-am-ness are mentioned in the context of the category of object-oriented cognitive *samādhi* that relies on tangible or subtle objects for it to be constituted. The yogi consciously chose objects from a series of possible objects, such as those presented in the third chapter of the *Yogasūtra*, while the sense of happiness and I-am-ness (*asmitā*) are objects that the yogi did not choose consciously or intentionally, but rather arise by themselves to the surface of the mind and become the object of meditation.

At the climax of the cognitive *samādhi*, upon accomplishing integration with the object of meditation, a wave of intoxicating emotion arises, which is both physically and mentally pleasurable, and this floods the mind. Such a wave may cover and obscure the uninvolved gaze, *vairāgya*, and may lead the mind to pursue that sense of happiness, to try to recreate it, again and again, falling under its grip. Such a response may again ignite mental and psychological processes that seek to retrieve and restore the sense of happiness, which is not the one mentioned in the context of Brahman knowledge. However, the presence of a teacher or friend, or awareness of the road map outlined by Patañjali, may help a yogi make this feeling the object of inquisitive meditation. Simultaneously, establishing the uninvolved inner gaze and settling further into a meditation devoid of conceptualisations can ensure that there is only a witnessing gaze that is able to contemplate the intoxicating feeling without being drowned in it.

As the uninvolved gaze stabilises and becomes more established, the sense of happiness loses its appeal for the yogi that is concentrating on it, such that conceptualising processes no longer interrupt the concentration. At this point, the sense of I-am-ness arises and it becomes the object of meditation, the presence of uninvolved awareness directed this time towards the sense of I-am-ness. At the climax of this meditation, the clear discerning gaze emerges. The yogi, who had previously been able to discern between the feeling of happiness and the sense of I-am-ness, and who was able to give up the former, now experiences the sense of I-am-ness which emerges with the uninvolved gaze. The uninvolved gaze reaches its full maturity with the internalisation of the insight – 'I am not who I think I am, I am not the source of awareness'. The meaning of discerning insight is the realisation of the true nature of the sense of I-am-ness and the understanding that it is distinct from the true Self. Such insight allows the *buddhi*'s nature, the intellect, to be grounded in a flowing state of serenity and to see clearly and openly things as they actually are, as 'truth-bearing' (*ṛtam bharā*),[38] and devoid of any mental processes and causes of distress that usually distort the perception of things and entail suffering.

Henceforth this discerning insight turns into a *saṃskāra* that blocks other *saṃskāras*. However, even this insight must be dispensed with; its power must disintegrate and dissipate, allowing the objectless *samādhi* to emerge, a state identical to liberation. In this process, the discerning gaze becomes clearer and culminates with the rise of supreme discerning insight. This event is not momentary and fleeting but a knowledge that accompanies the yogi in his or her daily existence. However, the yogi will have to relinquish this insight for the sake of establishing an objectless meditation, which is accompanied and enabled by the uninvolved gaze. Such a gaze takes place this time by itself, being a *para-vairāgya* (ultimate uninvolved consciousness) independent of an object, and completely overlapping with an objectless meditation.[39] In such a mental state, the mind remains still and tranquil independently of any object or refined *saṃskāra* of wisdom, whatever it may be.

Here I am interested in turning the spotlight on the clear discerning gaze that culminated in the rise of discerning insight. I will try to address the questions I have raised so far regarding the release of the imaginary and confusing entanglement of the sense of I-am-ness as a component of the world of phenomena, and the true Self, the principle of pure awareness. Undoing this tangle guarantees liberation. What is the meaning of this confusing set of relationships and the statement 'I am not who I think I am'? After all, this statement goes against our most basic intuition and how we perceive ourselves.

Moreover, it is the sense of I-am-ness that formulates this feeling or statement about itself in the first place; according to Patañjali, such self-perception may also be contested, seeking certainty at the same time. A search of this kind can produce more and more discursive thoughts, and can begin to revolve around itself in a closed circle: 'How will I reveal the pure awareness or true Self inherent in me and that precedes everything?'; 'How am I supposed to achieve something that has always been in me (pure awareness)?'; 'How can I become what I already am?'; 'How do I dismantle the tangled and confusing connection between the sense of I-am-ness and the self which I really am?'; and 'How do I stop the sequence of identities that I adopt and settle upon, a sequence that binds me to mundane existence?'

As mentioned earlier, Sāmkhya philosophy offers analytical meditation to bring about discerning insight, based on an inquiry into the various components of the world of phenomena (*prakṛti*). This inquiry culminates when it is directed at the intellect, the organ of inquiry itself. When the essence of these components of the world of phenomena become familiar and known, the philosopher then understands that the true Self is not part of the world of phenomena. For the Sāmkhya philosopher, such an inquiry is demanding and lengthy, and it ends only after the discerning insight has been assimilated. This is due to the gap between the philosopher's intellectual understanding – that the causes of distress and patterns of behaviour are nothing but a mental activity that has nothing to do with the true Self – and their phenomenal gaze, which causes them to feel, think, and act in ways that imply and disclose the dictating presence of the sense of I-am-ness. In most cases, the gap continues to exist because an intellectual understanding of its existence is not sufficient; such an understanding is usually not absorbed deep enough into the psyche but instead remains only at the level of thought. Such intellectual knowledge tends to seep in slowly. It takes a long time to assimilate into the mind and effectively integrate it, at which point this discerning insight has a natural effect that dilutes the causes of distress, and that gnaws away dormant mental imprints and habitual tendencies.

The map that Patañjali plots on the way to the discerning insight is complex, demanding, lengthy, and not necessarily linear, as one is sometimes forced to go back to one of the yogic limbs in order to stabilise an earlier stage and progress to the next. In his doctrine, Patañjali adds the psychological dimension, which is essential for perseverance in yoga practice and for its fulfilment. However, the gap between an intellectual understanding and day-to-day existence still remains, even among experienced Western yoga practitioners. Some have spent ten years and more in India or the Himalayas, practicing yoga and meditation under the guidance of a guru, having deep and lasting experiences of love and compassion, clarity and lucidity, visions of deities, a sense of wonderment and openness, and good health. Nevertheless, upon their return to the West, they experience difficulties and crises at work, in family life, in their intimate relationships, in their health, and in the management of their financial affairs.[40]

Why is it that practitioners who have had such sublime spiritual experiences, and have touched the heights of yoga and meditation, continue to experience such crises? After all, practicing at such a deep level was supposed to free them from distress and painful circumstances, which seems to be the spiritual promise.

The emergence of discerning insight allows the *buddhi*'s nature to reflect and see clearly and openly things as they actually are, as 'truth-bearing' (*ṛtam bharā*) without the distorting mental processes and causes of distress. Henceforth the discerning clear insight turns into a *saṃskāra* that blocks other *saṃskāra*s that produce karma, and hence enable liberation from suffering. However, the predicament experienced by such practitioners demonstrates that sometimes the mental imprints continue to exist within them, as do the habitual tendencies and stubborn patterns of behaviour that distort their perception of the objective world that cause them, and others around them, distress and suffering. As experienced as they are, they are forced to confront their shadow, to acknowledge what it is that prevents them from personal growth, harmonious relationships – with their families, with their friends, and with their communities – and the fulfilment of yoga.

I seek to see the *Yogasūtra* as a philosophical work which contains a profound psychological framework, and a guide of instruction for the yoga practitioner, for despite being concise, it offers a great wealth of material for contemporary thought. In my view, it remains a relevant teaching aid for contemporary practice not just a text for philosophical interpretation and contemplation. Returning to the original text of the *Yogasūtra* allows us to find new meanings hidden between its lines. I am interested in thinking along with the concepts in the *Yogasūtra*, delving into the discerning insight as a specific subject in the context of the psychology of yoga, and proposing a possible model of meditation related to it. This model places the sense of I-am-ness as the object of a meditation that we can begin cultivating with the intention of achieving immense psychological benefit.

Such meditation is mainly about contemplating the sense of I-am-ness, which adopts and sheds various characters and roles, and with which it identifies and becomes associated with to one degree or another. These parts of the ego, the sense of I-am-ness, resurface in the mind rapidly. We do not have a language rich enough to describe this process. At the same time, it is not necessarily possible to discuss the words, motives, and reactions of these various characters and the interrelationships between them. The theoretical basis for this meditation rests in part on the work of the psychologist Richard Schwartz. In his view, it is a mistake to see the sense of I-am-ness as an indivisible unit; instead it is a multifaceted entity that is composed of many figures and roles which coexist in modern life. Because our contemporary existence is also complex it accordingly requires sophisticated thinking, preparation, and action to live and manage life.[41]

We can call by name almost any character that our sense of I-am-ness wears and see it as a 'part' of our personality. Such a character or figure is not just a temporary emotional condition or a particular behaviour pattern but is a latent autonomous mental system with a range of emotions, expressions, abilities, passions, and worldviews. It seems that in each of us there exist several characters simultaneously interacting with each other, and they are different from each other in age, talents, temperament, and desires.

In the language of the psychology of yoga, the ensemble of characters that the sense of I-am-ness wears become a cluster of causes that lead to various configurations of distress. They are the sedimentary materials of the phenomenal gaze's conscious and unconscious, forming an infrastructure that conceals the true Self. Therefore, a meditation on a particular character of the sense of I-am-ness means an opportunity to quell this cluster of causes for our distress.

Many figures from one's self-identity may come up in meditation. They may emerge from memory in the form of conflicts or pleasant encounters we had in the past, and these each require processing precisely during meditation. Each of the characters becomes dominant and takes over the space of the mind whether it be the quarreller, the lover, the commentator, the judge, the time manager, the provocateur, or the empathic. Meditation on the sense of I-am-ness offers a method for dealing with our various 'parts' and includes practicing the opposite (*pratipakṣa bhāvanā*),[42] an approach proposed by Patañjali in sūtra 2.34, where he states: 'To cultivate the opposite is (to reflect upon the fact) that thoughts which contradict the *yama*s, such as violent thoughts and so on, whether executed, planned to be executed, or even approved, whether driven by greed, anger, or delusion, whether mild, moderate, or intense, result in endless suffering (*duḥkha*) and ignorance (*ajñāna*).'[43]

The sense of I-am-ness itself serves as a mature, intelligent, and skilled character and is the leader of the other characters. In the context of yoga, the sense of I-am-ness is the yogic figure that sits in meditation, who responds to the other figures that emerge, and that acknowledges and reconciles them. Under its influence, they are encouraged to step away from the front of the mind's stage and take a place behind the scenes. However, the yogi is required to give up this sense of I-am-ness as well – the mature, intelligent, and skilled figure of the yogi situated in meditation, even this figure must be renounced. The converging inner gaze is a process of ever-regressing self-observation. The sense of I-am-ness is the observer looking at the wise, mature and skilful figure, and the observer watching the observer looking at the wise, mature and skilful figure, and so on. This process ends when the mind exhausts itself or when the process is no longer relevant, and the mind becomes empty and clear. As noted, I will expand on the meditation aimed at the sense of self, and its theoretical and practical basis, in the fifth chapter.

The present chapter, ***Metamorphosis of a Gaze***, is the introduction to this book.

In the second chapter, ***The Sense of I-am-ness*** **Asmitā**, I will present the sense of I-am-ness as it is described in the *Yogasūtra* and in the seminal text on Sāṃkhya philosophy, the *Sāṃkhyakārikā*. The text was written by Īśvarakṛṣṇa (350–450 CE) as a final summary of this philosophy that originated with the sage Kapila (sixth century BCE). This includes the 'formation' of the sense of I-am-ness, how it evolves within the tangled and confusing relationships of the world of phenomena (*prakṛti*) and the true Self (*puruṣa*), and how it can be understood as a cause of distress within the psychological framework of yoga. This differs from classical New Age or psychological conceptions, such as Freud's understanding of the ego, which tend to equate their understanding of the ego with the yogic sense of I-am-ness. Drawing on Trungpa and Levinas, I will then explore the meaning and possible implications of giving up or surrendering the sense of I-am-ness. Finally, I present a concise discussion of the ways in which Western modern culture influences and shapes and affects the modern yogi's sense of I-am-ness or ego.

In the third chapter, *The True Self* Puruṣa, I will examine the true Self as the principle of pure awareness, as it is presented in the *Yogasūtra* and the *Sāṃkhyakārikā*. Although explanations of the true Self always prove to be deficient because it is something that is transcendent and ineffable, they can serve as a bridge to the otherness that is being invoked. Attempting to understand the meaning of the true Self also redirects the inner gaze of *pratiprasava* away from the objective world and mental processes toward establishing a clear discerning gaze. I will draw upon Patañjali's metaphorical expressions – such as the 'seer' and the 'owner of the true Self' – to discuss the concept of the Self. Most of Patañjali's metaphors are taken from the empirical world where there is a relationship of sensation, perception, cognition, and ownership or sovereignty, although in fact Patañjali does not provide a full definition of the concept of the Self in the text. In *Sāṃkhyakārikā* the true Self is described as an inactive, equanimous, and aloof witness that is not subject to causality, and is pure awareness. I will then discuss the concept of purity of awareness and its resemblance to the purity and transparency inherent in *buddhi*, the intellect, and examine the multiplicity of *puruṣa*s and the tension that exists between them and the *Sāṃkhyakārikā*'s definition of true Self as an inactive, equanimous and aloof witness. Finally I will discuss another 'type' of *puruṣa*, which can be a god or deity *(Īśvara)*. God is not mentioned at all in *Sāṃkhyakārikā*, not even implicitly, but is mentioned in the *Yogasūtra*, reflecting the theistic component of yoga. *Puruṣa* is detached from the world, while god is perceived as being pure awareness, a special *puruṣa* that 'bends' and 'touches' the pure aspect of the yogi's mind, becoming its sovereign. God does so without being involved in the world of phenomena. However, by acting upon yogis that are on their path to liberation in this way ontologically deviates from *puruṣa*'s usual characteristics. How this can be understood will also be examined in this chapter.

In the fourth chapter, *The Discerning Clear Gaze* Viveka-Khyāti, I will discuss discerning wisdom. Yoga practitioners pray, perform rituals, engage in physical and mental training, and cultivate virtues. Employing these practices they aim at eroding the binding and dormant mental imprints by contributing positive and mind-stilling mental imprints to their karma. These practices are, however, insufficient in themselves to release yoga practitioners from enslavement to their dormant mental imprints. This is because the identity of the sense of I-am-ness is always involved in these efforts and in their consequences. The obvious question is what kind of knowledge or insight can reveal the sense of I-am-ness involved in actions and their consequences? Because the sense of I-am-ness is itself entangled within the world of phenomena, it must be dismantled and stripped of its constituting identifications, and be completely discerned from the true Self, *puruṣa*. How can this knowledge be cultivated, or how can one come to settle or abide in such insight? In response to this question I sketch, map, and interpret yogic meditation, cognitive *samādhi*, and its categories.

In the fifth chapter, ***Meditation on the Sense of I-am-ness***, as mentioned earlier, I will expand on the theory and practice of yoga directed toward the sense of self.

In the sixth chapter, I will present the ***Concluding Observations*** for the study.

In ***Appendix:*** **Yogasūtra:** ***Authors, Texts and Readers***, I will discuss Philipp A. Maas's contention that the so-called Yogabhāṣya or Vyāsbhāṣya, which is considered to be the oldest commentary to Patañjali's *Yogasūtra*, is not an independent work but an auto-commentary.

Notes

1 A. R. Jain, *Selling Yoga: From Counterculture to Pop Culture* (New York: Oxford University Press, 2014), 6–7.

2 R. W. Perrett, *Hindu ethics: A philosophical study* (Honolulu: University of Hawaii Press, 1998), 64.

3 F. Zimmerman, *Jungle and the Aroma of Meats: An Ecological Theme in Hindu Medicine (Comparative Studies of Health Systems and Medical Care)* (Delhi: Motilal Banarsidass, 2011), 37–38.

4 I refer here to the distinction between Brahmanas practicing *śrauta*, who placed importance on the system of sacrifice and ritual actions, and the *śramaṇa* tradition, which placed emphasis on the spiritual striving towards liberation. This distinction, however, usually goes together with the hypothesis of Greater Magadha which has been put forward by J. Bronkhorst, *Greater Magadha: Studies in the culture of early India* (Leiden: Brill, 2007).

5 I say family man here because at the time the path of the yogi was not generally open to women.

6 P. Olivelle, trans., *The Early Upaniṣads* (Delhi: Oxford University Press, 1998), 69.

7 Y. Grinshpon, *Crisis and Knowledge: The Upanishadic Experience and Storytelling* (New Delhi: Oxford University Press, 2003), 17.

8 D. Raveh, *Philosophical Threads in Patanjali's Yoga* (Tel Aviv: Hakibutz Hameuchad, 2010), 15.

9 D. Raveh, *Exploring the Yogasutra: Philosophy and Translation*, annotated edition (London: Continuum, 2012), 9.

10 Tubb and Boose indicate a similarity between sūtra and kārikā literary styles in that both are essentially sign-posts in a line of oral argument and in the absence of that oral corpus the written works often have meaning for us only as they are expounded in a full scholastic commentary either by the author themself or by scholars or commentators. In these laconic works (sūtras and kārikās) the underlying motive is clearly a desire to facilitate memorisation of the chief points of a system. G. A. Tubb and E. R. Boose, *Scholastic Sanskrit: A Handbook For Students* (New York: American Institute of Buddhist Studies: Distributed by Columbia University Press, 2007), 1–2.

11 G. J. Larson, "Classical Yoga as Neo-Sāṃkhya," *Asiatische Studien – Études Asiatiques*, 52(3) (1999), 726.

12 D. G. White, *The Yoga Sutra of Patañjali: A Biography*, Princeton University Press (Princeton, NJ: Princeton University Press, 2014), 1–2.

13 P. A. Maas, "A Concise Historiography of Classical Yoga Philosophy", in E. Franco, ed., *Periodization and Historiography of Indian Philosophy* (Vienna: The De Nobili Research Library, 2013), 79–80.

14 C. K. Chapple and A. L. Funes Maderey, eds., *Thinking with the Yoga Sutra of Patañjali: Translation and Interpretation* (London: Lexington Books, 2019), xii.

15 Quoted from D. R. Harper, comp., "Theory," entry in *Online Etymology Dictionary*, https://www.etymonline.com/search?q=theory, retrieved 22 July 2021.

16 G. J. Stack and R. W. Plant, "The Phenomenon of the Look," *Philosophy and Phenomenological Research* 42(3) (1982), 363–364.

17 Raveh, *Philosophical Threads in Patanjali's Yoga*, 101.

18 D. Raveh, *Exploring the Yogasutra*, 130.

19 W. Halbfass, *Tradition and Reflection: Explorations in Indian Thought* (Albany, NY: State University of New York Press, 1991), 244.

20 'Steady yogic discernment (*viveka-khyāti*, namely awareness of the absolute difference between *prakṛti* and *puruṣa*) is the means of cessation [of that confusing connection].' Sūtra 2.26, Raveh, *Exploring the Yogasutra*, 131, square parentheses added by author.

21 Sūtra 2.10, Raveh, *Exploring the Yogasutra*, 130.

22 M. Klein, *Envy and Gratitude, and Other Works 1946–1963* (New York: Free Press, 1984), 181.

23 R. Mehta, *Yoga: The Art of Integration: A Commentary on the Yoga Sutras of Patanjali* (Adyar, India: Theosophical Publishing House, 1990), 115–116.

24 Raveh, *Exploring the Yogasutra*, 129.

25 F. Godrej, "The Neoliberal Yogi and the Politics of Yoga," *Political Theory* 45(6) (2016), 780.

26 Godrej, "The Neoliberal Yogi," 781.

27 C. Trungpa, *Cutting Through Spiritual Materialism* (Boston, MA: Shambhala, 1987), 15.

28 Raveh, *Exploring the Yogasutra*, 129.

29 E. Bryant, *The Yoga Sutras of Patañjali: A New Edition, Translation and Commentary* (New York: North Point Press, 2009), 129.

30 Sūtra 2.34, Raveh, *Exploring the Yogasutra*, 132.

31 E. Bryant, *The Yoga Sutras of Patañjali*, 52–53.

32 H. Āraṇya, *Yoga Philosophy of Patanjali: Containing His Yoga Aphorisms with Vyasa's Commentary in Original Sanskrit and Annotations Thereon with Copious Hints on the Practice of Yoga* (Calcutta: Calcutta University Press, 1981), 37.

33 Āraṇya, *Yoga Philosophy of Patanjali*, 37.

34 Raveh, *Philosophical Threads in Patanjali's Yoga*, 39.

35 Sūtra 3.9, Raveh, *Exploring the Yogasutra*, 134.

36 Sūtra 3.2, Raveh, *Exploring the Yogasutra*, 133, which in this context states: "*dhyāna* is [the] even flow of consciousness (in the course of *dhāraṇā*) toward it (toward the object meditated upon)."

37 K. Rose, *Yoga, Meditation, and Mysticism: Contemplative Universals and Meditative Landmarks* (London: Bloomsbury Academic, 2016), 104–105.

38 Raveh, *Exploring the Yogasutra*, 129.

39 See Vyāsa's commentary to sūtra 1.16 in Āraṇya, *Yoga Philosophy of Patanjali*, 39. Vyāsa employs the term *para-vairāgya* and explains it, although the term is not mentioned directly in the sūtra.

40 G. Ifergan, *The Psychology of the Yogas* (Sheffield, UK: Equinox Publishing, 2021), 89–90.

41 R. C. Schwartz, *Internal Family Systems Therapy* (New York: Guilford Publications, 1994), 33.

42 For a discussion of how the concrete yogic psychological method of "cultivating the opposite" (*pratipakṣa bhāvanā*) has been transformed into "imagining the opposite" see G. Ifergan, *The Psychology of the Yogas*, chapters 2 and 3.

43 Sūtra 2.34, Raveh, *Exploring the Yogasutra*, 132.

2 The Sense of I-am-ness *Asmitā*

The world of phenomena (*prakṛti*) exists in two modes: as potentiality and as concrete reality. 'Potentiality' refers to the unmanifested, intangible, and subtlest origin of all phenomena, including what later becomes the mental faculty, the psychological substratum and concrete reality through a process of causation or modification in which objects are not something newly produced from some discrete forces other than those that are inherent in their causes. For example, every clay pot exists within the potentiality of clay and every ice cube in the potentiality of water.

'Concreteness' in the context of the philosophy of yoga is the product of the contact between the true Self (*puruṣa*), pure awareness, and the world of phenomena in its potentiality mode (*avikṛta prakṛti*). This contact generates a process in which the physical world begins to form, solidify and change from a refined to a raw state. This is a process of creation or evolution (*pariṇāma*) manifesting the potentiality that underlies the world of phenomena. Such potentiality becomes visible and concrete (*vikṛta prakṛti*), and is characterised by modifications or causality, depending on the *guṇa*s and the prevailing circumstances that have the potential to generate a certain process of modification within *prakṛti*. Here, the broad meaning of potentiality is therefore a state in which no phenomena have appeared or materialised as yet, and what makes these phenomena appear and materialise is radiant pure awareness. However, there is also a particular meaning of potentiality, such that whatever appears or manifests still carries a particular unmanifested or dormant cause in potentiality mode that when certain circumstances occur, and stir that cause into action, a new process of modification will take place. To take an example, in the context of the psychology of yoga, the latent mental imprints of aggression, that do not manifest in certain pleasant circumstances, may be triggered and become manifest in more challenging circumstances. Nevertheless, the nature of the contact between the true Self (*puruṣa*) and the world of phenomena, and what instigated that contact, remains unclear, for it is difficult to grasp how a transcendent principle can become intertwined with the world of matter or phenomena.

Therefore, *prakṛti* also includes within it a huge range of mental or psychological states, abilities, and tendencies. How can mental states be an integral part of the material world? After all, the two seemingly oppose each other. According to the materialist perspective everything that exists is subject to physical properties; the mind is the brain, and there is nothing beyond matter, not even states of consciousness, for they too are derived from the neurophysiological activity.[1] Another perspective is that states of consciousness may exist that are related to events at the subjective ontological level and do not result from neuropsychological activity. Others argue that there is probably no difference between the mechanical activity of the mind and artificial intelligence.[2] In contrast, David Rudrauf, a neuropsychologist, suggests that 'mental functions might not be tied to fixed brain regions. Instead, the mind might be more like a virtual machine running on distributed computers, with brain resources allocated in a flexible manner.'[3]

The perspective of a Sāṃkhya philosopher is essentially different from these positions. According to such a philosopher, the mind stands for primordial matter, and is transparent like a pure crystal. Being transparent, it can contain the light of awareness and radiate it, just as it 'refracts' in a prism, so that phenomena and events can become perceivable for the individual. The light of pure awareness is something else altogether and exists beyond the mechanical–material mind that serves only as an organ through which the world of phenomena is 'experienced'. According to Sāṃkhya philosophy, this reflexive capacity of the mind is made possible thanks to the first evolute[4] of the world of phenomena, the *buddhi* – the seat of rational thinking, discernment, intuitive wisdom, and intelligence. The second evolute in the process of development from potentiality to concreteness within the world of phenomena is the ego, the phenomenal ordinary self (*ahaṃkāra*), which is self-conscious and associated with self-importance (*abhimāna*),[5] the 'I' who wills, acts, and determines. To understand what the sense of self or I-am-ness (*asmitā*) is in the psychology of yoga, it is advisable to first understand what the phenomenal self is according to Sāṃkhya philosophy.

According to the *Sāṃkhyakārikā*, the seminal text of Sāṃkhya philosophy composed from the fourth or fifth century CE: 'From *prakṛti* [comes] the great; from that, egoity; and from that, the group of sixteen; again from five of those sixteen, [comes] the five elements.'[6] What this means is that the world of phenomena gives rise to the great principle, the intellect, from which the ego (the phenomenal self) evolves. From the ego evolves cognition, the five senses and the five organs of action, and the five subtle elements. The five coarse elements evolve from the five subtle elements. That is, from the *sattvic* component of the ego there evolve eleven organs: cognition; the five sense organs – eyes, ears, nose, tongue, and skin; and the five organs of action – mouth, hands, feet, anus, and sex organs. From the ego's *tama*s quality, which is static, heavy, lethargic, solid, and coarse, evolve the five subtle elements: sound, touch, colour, taste, and smell. From these evolve the five coarse elements: ether, air, fire, water, and earth. The coarse elements, which are then subjected to the three *guṇa*s, can form a variety of experiential combinations at any given time, which can be, for example, harmonious, dangerous, disturbing, or confusing.[7]

The dynamics of existence and the set of forces operating in the world of phenomena and humankind are described through the three *guṇa*s or qualities. The dominance of each of these qualities produces different prevailing conditions in the mind: the dominance of *sattva* leads to purity, clarity, serenity, pleasantness, neutrality, or indifference; and *raja*s brings activity, agitation, passion, and longing; and *tama*s brings staticness, heaviness, and lethargy. These three qualities are in constant interaction with each other, a flux in which at any particular moment one of them tends to dominate the others. This can be visualised as a triangle whose three sides change constantly in length. As one side grows and lengthens, the others shrink, and the angles at which they meet the largest side become more acute. Thus, for example, a heavy sleep without dreams may occur when the quality (*guṇa*) of *tama*s dominates one's mind and body. The term *tama*s means 'darkness': a term that describes stagnation, passivity, and a heavy fatigue that obscures the mind. In such a mental state, a sleeping person is not aware that they are dreaming. Waking up from a heavy sleep such as this may leave remnants or residues, such as bad moods, pain, confusion, or joy, and for no apparent reason. These residues, which clearly indicate a previous mental activity, relate to the dream experiences and its contents, which may not be remembered upon waking.

In this seemingly orderly and organised cosmological worldview as presented in Sāṃkhya philosophy, a sense of certainty is established, and an understanding that what happens in the world and through the evolution of the phenomenal world, emerges for the benefit and liberation of the true Self. In a sense, in this play of consciousness, the psycho–physical organism (the product of the world of phenomena) becomes a vehicle through which the true Self comes to 'see' and 'experience' the world of phenomena.[8] Through the immensely impactful contact of the two principles, *puruṣa* as pure awareness and *prakṛti* in its potential state the evolutionary process of latter is somehow enabled. Simultaneously, *prakṛti* brings its primal evolute, the *buddhi* or intellect, which develops the indispensable knowledge that can enable the realisation that the two principles are actually radically different. Such a realisation is a synonym for liberation. So both principles, *puruṣa* and *prakṛti,* as radically different as they are, combine to mutually benefit each other's capacities. *Prakṛti* performs its activities so that pure *puruṣa* can see and experience the world of phenomena as the content of one's mind. *Puruṣa* expresses its nature by revealing itself as radically different or set apart from *prakṛti*'s evolutionary process. The simile employed in the *Sāṃkhyakārikā* is that of a lame man and a blind man that interact with each other, whereby the lame man stands for *puruṣa* and the blind man stands for *prakṛti.*

The Sāṃkhyan worldview described above can be expressed in a mythical language in which a primordial world of particles of light, project the light inward, into themselves. The potential world of phenomena lay unrealised or not yet manifested, and everything is still and motionless. A sudden shock, an inexplicable and unexpected contact, brought these two foundational principles together – light and the world of phenomena – in such a way that light impregnated the world of potential phenomena. This encounter is akin to creating a womb for the world, and with it bringing about the foundation for the development of the world of phenomena.[9]

However, this description does not have the capacity to adequately explain how the Sāṃkhyan world was created, how it actually happened. It does not seem to have the power to adequately explain the process of evolution, the developmental order, and the cause for the initial contact between the principle of awareness or the true Self, and the world of phenomena, the contact that generated the process in the first place. It is also difficult to know how each component of the cosmological developmental process integrates with the subjective element, which is individual personal awareness. Since Sāṃkhya is a system of liberation through

Self-realisation or pure awareness, it might be that this ambiguity may challenge the notion of liberation and perhaps even question its validity.

I believe, therefore, that a different reading is required, a reading that is not satisfied with the understanding of the metaphysical system of Sāṃkhya as it has often been presented. Instead I propose a reading that emphasises the psychological framework embedded within the *Sāṃkhyakārikā*. Evidently, twelve kārikās in this text indicate that there are subjective psychological elements such as pleasure, pain, confusion, or depression, so such a reading is possible and even necessary. Over 20 kārikās (out of a total of 72) deal with praxis, the application, realisation, or skilful practice of ideas, and psychology. At the basis of the classical interpretation of the *Sāṃkhyakārikā* is the term 'centralisation', which refers to the concentration of mental and physical activity under the control of the subject or individual – the phenomenal self (*ahaṃkāra*) or ego.[10] The *Sāṃkhyakārikā* enumerates the components of the world of phenomena and defines them, including the intellect (*buddhi*), in kārikā 23, which denotes the seat of discernment, decision making, the will, and intelligence.[11] By attributing these activities to an ordinary phenomenal self (*ahaṃkāra*), the intellect becomes an element belonging to the phenomenal self, that is, the seat of discernment, decision making, the will, and intelligence all become the property of that individual. Hence the intellect has a subjective dimension. It becomes subjective. This centralised process is evident in the addition of an 'I' to statements that refer to a particular decision, discernment, perception, or action. The reference to a subject converts metaphysical concepts into psychological concepts, and hence provide an understanding of the experiential dimension, of the subjective experience.

Consequently, it would be worthwhile suspending the metaphysical cosmological perspective of Sāṃkhya while holding onto the assumption that the purpose of Sāṃkhya philosophy is not only to describe and explain, but also to influence and lead one to liberation. Moreover, such a psychological reading would serve and enhance our understanding of the psychology of yoga. After all, yoga as a sister school of Sāṃkhya philosophy was based on its metaphysics, and proposes a psychological method for the application of its philosophy.

Before I review in detail the concept of the phenomenal self according to the *Sāṃkhyakārikā* and the *Yogasūtra*, I will briefly focus on the *buddhi*, the intellect, the primary evolute that precedes the phenomenal self in the evolution of the world of phenomena. According to kārikā 23, the *buddhi* is the conscious, intentional will that directs, clarifies, and identifies (*adhyavasāya*) the truth or validity of information received during a sensory encounter with an object, determines its identity, and decides if any action is needed. According to Krishna Chandra Bhattacharya,[12] *buddhi* is knowledge. Knowledge is expressed in a will that is driven by intention and purpose, and by feeling. The root of knowledge lies in a subjective sense of certainty (*niścaya*), which can be formulated as a primal existential declaration: 'I am I'. Certainty in itself is nothing but the capacity to identify and make judgments, to undertake a determination, or the ability of a subject to make a decision concerning an object. That is, the *buddhi* is a font of knowledge that can identify and distinguish between objects, a knowledge that is founded on self-identity. This identity is objective and, for the subject, it is a certainty.[13]

Thus, clarity, determination, and decisiveness are synonymous with the *buddhi* itself. Its four main characteristics when the *buddhi* is dominated by the *sattva* quality are: virtues (*dharma*); discerning wisdom (*jñānam*); dispassion as a mental state that culminates in uninvolved contemplation (*vairāga*); and control, sovereignty or power (*aiśvaryam*). When the *tama*s quality is dominant in the *buddhi*, the opposite of these four characteristics manifest and dominate one's existence. One can cultivate dispassion towards sensory pleasures by actually avoiding sensory contact with objects of desire, and by developing the ability to discern between the various passions, and their respective intensities in relation to such objects. This capacity enables the Sāṃkhyan practitioner to know which passions he or she has succeeded in conquering and which it is better to avoid. This dynamic process leads to a weakening of cravings and a reduction in the tendency to pursue objects of desire.

Avoidance is not the exclusive method of weakening habitual tendencies to pursue objects of desire. Suppose one attempts to refrain from any engagement with mental content or any object. In that case, the very act of such avoidance is a strategy that may be a hindrance to engaging the pure *buddhi,* including the discerning wisdom that it encompasses. Therefore, cultivating indifference or uninvolved awareness to the presence of particular objects of desire may enable the practitioner to relinquish a previously held avoidance towards that particular object, thereby weakening altogether any habitual tendencies to pursue such objects.

The prevalence of the four main characteristics of the intellect (*buddhi*) – virtue, intelligence, dispassion, and control – indicates the degree to which an individual has managed to cultivate the *sattvic* qualities of their intellect. If so, how can the intellect act to cultivate and realise these sublime qualities? After all, these psychological qualities refer to an individual rather than the intellect's metaphysical dimension. They cannot be realised without an agent acting to cultivate them. For Bhattacharya, certainty and the capacity for clarity, determination or decisiveness, are synonymous with intellect and refer to the will. Knowing does not necessarily lead to willing, but willing, by itself, presumes knowing (which precedes it) in the sense that one knows 'this thing must be done'. Such knowledge implies the existence of an understanding that 'I am completely real', and that 'I am this entity, different from the others'. This is in contrast to the primal existential cry of the intellect, 'I am I'. That is, knowledge is inherent in the will, which points to the inner meaning concerning the formation of *ahaṃkāra*, the ego as the agent that evolves from the *buddhi*, the intellect.[14]

There is some difficulty in writing about the ego since, as in a closed circle, the one who writes about the ego is the ego itself. After all, yoga aims to break out of this cycle of misconception that sees the ego as the true Self. This perception is so deeply ingrained in the personality or ego, and is like a transparent screen that is always there even though we do not see it and are not aware of it at all. And yet, the true Self – pure awareness – diffuses through the intellect, alongside that misconception, and the act of writing (by the ego). The shards of pure awareness that have diffused through the intellect may exist and manifest in perception or writing as inspiration or insight that enables a fresh and new perception of a given state of affairs. Such insight may erode the misconception and enable a gradual replacement of one truth with another, being a relevant insight that more accurately reflects reality. Any such insight slightly reduces one's suffering.

I will now return to the *Sāṃkhyakārikā* to clarify the notion of the ego. According to kārikā 24, the ego (*ahaṃkāra*) is defined employing the term *abhimāna*, which literally means self-importance, self-perception or pride.[15] In the context of this kārikā, its meaning is opinionated and intentional self-expression. Self-importance or opinionated and intentional self-expression indicates a self-centred, selfish phenomenal self. Such an 'I' is driven by egocentrism, and tends to typically say things like: 'What do I get out of this?'; 'It is my right to choose'; or 'Only I can do the job'. Egocentrism is the worldview from the sole perspective of the phenomenal self, a state of mind where a person sees themself as the centre of the world, as if they were the axis around which all situations and actions revolve. *Abhimāna* as self-importance is the erroneous extension of the label 'I', which may also lead to projections onto objects, other people, and matters that are completely extraneous to it, taking ownership over them.

Suppose the intellect – the *buddhi* – is the seat of knowledge and the capacity for clarity, determination, or decision-making in matters concerning willingness. In that case, the phenomenal self is the concrete self-expression for that certain willingness. That is, the existential, ordinary phenomenal self is not only one who wants to act in one way or another, but perceives itself to be the one who acts. The meaning of willing for the phenomenal self becomes 'I wish' or 'my will', and its confident and determining knowledge becomes 'I know and determine'. That is, the essence of the phenomenal self – *ahaṃkāra* – is the erroneous identification with the true Self and itself as a finite, limited, and mortal entity, an entity distinctly separate from others.

A central characteristic underlying the definition of the phenomenal self is the ingrained tendency to appropriate objects when it comes into contact with them. This sense of ownership then becomes inseparable from the experience of the object. Empirical awareness is also personal and appropriated. Everything the phenomenal self knows, feels, and thinks is associated with itself and ostensibly stems from introspection: 'my pain or pleasure', 'my knowledge', or 'my act'. Appropriation lends the phenomenal self a feeling of otherness, uniqueness, difference, and of being a personality in itself. Moreover, the sense of ownership promotes the phenomenal self, the ego, to feel responsible for the consequences of its actions and for control over its actions.

The term *ahaṃkāra* has several meanings: (1) the perception of the phenomenal self as an individual subject; (2) I (*aham*) the performer, the producer, the performer, or the doer; (3) selfishness in the sense of being a self-centred and self-absorbed person; (4) arrogance and pride.[16] From these meanings we can learn about the creative process or the developmental process through which *prakṛti* evolves. The *buddhi* projects onto the world the phenomenal self, and the phenomenal self imposes on the world its worldview, and thus the individual solidifies itself. For example, longing, the craving for certainty, confidence, pleasure, and eternity, lend to the phenomenal self a subjective sense that it is a solid and lasting reality, even though it is nothing but a collection of these habitual tendencies and impressions. Thus, the individual is established and acts out of identification with a personal set of beliefs, feelings, and emotions, and out of involvement and attachment to events, situations, and phenomena in daily life. The phenomenal self is thereby an agent of intentional, physical, and mental activity. It projects itself on reality and casts its worldview onto it, and it is also the one who produces and shapes the personality.

How is the ordinary phenomenal self affected by the three qualities? *Sattva* is the ability to reflect objects in the intellect. This ability is embedded in the processes of perception and sentience in the phenomenal self. *Raja*s is the dynamic aspect of existence, controlling the organs of perception and action as it allows body and mind to move and interact with the environment. *Tama*s is the static aspect of existence, which controls the material world, including body and mind, and makes these fixed and stable.

I will now examine the process of the formation of the psycho-physical entity and present the third component of consciousness, known in Sāṃkhya philosophy as the 'inner organ' (*antaḥkaraṇa*). According to kārikā 27, this component is '*manas*', which translates as 'cognition', a conscious representation of objects.[17] I chose this translation to emphasise its cognitive dimension, being the component that is responsible for processing information received from the senses when coming into contact with an object. This translation is consistent with the definition that appears in the kārikā as mentioned earlier, according to which cognition grasps the nature of both the organs of sentience and action. Cognition embodies the principle of sorting, considering, and ascertaining. Its range of activities is attributed to the interaction of the three qualities.

What is meant by the fact that *manas* embodies the principle of sorting, considering, and ascertaining? These capacities are involved in the initial process of determining an object's identity, wondering about its nature. *Manas* is thus a collection of rational functions that establish some understanding about a particular object; the *buddhi* or intellect is the final determinant that knows what the object is based on the input provided by the rational processes of *manas*. For example, the banana in front of me – is it ripe or not? Cognition will process, sort, differentiate, and compare this particular banana to similar bananas it has encountered in the past, and consider and ponder these comparisons until it gives rise to a definite determination or knowledge in the intellect. These processes almost always occur in the blink of an eye. That is, when sensory contact is made with an object, the information or impressions are received in cognition and are transmitted to the phenomenal self, which perceives the object through personal experiences and acquires ownership of how the object is experienced. From the phenomenal self, the information passes on to the intellect that will determine and decide what is known about the object and the action to be performed by the phenomenal self regarding that object. At the same time, it will reflect the object to the true Self – to *puruṣa* – who is but a non-active witness.

This process is immediate and continuous, and takes place in direct contact with a sensory object and indirectly, relying on previous perceptions of an object from memory.[18] Such a process may be slowed down if one of the components of the internal organ's functions is delayed. For example, when impressions of a particular sensory object are obscured by a fog, or when encountering a new object that has never been seen before, or when some information temporarily escapes our memory. In these situations, the apparatus of cognition will take some time to find and process the required information, and only after initial sorting, this information will be transferred to the phenomenal self and from there to the intellect.

In his *Yogasūtra*, Patañjali labels the 'inner organ' (*antaḥkaraṇa*) of the Sāṃkhyan worldview as *citta*, which stands for the common Western concept of the mind.[19] The term *citta* originates from the root *cit*, which means identifying, observing, perceiving, or illuminating. Although Patañjali does not directly define the concept, his text seems to implicitly represent it as the psycho-mental mechanism, which encompasses all of the mind's mental and physical functions. The *citta* comprises the three main subsystems of the Sāṃkhyan internal organ: the intellect, the phenomenal self, and the cognition apparatus. In yoga, the phenomenal self is termed '*asmitā*'.

Asmitā is the first person of the root 'to be'. The suffix 'ta' represents an abstract noun as a feeling or sensation. It means 'I am', 'I exist'. Patañjali mentions *asmitā* a few times in the *Yogasūtra*. Firstly, in the context of the highest meditative concentration, which leans on an object in order to be established, the yogi is self-aware only, in the sense that the object of meditation is experienced within the most interior domain of oneself, the meditating or observing self. That is, in this highest concentration, the mind is like a transparent pure crystal, entirely taking on the colour of the object it beholds, reflecting it. In such a concentration, there is no room for distracting thoughts. There is only one thought, and it is concerned with the phenomenal self, identified with the *sattvic* quality of the *buddhi*, and this thought is – 'I am I'. This thought is without the usual characteristic of the phenomenal self that tends to appropriate feelings, thoughts, desires, objects, the body, and the activities concerning them. Instead, the one thought 'I am this being' or 'I am completely real' is the one that occupies the mind, lending it a solid and real subjective sense of certainty and identity.[20] In the highest concentration on the sense of I-am-ness, the distinction between the sense of I-am-ness and the true Self becomes clear. The sense of I-am-ness in the context of the causes of distress is an erroneous subjective self-perception, a component of the psycho–physical entity in the world of phenomena, *prakṛti*, which is either unaware of the true Self or ignorant of the fact that it is something quite distinct from the true Self.[21] In chapters 4 and 5 I will expand further on the discerning insight and meditation on the sense of I-am-ness, and dwell on the meaning of this supreme concentration that leans on the phenomenal self itself.

The 'layers' of the mind according to the psychology of yoga

The upper layer of the mind is made up of five causes of distress or affliction, the five *kleśa*s that bind individuals to their sense of identities and entangling identifications with the world of phenomena, from memories and beliefs to objects, people, and events. They solidify the existential, ordinary, phenomenal self, and lock individuals into a vicious cycle of suffering. While the mental processes mentioned in sūtra 1.5 are primarily concerned with cognition and the perception of objects in waking and sleeping states, the causes of distress are the five main forms of psychological reaction to the world of objects and events. The five causes of distress referred to in sūtra 2.3 are: partial and relative knowledge based on wrong cognition (*avidyā*); the sense of I-am-ness as a solid personality, the phenomenal self (*asmitā*); attraction or acceptance (*rāga*); aversion or rejection (*dveṣa*); and fear of death (*abhiniveśa*). In sūtra 2.2, Patañjali notes that it is possible to minimise the causes of affliction and thereby assist the aspirant yogi on the path to liberation.[22] What, then, makes our psychological reaction to the world of objects and events into a source of distress?

Avidyā

I will start with the first *kleśa*, *avidyā*. It stands for the absence of Self-awareness, which is perhaps not total ignorance but distorted knowledge, and stems from the inability to discern between the principle of awareness and the world of phenomena, the latter of which includes also all of the physical, psychological, and mental components of the phenomenal self. The state of *avidyā* conceals the principle of pure awareness and covers it by establishing a false identity, the sense of the ego. In sūtra 2.5, it is said that *avidyā* is a mistaken identification, whereby the temporal is seen as eternal, the contaminated as pure, sorrow as joy, and the ego as the true Self.[23] This kind of erroneous identification causes an individual to perceive their existential–phenomenal self as the true Self. As we have seen, one can extricate oneself out of this deceptive error by means of the yogic insight or discerning wisdom (*viveka-khyāti*).

Avidyā, absence of Self-awareness, has psychological consequences for the four other causes of distress, to the extent that even experiences of joy and pleasure can be misleading, since they are also bound up in suffering. Pleasure means attachment to gratifying objects. Attachment leads to action aimed at replicating that sense of pleasure. Karma is then created and becomes the basis for the next action, which will be triggered when the desire resurfaces, seeking again pleasurable objects and occasions where the desire may be satisfied. However, satisfying this desire will create further karma that will be the basis for the next action, seeking and replicating the desired sense of pleasure. Such repetition of actions and reactions locks the person into a vicious cycle. For the discerning yogi, existence in *avidyā* involves pain and sorrow.

Let us try to understand the nature of *avidyā* employing the familiar metaphor of a person sleeping at night, dreaming a nightmare and reacting with fear and anxiety. A cold sweat covers their skin. After they have dwelled for a certain amount of time in the grip of the nightmare, its intensity and density start to decrease, and the person realises, to their relief, that it was only a dream. They then wake up as this actual insight liberates them from the painful grip of the dream.

The inability to recognise the dream as a dream is a product of ignorance (*avidyā*), a misconception of actual reality perceived through a subjective interpretation that creates a mentality of its own to which we are born, capable of perpetuating painful experiences. According to the metaphor, because of the inability to recognise the dream as a dream – or rather, because of the mistaken perception of the dream as reality – the dreamer unconsciously undergoes a painful experience in which he or she is overwhelmed with anxiety and fear. Identifying the dream as a dream can enable the yogi to achieve a momentary glimpse into discernment between the dream and the principle of awareness, and between the ordinary phenomenal self and the true Self. The yogi realises at once that this is only a dream and experiences a profound insight that frees them from the false perception of the dream as a concrete reality, along with the anxiety it caused.

Despite the insight that it is only a dream, the yogi's initial reactions of fear, anxiety, and the cold sweat caused by the nightmare remain etched in their mind.[24] In other words, the yogi will carry these emotions as subliminal imprints (*saṃskāra*s) and, in order to realise yoga, one will have to empty one's mind of them as well. Hence, the next step on the yogi's journey is the refinement of the discerning wisdom, so that when the insight arises immediately and spontaneously upon dreaming, neutralising the power of the *saṃskāra*s, it can then become enduring and abiding as discerning wisdom.

Asmitā

The next cause of affliction is the sense of ego: *asmitā*. According to Patañjali, this feeling crystallises as the seer becomes more and more identified with the power of seeing. Hence, the sense of I-am-ness or personality is nothing but the product of this mistaken identification between the one who sees and what is being seen. Here, according to Patañjali, the seer is synonymous with the true Self, the *puruṣa*, the primordial presence of awareness, otherness, which is neither objective nor subjective. In contrast, the power of seeing belongs to the ever-changing mind as an apparatus of dynamic perception for the intellect, the *buddhi*. The *buddhi* perceives the world of phenomena and presents its image (after its impressions have been received through the senses and processed by the cognitive faculty) to the true Self. There is a relationship of priority between the *buddhi* and the sense of I-am-ness. Ignorance, which the *buddhi* is subjected to, undergoes individuation within the ego, and the ego produces its own distinct self-identity.

The core of Selfhood is innate and pervades one's mind. Thus, the different states of mind of the ego are mistakenly perceived as attributed and belonging to this principle of awareness or the true Self. If the intellect (*buddhi)* is in a state of peace, joy, and reflection (*sattva*), it will seem that it is the true Self that is the happy, clear, and peaceful one. If this peaceful quality is distorted by the arousal of another quality characterised by fervour and passion (*raja*s), the sense of serenity will be replaced by a craving for pleasure and certainty. This causes the misconception that it is the true Self who is craving for pleasure and certainty. In the same way, if one's mind is stagnant, lethargic, and passive (*tama*s), then a misconception will arise that it is the true Self who is experiencing dissatisfaction or boredom.

These are all states of mind that we attribute to ourselves, but in reality there is no connection between such states of mind and the true Self. Nothing can be imposed on the true Self. 'Intelligence of mind' (*buddhi*) is confused with the true Self, which is pure awareness and exists beyond the body and mind, and whose energy is experienced as thoughts. This misconception is something we are born into; the confusing interwoven connection between the true Self and the world of phenomena – of which the mind is an integral part – already exists from the very beginning.

With the thought 'I breathe', the true Self is identified with the activity of the breath and with the person who actually breathes. Therefore, according to yogic principles, we must abandon that thought. We must relinquish the notion that there is an agent, a performer, an individual subject within whom arises a sensation that can be expressed by the statement 'I am the doer, I am the performer – *I breathe*'. There is only the action and the objects *as they are*. Such existential, profound misidentifications lie deep within the personality. We take them as self-evident. For the yogi, these identifications constitute a fundamental and profound misunderstanding, and they are the reason that existence is filled with suffering, sorrow, and pain.

But it is only the inherent principle of awareness or the true Self (*puruṣa*) that provides one with the power of perception. The sense of self simultaneously arises as an inseparable part of the mind which is certain that it is not only a device of dynamic perception, but also the source of initial awareness (*puruṣa*) which enables seeing. Seeing them as one indistinguishable unit produces *asmitā* – the sense of ego.

The principle of awareness or the true Self (*puruṣa*) is like sunlight shining on a stained and faded mirror, which is analogous to the mind (*citta*). Although this light does not demonstrate any special preference, prejudice, or bias toward skin colour, gender, or origins, the objects in front of the mirror are reflected in a distorted way, through the grime and faded areas of the mirror. Thus, the stained, faded areas of the mirror may stand for one's concepts, beliefs, judgments, psychological tendencies, and patterns of behaviour, whether conscious or unconscious, positive or negative, through which the world of phenomena (*prakṛti*) is distortedly reflected in one's mind. Because we are so habituated to perceiving the world in this way, without complete clarity of mind, we suffer. We are sure that the source of the light that fills our minds is the ego (*ahaṃkāra*), just as the mirror that reflects the light is mistaken for the source of light. Yoga in action draws attention to that mirror by focusing and polishing it.

The mirror opens up a space in front of us in an ongoing present, and at the same time reflects the observer reflected in it, including everything behind it, its shadow and its memories. If a person turns their back on the mirror, taking into account the awareness they have acquired and gained through it, they know where they are going. Indeed, the act of polishing the mirror represents the unfolding, continuous, and stable understanding that the mirror's natural function is merely to reflect – it remains empty of any object. This understanding frees the mind of mental processes and empties it of any content that an object may invoke. The mind then stabilises and abides in an empty yet clear and natural state. In order to purify the mind of its contents, one may shift and direct one's gaze from the world of sense objects, such as buildings or ideas and the contents and reactions they evoke, to the root of the mind itself. This allows one to discern between the source of light, representing the true Self, and the mind that reflects it as a mirror.

The special status of discerning insight, as a clearing of the confusion between the true Self and the world of phenomena, demands that we once again dwell on the meaning of yoga as a union or unification. It is not exactly a union between the pure subject, the true Self, and the world of sense objects, or the union of the true Self as the principle of awareness and the body, but rather it starts with the realisation of their radical difference. Understanding the separateness or duality of these two principles – of pure awareness and matter – resolves one's confusion and consequently alleviates one's suffering. Although radically different in terms of ontology, the true Self is not divorced from the natural processes that take place within the world of phenomena, those processes that reflect the Self's inherent effulgence and sense objects as the different animate and inanimate forms of communication.

Liberation means giving up the sense of I-am-ness, all that is known, both pleasant memories and painful experiences that have been accumulated and which have been etched in the ego. All this is in order to become acquainted with unfamiliar otherness, the true Self, which cannot be conceptualised but can only be abided within. Such relinquishment has a profound psychological–emotional dimension. It is the horrific demand of yoga, a demand that can be learned from the words of Chögyam Trungpa, the Tibetan meditation teacher. In a documented oral dialogue, when asked by a student, 'Why is it so hard to let go of one's ego?', Trungpa responds:

> People are afraid of the emptiness of space, or the absence of company, the absence of a shadow. It could be a terrifying experience to have no one to relate to, nothing to relate with. The idea of it can be extremely frightening, though not the real experience. It is generally

> a fear of space, a fear that we will not be able to anchor ourselves to any solid ground, that we will lose our identity as a fixed and solid and definite thing. This could be very threatening.[25]

Thus, according to Trungpa, the student has a primal fear of losing his or her identity and reference points. In order to emphasise the intensity and possible impact of the fear of absence, Trungpa repeats the notion of fear several times, using expressions such as 'terrifying experience', 'extremely frightening', 'fear of space', 'afraid of the emptiness', and 'very threatening'. At the same time, Trungpa also reassures the students by letting them know that in the real experience of emptiness one will not feel threatened or experience fear. Trungpa addresses the Buddhist notion of emptiness not only as the renunciation of the identity of the phenomenal self, but also as the renunciation of the true Self. Although the purpose of yoga, to abide within the true Self, is diametrically opposed to Buddhism, the merger with the true Self also threatens to strip the yogi of their phenomenal self, of the ego's sense of identity and, as such, may also evoke the emotions associated with fear that Trungpa had spoken of that stem from the abandonment of identity.

The demand to give up one's ego or sense of identity may confront the yogi with terror. According to the modern French philosopher Emmanuel Levinas (1906–1995), the initial response to coming face to face with the anonymous being, the '*il y a*' ('there is'), is the experience of horror. Levinas believes that *il y a* is independent existence; it is primordial and independent of the world of phenomena, and transcends both subjectivity and objectivity, interiority and exteriority. Although it is not a pure absence or nothingness, it cannot be perceived in discursive thought, for in *il y a*, discourse does not exist at all. It cannot be extinguished, it is anonymous and impersonal, and it pursues the identity of the ego in order to empty it of all that is personal. The *il y a* is the primary identity, the nucleus of the individual's Self, and precedes psychological and social aspects that shape the individual personality in relation to events and phenomena. When *il y a* invades the individual, it is impossible to escape; it is impossible to take shelter in facets of human identity or to retreat into that identity as if into a shell, because the invasion leaves the individual completely exposed and causes them to react with horror.[26] Levinas's notion of horror is not dissimilar to Trungpa's notion of the fear of losing one's identity as a fixed, defined state.

Most contemporary commentators believe that sense of I-am-ness is the ego, the empirical or phenomenal self that depends on the senses to perceive and cognise. The ego, the bedrock of objective knowledge, actions, and feelings, is intentional and continuously changing. When in contact with sense objects, tangible or subtle, the ego grasps and refers to them with a sense of identification and ownership. Everything the ego experiences is known to itself as its own – 'my pleasure' – or something it identifies with – 'I am angry'. This sense of ownership or identification differentiates the individual as a unique being defined by personal boundaries.[27]

In Freud's view, the ego's role is to reconcile instinctual impulses, desires, and tendencies with morality and society's demands. New Age commentators believe that the ego is about expressions of pride and excessive self-esteem or selfish conduct based on mistaken identity. Therefore its effect on the body and mind is negative. Such interpretation is somewhat consistent with the definition of the phenomenal self, the *ahaṃkāra*, saturated with a sense of self-importance, self-perception, or pride – *abhimāna*. However, it values the ego as a negative factor in a one-sided and reductive manner. Unlike this New Age definition, the phenomenal self in yoga asserts responsibility and ownership of its actions and chooses where to turn the gaze: towards the world of conditioned phenomena or Self-realisation through dismantling misconceptions imposed on the true Self. This pride to which the concept of *abhimāna* refers can be interpreted in a modern perspective also in the sense of respect: the self-respect of the yogi, consideration for his or her own needs, assertiveness, respect for the other, and consideration for them. These may be sources of strength and power to overcome the causes of distress and ignorance, of course, assuming that the yogi chooses to turn their back on the destructive aspects of pride, including arrogance or selfishness.

Nevertheless, the sense of I-am-ness is not an enemy that should be avoided or repressed. Its function is temporary, and it is a positive and substantive one. Without it, it is impossible to build hospitals, develop productive agriculture, construct homes, create art, educate values, or alleviate the burden of human suffering.[28] The sense of I-am-ness is the most significant factor in one's decision to embark on the path of yoga and to search for liberation. After all, the true Self is already liberated, it is even free from the need for yoga as it abides in yoga from the very beginning.

How, then, does contemporary Western modern culture influence and shape the yoga practitioner's sense of I-am-ness? How do these influences bolster the sense of self-identity as I-am-ness, producing various residues within it that accumulate karma and encourage its habitual tendency to aggrandise and sustain itself? And how can dealing with these influences through yoga dilute the sense of I-am-ness in order to clear and still the mind on the way to realising the true Self?

Western liberal society emphasises the realisation of the individual's potential and all of the possibilities for personal well-being. These values are closely related to the autonomy of the individual, and maximising the sovereignty one has over one's life; what is emphasised is personal conduct that relies on every possible resource, including emotional, mental, and physical mechanisms, that can be turned into an advantage in the world. Cultivating these values is seen as a goal in itself, creating a system in which the individual acts, reflects on its actions, and values its abilities for independence and freedom. Anyone who does not reach their full potential is perceived as being someone engaged in an act of self-betrayal.[29] What is considered important is the individual's investment in educational activities, training, leisure, and consumption. The individual is encouraged to plan programs that will increase their own future value, improving their health and status, and augmenting their economic, mental, and social well-being. These achievements depend on the efforts of the individual; they are seen as being a matter of personal responsibility. An individual's health is seen to derive from the choices they personally make. It seems that these values of contemporary yoga – responsibility, personal conduct, investment in the individual, and realising the possibilities for personal well-being – reflect the principle that personal investment in the present will lead to personal well-being in the future – whether physical–psychological or as a liberation from suffering and misperception of the phenomenal world.

Contemporary yoga offers the individual a wide variety of physical and spiritual streams. It allows people to shape their identity and lifestyle with various options and different yoga frameworks that exist in the 'market'. These may be psychologically articulated into statements such as 'My egoism is rational', or 'I have a right to happiness, freedom, and inner peace'. In many yoga classes, the language is saturated with expressions emphasising personal choices, such as 'Thank you for coming to practice today', or 'This is your time'. Contemporary yoga considers the individual responsible for making choices, and accepting the consequences and the risks involved in making those choices. For example, in the registration forms for yoga classes, practitioners are asked to release the teacher from any liability for injury or accidents during the class.

There is no doubt, therefore, that physical yoga has become a commercial, lucrative, and profitable product. Yoga magazines and newspapers feature an extensive array of lessons, special programs for teachers and stylishly designed yoga clothes, and alternative Western beauty and consumption standards. The practitioner, the 'consumer', chooses the yoga stream or style of physical yoga to which they are best suited in order to 'reach the practice mat', and to take responsibility for their body and its limitations. Therefore, the practice of yoga is perceived as an investment in the individual, a form of human capital, and a long-term investment. It is clear, therefore, that in the way yoga is presented and practiced in the West there is an overlap between its content and the values of Western liberalism.

Godrej believes that many yoga practitioners may be perfect representatives of neo-liberalism: autonomous, self-disciplined, driven by sensible choices, responsible for their health, comfortable with competitive market conditions, interested in driving the free market economy and investing in themselves.[30] I suppose some readers will argue, and rightly so, that there is nothing wrong with striving to be a self-disciplined person responsible for one's own health and investing in one's own well-being. However, we must not forget that neo-liberal culture produces inequality and a form of passive citizenship that is reduced to a person's self-concern. It sanctifies consumption and entrepreneurship, and elevates the atomised individual as a solution to all social problems, while liberating the individual from a broader sense of political, economic, and social responsibility. According to such a culture of self-concern, problems such as unemployment, poor health, and poverty indicate a lack of responsibility and a lack of self-control, rather than indicating an unjust socio-economic order.[31]

In this kind of culture, yoga practitioners may indeed be the perfect representatives of neo-liberalism. They may find themselves inadvertently encouraging and directing consumption and passive, undemocratic, and unequal political behaviour. They may encourage a form of self-discipline that makes the individual responsible for promoting their health through the consumption of yoga options, and to equate success in life with self-control. Many may be in denial or completely unaware of the truth of their complicity in this socio-economic order, in which the poor, the unemployed, the overweight, and the unhealthy are blamed for their condition; likewise, they foster the perception that a lack of equality ostensibly derives from personal choices and a lack of cultivation of the discipline required to achieve self-fulfilment. The activity that leads to the optimisation of the body and its health becomes the marker for a productive and diligent citizen. Self-improvement and self-help have become a civic duty and are effectively used as a form of resilience mitigating against social injustice, gender inequality, or crime. This kind of mind-set contributes to a pervasive political indifference, a disregard for social injustice, and a focus on the freedom to consume, to choose the yoga that best suits you, and to acquire the associated merchandise. Such a practitioner may be so immersed in themself and in their practice that they have no ability or interest to see the broader socio-economic picture. In a neo-liberal culture, these are the sedimentary materials that underlie and dominate the phenomenal gaze of the yoga practitioner, in such a way that they have become transparent and invisible to the practitioner. They thereby betray the true intent of yoga, which should seek to cultivate and achieve a clear discerning gaze free from such occluding materials.

Of course, these statements are not valid for all contemporary yoga practitioners. As expressed in texts such as the Bhagavad Gītā or Patañjali's *Yogasūtra*, the ethics and psychology of yoga may be useful to challenge and dismantle the neo-liberal concepts to which one adheres. These concepts and the perceptions they encourage are like a kind of 'garment' that clothes the ego, mental layers that solidify and bolster it. Cultivating the moral rules of yoga – such as *satya*, the pursuit of truth, sincerity, *aparigraha*, non-possession, or non-accumulation of possessions – may encourage attitudes and behaviours that inhibit neo-liberal values and neutralise its cultural effects. This is the case, for example, in the practice of *vairāgya*, as dispassion or uninvolved awareness, and particularly *pratyāhāra*, where the senses are withdrawn from sense objects. Another effective practice is to cultivate *ahiṃsā* – non-violence, an unwillingness to engage in aggression. *Ahiṃsā* was one of the significant foundations of Gandhi's teaching and way of life. It challenged a world saturated with violence and generated a search for new social and moral structures that would replace the striving for material possessions, consumption, and competition. Gandhi translated the yogic value of non-violence into an active strategy. *Ahiṃsā* gained broad solidarity in India, brought about political, social, and economic changes, and eventually led to India's independence and liberation from British rule.

When individuals tread the path of yoga, they carry their personal history with them, their character, their internal conflicts, and an array of defence mechanisms. In addition, they also bring with them the socio-cultural influences that are prevalent around them, which shape a range of self-perceptions, values, and beliefs through which they see the world.

Even when the individual treads the path of yoga, they must consider the place of the ego in their yoga practice as well. Trivedi argues that the approach of yoga promotes a personal or subjective attitude towards the goal, whether it be well-being or liberation, and therefore the reader or practitioner of yoga will have a greater tendency to believe that they are 'agents of action' on their journey toward silencing the mind; as goal-oriented beings they are able to monitor their environment, select and carry out goal-directed actions effectively, and take responsibility for the results. The sense of being an agent of action therefore implies the ability to perceive and change one's environment. The basis for this perception is the ego. Unlike yoga, Sāṃkhya philosophy is characterised by an impersonal and passive approach towards its purpose and the mind. The reader or practitioner of Sāṃkhya will therefore be less inclined to see themself as an agent of action.[32]

Trivedi's quantitative analysis of key concepts related to the individual subject in the *Yogasūtra* and *Sāṃkhyakārikā* has led him to produce a catalogue which indicates whether these occur 'slightly' or 'more' in the text. This catalogue of vital yoga concepts is sorted according to the frequency of their appearance and dominance. For example, practice is a dominant theme in the *Yogasūtra*, and the concept of a phenomenal self is often attached to the theme practice. Trivedi links the concept of centralisation to the idea of an active agent. He sees the phenomenon of centralisation as an expression of the projecting of metaphysical concepts on an individual ego, as expressed by adding an 'I' to a particular statement concerning practice, belief, or action. That is, 'the *buddhi* has the potential for purity', may be converted to 'the *buddhi* of the individual has the potential for purity'. Such a change also makes it possible to project a particular practice and state of consciousness onto the individual, as expressed in the sentence 'the individual's *prāṇa* is in harmony with the mind' (as opposed to the sentence '*prāṇa* is in harmony with the mind'). It would be worth noting sentences that have a centralisation associated with the ego because adding 'I' to metaphysical concepts turns them into psychological concepts that pertain to the individual. Hence an insufficient understanding of yoga practice driven by the phenomenal self may solidify the ego and intensify its tendency to believe that it is a true Self as an agent of action. This feeling may be tremendous and intoxicating, and accompany its actions and yoga practice. Eventually, such a practitioner will feel unwanted feelings of pride, competitiveness, arrogance, and power. These are, of course, signs on the roadmap of yoga that indicate the ego itself.

Rāga and *dveṣa*

The next causes of distress (the *kleśa*s) are pairs of opposites: attraction and desire (*rāga*), or 'moving toward', as opposed to rejection and aversion (*dveṣa*), or 'moving apart'. In sūtra 2.7, Patañjali writes: 'Attraction stems from a pleasant experience'. And in sūtra 2.8, he adds: 'Rejection arises from a painful experience'. It can be said simply that *rāga* is the desire for pleasurable events and objects of desire, and *dveṣa* is the avoidance or rejection of unfortunate events and objects that may cause suffering.

The inner movements of attraction and avoidance, which occur in the mind of the individual, are closely related to the events and objects of pleasure and pain stored in one's memory and the circumstances in which they have occurred. For example, pleasant memories of the past will impel one to replicate these moments of pleasure in the present and future. We are attached to them, whether consciously or unconsciously, because of the hold the past has on us. Unconscious attachment is related to the dormant subliminal imprints and their emotional burden, and they have the potential to activate the phenomenal self, the ego, and motivate it to act out. Psychologically, the sense of the ego precedes attachments, for the 'I' is the beneficiary or the one experiencing distress. The yogi transcends these two causes of affliction by freeing themself from their grip.

Attraction and rejection as mental movements are expressed in varying intensities and emotional qualities. Attraction may range, for example, from relief to joy, or from lust to arousal. Rejection, too, may be expressed as a range of emotions: for example, from being scared to terror, and from irritation to rage. Attraction and rejection are a pair of complementary opposites. When desire for a particular object develops in the mind, it can simultaneously generate a wish to reject the object of desire, and vice versa. For example, if we are on a diet, craving a favourite food such as chocolate also engenders the wish to avoid it. In certain circumstances, attraction and rejection may coexist as 'mixed feelings', such as the mix of love and hate that a young person may feel toward high school, or a love that is accompanied by pain due to longing or dependence on a lover. In the experience of mixed feelings, a basic friction is created between the *kleśa*s, and it is expressed as an internal conflict that produces pain and tension. It is this vast range of emotions that makes the suggested psychological reading of the *Yogasūtra* and the *Sāṃkhyakārikā* valid and significant.

Abhiniveśa

And here we come to the last *kleśa*, the fear of death (*abhiniveśa*). Sūtra 2.9 reads: 'Clinging to life affects even the wise; it is an inherent tendency.'[33] That is, even the wise have a basic instinct of self-preservation. Patañjali teaches us about wisdom using the Sanskrit root *vid,* which means 'to know', hence the wise ones within the context of this sūtra are scholars. Their knowledge was acquired through a valid and correct means of knowledge derived from inference (*anumāna*), testimony (*āgama*), and direct perception (*pratyakṣa*). These processes are mentioned in sūtra 1.7 as mental processes that should be brought to stillness. Thus, the wise ones will be equipped with the 'right' knowledge, but their mind will still be preoccupied by subtle processes that should be brought to cessation. *Abhiniveśa* is one of these mental processes.

The cessation of these processes also concerns the *kleśa* of the instinctive will to live, and it is contrary to our most intuitive self-perception. The contradiction between the desire to still the mind and the instinct to live teaches us about the temporality of things and events, including of life itself. What has come into being will also decay, and everything must be completely relinquished for the sake of Self-realisation. Without a deep understanding of this truth of impermanence, life is characterised by an anxious search for certainty and caught up in a constant cycle of becoming, of change and decay. Life is bound up with the fear of death, which feeds the other causes of affliction: attachment, aversion, and the sense of I-am-ness.

As stated in sūtra 2.6, the sense of I-am-ness or personality is nothing but a product of the misidentification between the seer and the power of seeing. The seer is a synonym for the true Self (*puruṣa)*, while the power or mechanism of sight is the ever-changing mind. It is an apparatus of vision or dynamic perception, and its faculty of intelligence is the *buddhi.* The *buddhi* perceives the world of phenomena and reflects its image (after its impressions have been received through the senses and processed by the cognitive faculty, *manas*) to the true Self, the seer. The *buddhi* precedes the sense of I-am-ness in that the former's mistaken identification solidifies and undergoes individuation, and the ego produces its own distinct self-identity. Within this development, the ego experiences itself as a living creature, and with this experience arises the fear of death.

Mental imprints

The underlying psychology of the *kleśa*s is a vast expanse of *saṃskāras*, dormant mental imprints that are etched in one's mind and remain concealed. These imprints have the potential to become active when triggered by external or internal stimuli, which may cause the mind to act. The action that is the outcome of these mental imprints is what is called karma.

In the *Bṛhadāraṇyaka Upaniṣad,* one of the early Upaniṣads which are ancient Sanskrit texts of spiritual teaching and ideas of Hinduism,[34] a description of the concept of karma is presented in the context of morality. Karma, according to this description, is what determines a causal and moral relation between action and consequence in a given social situation: 'What a man turns out to be depends on how he acts and on how he conducts himself. If his actions are good, he will turn into something good. If his actions are bad, he will turn into something bad. A man turns into something good by good action and into something bad by bad action.'[35]

According to this principle, one's personal fate and all that transpires in one's life, family relations, and broader social environment are the consequence of all of one's actions. There is no system of reward and punishment imposed on a person by any divine entity, and there is no system that tests the righteous and the wicked for their morality and faith. This means that one's current ethical or non-ethical actions are directly influenced by one's previous actions and their consequences, and these will also determine the quality of one's future actions. Thus, the residue from actions, experiences, and past events accumulate into mental imprints. The mental imprints are like undercurrents beneath the layers of mind, and they feed the *kleśa*s when certain circumstances transpire that are the basis for further actions. Their consequences will reproduce mental imprints, and these will activate and manifest through the five mental processes (*vṛtti*s), or as the causes of affliction. As noted, such mental processes or causes of affliction are preceded by mental imprints. The potential of mental imprints to spur action is based on an idea of causation that is conceived as a kind of circular process that has no apparent beginning.[36]

The *saṃskāra*s are the hidden imprints in our unconscious, the residue of our daily experiences – internal and external, desirable and undesirable.[37] These imprints are assumed to be our basic self-perceptions, attitudes, and beliefs that lie in the depths of our memory, and are composed of emotions, sensations, and thoughts about past experiences or events.[38]

The mental imprints are interrelated, and organised into configurations, attributes, and tendencies. Their configuration will depend on the intensity of the mental imprints and their respective intensities in creating certain habitual tendencies, attitudes, thoughts, desires, and images. Making a decision, for example, may seem to be a completely conscious process, but it is in fact influenced by mental imprints and the way they are organised. The formation of mental imprints is at the core of one's character, behaviour, and way of thinking. These configurations are termed *vāsanā*s.

The *vāsanā*s, the tendencies of one's personality and imprints of thought and behaviour, are related to the causes of affliction, the *kleśa*s, as these affect human behaviour. The intensity of each *kleśa*, its effect and the feelings it engenders in various circumstances, all shape the *vāsanā*s. They are a collection of modes of behaviour driven by rejection, attachment, fear of death, identification, and the emotions that are associated with them. *Vāsanā*s are expressed and manifested by means of the causes of affliction. For example, a particular person may develop a tendency to be submissive and obedient to avoid rejection and develop a sense of belonging. The greater that person's fear of social rejection, the more significant could be their submissiveness and obedience.

Psychologist John Welwood describes the case of a patient who regularly experienced anger and frustration in her marriage.[39] In a state of despair, she turned to her guru for advice. He advised her not to be angry with her husband but to treat him with generosity and friendship. On the face of it, this advice is in line with Patañjali's teachings: 'Through practice of friendliness [*maitrī*], compassion [*karuṇā*], joy [*muditā*], and equanimity [*upekṣā*] toward the happy, the suffering, the virtuous, and the unvirtuous (respectively), consciousness is clarified.'[40]

She felt relieved by the guru's advice, for it suited her defensiveness against feelings of anger. Anger frightened her; she felt threatened by it and refused to deal with it. The instruction to express feelings of friendship and compassion was for her a spiritual bypass. But this only intensified her sense of helplessness and her frustration with married life.

The guru's advice was compatible with interpretations that consider *pratipakṣa bhāvanā* a method of adopting a contrary position to negative and destructive impulses in order to extinguish them and replace the negative tendency with another mental attitude. This is in contrast to what I view, following Vyāsa,[41] to be a more accurate interpretation of *pratipakṣa bhāvanā* based on the principle of thinking or reflecting on the consequences of one's negative thoughts and actions, and the distress they may cause. However, the guru's method was not effective for Welwood's patient.

According to Welwood, the advice was given to her without taking into account her difficulty in suppressing and managing her intense anger. It turns out that she had been abused by her father in childhood. Whenever she expressed anger about the way he treated her, he would slap her and send her to her room. He wanted to silence her expressions of anger and delegitimise them. Because of her fear of her father, she learned to suppress her anger, and instead tried to please others and be a 'good girl.'[42]

Her father's severe reaction left an intense impression on her, and as a result certain *saṃskāra*s were etched in her mind, such as 'when I'm angry, I'm in danger', 'I'm unwanted when I'm angry', and 'I'm not loved when

I'm angry'. These *saṃskāras* led to a *vāsanā*, a behaviour pattern of avoiding anger and confrontation. This pattern made her submissive, always seeking to please others in order to gain their affection and feel a sense of belonging. According to Karen Horney, the suppression of emotions and impulses associated with fear and aggression can therefore be an attempt to avoid confrontation, since confrontation may jeopardise affection and approval. Confrontation may also harm the attempt to create harmonious unity.[43]

I have so far examined two terms associated with the phenomenal self: the *ahaṃkāra* of Sāṃkhya philosophy and the *asmitā* of Patañjali's yoga. These may be perceived as synonyms, of similar significance. Patañjali does not use the term *ahaṃkāra* at all, while Vyāsa[44] uses it twice which implies that he sees the two terms as synonymous. If there is indeed a difference between the two concepts, it is in my view a difference of emphasis. The notion of *ahaṃkāra* emphasises the action and misconception of the performer of the action, while the notion of *asmitā* emphasises the sense of identity that is supposedly separate from other entities or the identification with feelings, sensations, and beliefs.

The phenomenal self is like a parent who identifies with their children, who for example ties themself to their achievements and sometimes even takes ownership over them. It is also like a soldier who identifies with their homeland to the point of being willing to sacrifice their life for it. In everyday language it can be said that the individual believes that there is a tangible centre or focal point of being that they call 'I'. The phenomenal self is likened to an autonomous centre of command or control, it is the ego, a constant focal point of identity that represents the individual, and they feel that it owns their body or mind. To identify with this centre or with the phenomenal self, as if it were the true Self, entails a sense of connection to people, feelings, emotions and ideas to the point of feeling that It is similar to them and a belief that they represent It.

However, this centre is nothing but an existential apparatus associated with the causes of distress: ignorance, attraction, rejection, and the fear of death. The phenomenal self is perceived as autonomous, and takes command and ownership even though complete control over reality is impossible. Similarly, the phenomenal self feels that it is separate from others and also in its very interiority as if there is a constant internal dialogue about desires, aspirations, actions, and feelings.

The phenomenal self undergoes a vast sequence of experiences and events (this is due to the endless activity of the *guṇas*), so it continues to develop and identify with the feeling that it is the one who does and acts, and that everything occurs and happens to it and for it. This endless activity creates the illusion of one continuous and incessant movement so that the phenomenal self solidifies and condenses. In such a condition, it has no interval or time window for understanding the identification error in which it is situated. It does not become aware of its true Self which remains concealed by the thoughts, actions, and events that seemingly define its identity.

Notes

1 M. Burley, *Classical Samkhya and Yoga: An Indian Metaphysics of Experience (Routledge Hindu Studies Series)* (London: Routledge, 2012), 115.

2 M. Jakubczak, "The Sense of Ego-maker in Classical Sāṃkhya and Yoga: Reconsideration of Ahaṃkāra," *Cracow Indological Studies* 10 (2008), 246.

3 D. Heaven, "Location of the mind remains a mystery," *New Scientist*, 22 August 2012, available at https://www.newscientist.com/article/dn22205-location-of-the-mind-remains-a-mystery/#ixzz5xf8iUeuv, retrieved 7 August 2021.

4 This refers to the first component or product of the world of phenomena (before it comes into being, the world of phenomena exists only as a potentiality).

5 Kārikā 24 in Burley, *Classical Samkhya and Yoga*, 169.

6 Kārikā 22 in Burley, *Classical Samkhya and Yoga*, 168.

7 Kārikā 38 in Burley, *Classical Samkhya and Yoga*, 172.

8 Kārikā 12 in G.J. Larson, R.S. Bhattacharya and K. Potter, eds., *The Encyclopaedia of Indian Philosophies, Volume 4: Samkhya, A Dualist Tradition in Indian Philosophy* (Princeton, NJ: Princeton University Press, 1987), 154.

9 Y. Grinshpon, *Silence and Liberation in Classical Yoga* (Tel Aviv: Ministry of Defense, Israel, 2002), 92.

10 H.P. Trivedi, "Sense of Agency: The Mind in Samkhya and Yoga" (MA thesis, The State University of New Jersey, New Brunswick, NJ, 2017), 7.

11 Larson et al., eds., *The Encyclopaedia of Indian Philosophies*, 157.

12 Bhattacharya (1875–1940) was a scholar and academic who focused on the concept of freedom in reference to reason, desire and emotion.

13 K.C. Bhattacharya, *Studies in Philosophy*, vol. I (Delhi: Motilal Banarsidass, 1983), 183.

14 Bhattacharya, *Studies in Philosophy*, vol. I, 184.

15 M. Williams, *A Sanskrit-English Dictionary Etymologically and Philologically Arranged with Special Reference to Cognate Indo-European Languages* (Varanasi: Indica, 1996), 124.

16 Williams, *A Sanskrit-English Dictionary*, 124.

17 Burley, *Classical Samkhya and Yoga*, 169.

18 Kārikā 30 in Burley, *Classical Samkhya and Yoga*, 170.

19 G. Feuerstein, *The Philosophy of Classical Yoga* (Rochester, VT: Inner Traditions, 1996), 58.

20 Bhattacharya, *Studies in Philosophy*, vol. I, 183.

21 Bryant, *The Yoga Sutras of Patañjali*, 187.

22 Raveh, *Exploring the Yogasutra*, 130.

23 Raveh, *Exploring the Yogasutra*, 130.

24 This metaphor is a paraphrase of the famous Indian illustration of the rope and the serpent: in the dim night light, the rope is perceived as a snake that a person carries in his memory from another event and is terrified. Although the person has identified the rope and breaks free from the fear, such a reaction may be recorded or etched into their mind.

25 C. Trungpa, *Cutting through Spiritual Materialism* (Boston: Shambhala, 1987), 22.

26 G. Ifergan, *The Man from Samye: Longchenpa on Praxis, Its Negation and Liberation* (New Delhi: Aditya Prakashan, Aditya Prakashan, 2014), 133–134.

27 M. Jakubczak, "The Collision of Language and Metaphysics in the Search for Self- Identity: on 'ahamkara' and 'asmita' in Samkhya-Yoga," *Argument: Biannual Philosophical Journal*, 1(1) (2011), 47.

28 Raveh, *Philosophical Threads in Patanjali's Yoga*, 84.

29 Godrej, "The Neoliberal Yogi", 779.

30 Godrej, "The Neoliberal Yogi", 785.

31 Godrej, "The Neoliberal Yogi", 785.

32 Trivedi, "Sense of Agency," 2.

33 Bryant, *The Yoga Sutras of Patañjali*, 191.

34 Works composed in India from the middle of the first millennium BCE.

35 P. Olivelle, trans., *The Early Upaniṣads* (Delhi: Oxford University Press, 1998), 121, chapter 4, section 4, verses 5–6.

36 N. Mishra, "Saṁskāras in Yoga Philosophy and Western Psychology," *Philosophy East and West*, 2 (4) (1953), 309.

37 G. Feuerstein, *Encyclopedic Dictionary of Yoga* (New York: Paragon House, 1990), 309.

38 Mishra, "Saṁskāras in Yoga Philosophy and Western Psychology,", 314.

39 John Welwood, "Embodying Your Realization: Psychological Work in the Service of Spiritual Development," (unpublished manuscript, no date), https://www.johnwelwood.com/articles/Embodying.pdf, retrieved 23 October 2022. John Welwood (1943–2019) was an American clinical psychologist, one of the leaders in the East-West California Institute of Integral Studies program, University of San Francisco. Since the 1980s he had been integrating Buddhist psychology and meditation in his treatments.

40 Raveh, *Exploring the Yogasutra*, 129.

41 H. Āraṇya, *Yoga Philosophy of Patanjali: Containing His Yoga Aphorisms with Vyasa's Commentary in Original Sanskrit and Annotations Thereon with Copious Hints on the Practice of Yoga* (Calcutta: Calcutta University Press, 1981), 216.

42 Welwood, "Embodying Your Realization," 4–5.

43 Karen Horney (1885–1952), a psychoanalyst, Freud's successor and sharp critic, describes the possible characteristics of such a character in her book: K. Horney, *Our Inner Conflicts: A Constructive Theory of Neurosis* (New York: W.W. Norton, 1992 [1945]), 56–57.

44 See Vyāsa's commentary to sutras 1.45 and 3.47 in Āraṇya, *Yoga Philosophy of Patanjali*, 102, 328.

3 The True Self *Puruṣa*

There is a particular difficulty in writing about the true Self, *puruṣa*, for Patañjali sees it as a transcendental isolated Selfhood. Is it possible to write about such an eternal Self that cannot be equated with the human body, mind, personality, perceptions, thoughts, senses, and actions? What does it mean to conceive of a true Self that is not subject to time, space, and causality as they are known to us; that is essentially ineffable, such that any characteristic or adjective ascribed to it would be nothing but an imposition? In short, we cannot attribute qualities normally associated with the self to the true Self as if it were something finite or changeable. At the same time, we may ascribe qualities of the true Self to something other than it. For example, when I say 'I breathe', the true Self may be mistakenly identified with the breath and the body, which is not possible because it is beyond change and temporality. This statement links the Self with these objects, and such a confusing identification is a form of ignorance, a mistaken entanglement between the true Self and the world of phenomena. In this case, the breath and breathing body's action are ascribed to the true Self, even though the true Self is something quite separate and distinct from them, and is neither dependent on nor conditioned by them. Unlike the transient body, the true Self is an eternal absolute otherness. That is, the use of language and explanations that seek to explain and point to the true Self will be nothing but a collection of mental processes referring to the true Self. If someone says that they use language as a conventional means to give us some idea of the Self such that they can 'point' to it, what exactly would their finger be pointing at?[1]

Yet an intentional avoidance of talking about the Self only because it is an ineffable otherness is itself a mental activity imposed on the Self, mistakenly attributed to it. Any attempt to avoid conceptualising and examining mental activity without distinguishing between the conceptualising mind and the true Self, indicates that the avoidant's mind is still fixed in a given state in a mental process, even though the true Self is independent and free from the mind. In any case, although explanations about the self are not possible, they can still serve as a 'bridge' to the otherness as *pratiprasava* – changing the direction of one's gaze from the world of objects and mental processes towards the mind itself, to its root. One is then oriented toward mental collectedness or composure, and this process is gradually cultivated and perfected over time. The culmination of the process is the dissolution of the phenomenal everyday mind into its source, into the basis of the world of phenomena (*prakṛti*). Usually, the mind is directed outwards – to the world of objects – or toward the inner, mental, and psychological world. Turning towards an object or to a stimulus is usually a conditioned response, such that it is as automatic as the attraction of a metal object to a magnet. Such an encounter may generate a range of conditioned thoughts and behaviours as a reaction. However, once the mental imprints have been desiccated such that they can no longer germinate, the potential for a conditioned reaction is removed and complete stillness is achieved. The yogi's mind returns to the source of the world of phenomena, to the source of materiality, and dissolves in it. At this point the true Self dawns and settles into its nature.

How does Patañjali use the term *puruṣa*? Patañjali uses the notion of Selfhood eight times and also presents synonymous expressions for the Self, mostly of a metaphorical kind, and mostly taken from the empirical world where there is a relationship of sensation, perception, cognition, ownership, and possession. However, he does not provide a full definition of the concept of the true Self in the text of the *Yogasūtra*. Feuerstein believes that, in Patañjali's time, this concept and its meaning were familiar and exceptionally clear, and therefore there was no need to define it. One can learn about the meaning of the true Self as it is depicted in the *Yogasūtra* from the meanings given to it in earlier texts, such as the *Mahābhārata*. In these texts, the 'transcendental identity' of Person or Selfhood is an absolute otherness distinct from the world of phenomena, devoid of features or qualities (*nir-guṇa*), which cannot be literally explained.[2] Moreover, the mind is a developmental product, an evolute that emerges from the world of phenomena, and therefore the true Self is fundamentally different from it.

Patañjali adopts several synonymous and metaphorical concepts from the empirical world – the perception and processing of information obtained through the senses, interpretation of this information, and ownership over these processes. Thus, he seeks to conceptualise what cannot be described or characterised. From such synonymous and metaphorical concepts, the meaning of the true Self becomes apparent but not actual knowledge about the true Self. This is similar to a discourse on a rose, in which essential and detailed information about a rose may be presented but which is incapable of directly conveying the actual smell of its fragrance.

The concepts that link *puruṣa* to vision or sight are the seer (*draṣṭṛ*),[3] the power of the seer (*dṛk-śakti*),[4] the gaze (*dṛśi*),[5] and the pure gaze (*dṛśi-mātra*).[6] According to Vyāsa's commentary,[7] these concepts suggest that *puruṣa* is a pure force of consciousness (or the potential for such a force), a root of awareness that is inherent in every person. It is still, precedes all mental activity, and is free from the world of objects. It is a primordial and independent awareness of the world of phenomena, transcending subjectivity and objectivity. Such awareness is not a pure absence or nothingness, and it cannot be perceived in discursive thinking because there is no discourse in the first place in primordial awareness. Although there is no possible discourse in it, it cannot be turned off.

A key sūtra presenting *puruṣa* as a seer is sūtra 2.17: 'The conjunction (*saṃyoga*) of seer (*draṣṭṛ*) and seen (*dṛśya*) is the cause of that which is to be prevented (i.e., the cause of suffering).'[8] *Puruṣa* 'sees' through the transparent and reflexive intellect (*buddhi*), the faculty of the mind that is closest to *puruṣa*; what is 'seen' is the world of objects. Seeing the objects, *puruṣa* becomes their owner–master. Even though these objects do not exist in the seer at all, *puruṣa* owns them. Despite being external to *puruṣa*, the objects are perceived to be entirely concrete in the mind where vision takes place because of the pure awareness shining on them. Had it not been for the *buddhi*'s capacity for reflection having been enabled in the first place by *puruṣa*, the objects would not have appeared or been seen.

This sūtra's central theme is the erroneous and confusing connection between pure primordial awareness and the world of phenomena. To clarify these concepts and the link between them, I seek to return to the metaphor of the sun and the mirror. The sun is the source of light likened to the pure primordial awareness (the seer) that is inherent in every person. The sun is a constant source of light and heat, independent of what is happening in our world. Heat and light radiate from it, hence its power, as it is impossible to separate the sun from its rays. The sun and its rays are likened to the principle of a pure radiant awareness that is independent of our inner and outer worlds.

The mirror's inherent capacity to reflect is likened to the mind. It represents seeing and seen; the visible world of phenomena can be seen because sunlight is projected onto a mirror, which then projects the light onto the objects that are in front of it, and which are in turn reflected in the mirror. *Puruṣa* too – being as aforesaid pure primordial awareness – shines in the mind, enabling it with the power of perception. However, the mind is not just an instrument or an agent of cognition. Although in practice it only reflects, it mistakenly assumes that it is the source of primordial awareness. In this respect the mind can be likened to a mirror that is stained, hazy, and dusty, where the dust and stains stand for one's concepts, beliefs, judgments, psychological tendencies, and patterns of behaviour, whether conscious or unconscious, positive or negative, through which the world of phenomena (*prakṛti*) is distortedly reflected in one's mind. These occluding substances can lead to distorted perceptions, whether these be in regard to one's own body, or any other object that stands in front of the mirror. What is reflected is therefore distorted in the mind and becomes a source of suffering. The person bound to their sense of I-am-ness is wrong to think that he or she is the one who suffers, because the true Self has nothing to do with this suffering.

Puruṣa 'sees' through the intellect's (*buddhi*) capacity to reflect, which is the mental faulty that is closest to, and shares a tangential point with, *puruṣa*. This tangential point is the lucid transparency of the *buddhi* and the inherent purity of *puruṣa*. I will expand on this later in the discussion. The 'visible' or 'seen' is the world of objects. 'Vision' (*darśana*), in its ordinary sense as perception, is linked to our immediate experience, which occurs when we come into contact with objects. Vision also has another important aspect: insight, as a product of philosophical study, and in meditation and yoga practice. The yogi understands that this kind of vision is a conscious skill of perception in action that culminates in and is reflected through the vision of otherness, *puruṣa* as pure primordial awareness. Furthermore, in the context of the metaphor of the mirror and the sun, the sun is reflected in the mirror that is facing it.

In the context of seeing the otherness, a reading of kārikās 59 and 64 of the *Sāṃkhyakārikā*[9] reveals that the movement of the world of phenomena can be likened to that of a dancer. The dancer appears before the royal witness, the pure primordial awareness (*puruṣa*), and dances before his eyes. Her dance ends when the witness finishes watching her. The actual dance is likened here to the profound philosophical study of Sāṃkhyan analytical meditation, a study whose physical and mental expressions are like a philosophy of negation in action, of all that is not the pure primordial awareness. The dancer, who is likened to the material principle of the world of phenomena (*prakṛti*), engages in a dance that consumes itself; that is, the physical and mental activity is consumed and dismantled. She does not do so for the sake of admiration, applause, or affection. Her dance is like the creation of a series of dynamic sculptures in space. It emerges from a deep yogic meditative concentration entailing a series of movements that leave no residue in the space in which they are performed. The dance activity that consumes itself without any expectations of admiration and applause will therefore not create karma. At the end of the dance, after being seen by *puruṣa*, or rather after seeing him watching her as a witness who sees her, the dancer descends from the stage and converges herself into a state of silence and rest.

Expectations of admiration or applause may arouse the dancer to dance again to recreate the pleasure that accompanies admiration. It is also possible that the expectations for admiration infused within the dance may lead to the production of karma; this would create the foundation for subsequent action when the longing for admiration arises again. These actions may set the dancer into a vicious cycle, in *avidyā*. And so the personal destiny of a person – and perhaps everything that happens in a person's life, in their family and social environment – is nothing but a product of all of their physical and mental actions. Dancing as a negation in action illustrates what it means to dismantle the mind's conditioned and compulsive conceptualisation processes, which occupy and dominate the mind, which prevent it from achieving a clear and direct perception of reality. In this process, the Sāṃkhyan philosopher focuses on the elements of the world of phenomena (*prakṛti*) and examines them one by one. Stemming from a profound insight, the philosopher knows that all of the elements are subject to the constant activity and interactions of the *guṇa*s, in that these are frequently changing in terms of volume, shape, form, or intensity. These frequent changes produce mental processes that dominate and occupy the mind, and thereby distort its perception of reality, thus obstructing any possibility of realising the true Self or pure primordial awareness.

While the metaphor of the dancer stands for negation in action, in which the Sāṃkhyan philosopher dismantles the mind's conditioned and compulsive conceptualisation processes, for the yogi this represents a deep meditative absorption of stilling the mind. With the attainment of supreme stillness in which the mind is denuded of its beliefs, expectations, implications, or defence mechanisms, comes the realisation that '"I" am not (awareness), (awareness) does not belong to me, the "I" is not (awareness).'[10] With this realisation, the mind understands that it is not the source of primordial awareness, just as the mirror that reflects light is not the source of light. Yoga in action shifts the attention to the mirror, focuses it on itself, and polishes it to the point where it is completely free of distortions (including freeing itself from this metaphor that it is like a mirror). The polishing of the mirror, and the continuous and stable understanding that the mirror's natural function is only to reflect since it is itself empty of any object, is what it means to have a mind that has been emptied of mental processes. Such a mind is emptied of the contents that are ignited by the objects it perceives, and it gradually stabilises into this empty yet clear state. To clear the mind of its various contents, it is necessary to shift the gaze from the world of objects and what they generate in mind, to the mind itself. In this way, what is revealed is the distinction between the source of light, which represents the true Self, and the mind that reflects It as a mirror.

These insights – '"I" am not (awareness), (awareness) does not belong to me, the "I" is not (pure awareness)' – reflect the discerning insight. It means that *prakṛti* does not need to behave as if it is *puruṣa*, since continuing to act in this way entails the continuity of ignorance. Such a mind would be preoccupied and dominated by this insight itself. The eyes of the witness (as *puruṣa*) watching the dance reflect the dancer's eyes (as *prakṛti*), that is, the dancer sees her eyes reflected in those of the witness. This interplay of reflections signifies that the discerning wisdom, which is presented as the abysmal difference between them, between *puruṣa* and *prakṛti*, is complete, pure, and devoid of any perceptual error, and not involved with any other activity or objects of the senses. According to the two metaphors – the sun radiating light on the mirror and the dancer dancing in front of the witness who watches – the capacity for reflection is the essential and primary constituent in the world of phenomena that is directed toward pure primordial awareness. The *sattvic* component of the mind – the quality of transparency and purity – contains the reflection of *puruṣa*, but because it remains under the influence of ignorance, continues to produce misconceptions.

Commentators disagree on the issue of reflectivity. For Vyāsa, *puruṣa* is the basis for empirical knowledge due to its reflection in the mind; it is the 'owner' of empirical knowledge. In contrast, Vācaspati Miśra argues that the mind is the basis for perceiving the world of phenomena and its knowledge because *puruṣa* is reflected in the mind. However, the world of phenomena does not serve as an object for *puruṣa* because it is devoid of any tendency to objectification. The two commentators have different perspectives, and the difference stems from the different emphases they give to these two primary principles that make up existence. Vijñānabhikṣu accepts the opinion of Vācaspati Miśra and adds that this reflection is double (*pratibimba*).[11] This idea of double reflection is intriguing and its essence is the mutual reflection between intellect and *puruṣa*. That is, *puruṣa* is reflected in the intellect, and the intellect is also reflected in *puruṣa*. The intellect reflects objects in front of it and *puruṣa*, and it in turn is reflected in *puruṣa* so that *puruṣa* becomes the bearer of knowledge. However, *puruṣa* does not go through any process or lose its status as a pure and unchanging witness. Its power of awareness is intrinsic, just as the diverse and dynamic reflections in the mirror cannot affect the sun itself or change it.

I am interested in examining the interpretations of sūtra 2.20[12] that have been made by these commentators in regard to the reflection of *puruṣa* in the intellect. I will do so with reference to the enigmatic kārikā 66, which is directly related to the simile of the dancer and the king, the witness spectator watching her: 'the indifferent one (namely, awareness), thinks, "I have seen her." The other (namely, materiality) thinks, "I have been seen," and ceases. Though the two continue to be in proximity with one another, no new transformations take place.'[13] This simile of Īśvarakṛṣṇa, author of the *Sāṃkhyakārikā*, is enigmatic both because of the way he presents the matter of reflection as 'his eyes that reflect her eyes', and because of the personification of the ontological principles of Sāṃkhya, *puruṣa* and *prakṛti*.

What is the meaning of 'his eyes that reflect her eyes'? In the intimate moment, still, clear, and naked of any mental content, the dancer is fully revealed to the pure witness, as is the power of awareness that emanates from him. At the same time, the dancer's face is turned towards the witness, thereby seeing herself reflected in his eyes. She uses a passive form of language, 'I have been seen', in the sense that seeing *puruṣa* does not result from any voluntary action or coercion, and she does not act physically or mentally in order to be reflected. The thought 'I have been seen' is a non-verbal recognition and is only given as a verbal expression in the text by the writer. This is likened to a mother that recognises her child without any notion occurring in her mind, such as, 'here is my son'. *Puruṣa*, being a pure witness from whom the power of awareness always emanates and is projected, is like a 'seer' who is always there, just like the sun that always radiates light.

Although the power of awareness derives from *puruṣa*, from which it is always emanated and projected, Sāṃkhyan philosophers tend to oppose the idea that *puruṣa* is aware of any specific object, phenomenon, or event, or alternatively that a process of objectification takes place at all. That is, *puruṣa* does not 'perceive' the world of phenomena as the mind perceives it. Being a pure and utterly indifferent witness, *prakṛti* – or in this context the dancer – is the one on whom *puruṣa* casts Its light (like the light coming from the sun that is always there), and it is not *prakṛti* who sees It from any active or intentional act. Consequently, the thought 'I have seen her' is attributed to the spectator, to *puruṣa*, in the sense that this power of awareness is always present and radiated, just like the sunlight falling on a mirror. The statement therefore does not arise, or is not consciously articulated, within *puruṣa*, but rather is a personification of Its power of consciousness. And so in the intimate moment, still, clear, and naked of any mental content, the dancer as the mind is exposed to the pure witness. The power of consciousness emanating from It is projected onto the dancer by Itself with no particular intention of being aware of her. When her face is turned toward It, she sees herself reflected in Its eyes. The confusing identification between *puruṣa* and *prakṛti* – that is, the connection between pure primordial awareness and the world of phenomena – needs to be understood as a misidentification so that its formation can be dismantled, but also to understand the power relations between possessions (*prakṛti*) and owner (*puruṣa*).[14]

I would like to understand the essence of *puruṣa* according to the synonyms and metaphors that Patañjali attributes to It. How is *puruṣa*'s ownership (*svāmin*, *grahīt*) expressed? Despite *puruṣa*'s indifference, in the sense that It does not perform any appropriating action in the world of phenomena, It is presented as the owner of phenomena since It is reflected as a pure primordial awareness in the mind. There, in the mind, sight occurs as an active experience when in contact with any object. Were it not for this reflection, objects would not be perceived and experienced. *Puruṣa* is, therefore, an exclusive 'seer'.

The pure primordial awareness itself is reflected and contained in the ordinary mind directed towards a particular object, and in the ideas and images we have about it. One way or another, it is impossible to perceive or experience them without *puruṣa*, the primordial and pure awareness, which illuminates the contents of mind reflected in it. However, at the same time, the ordinary mind sees *puruṣa* as having a mental content or intention, thus mistakenly thinking that it is itself the source of awareness: 'I am *puruṣa*' or 'my *puruṣa*'. Thus, it would continue to produce mental processes (*vṛtti*).

The view that holds *puruṣa* as the owner of *prakṛti* poses a certain tension. Usually, the creation of an object naturally confers ownership of it. A theological equivalent of this kind of relationship appears, for example, in the biblical phrase 'Blessed be Abram by God Most High, Possessor of heaven and earth',[15] from which we learn that the Creator is the owner of creation, and it is his property. As a result, if the mind, the vital component of *prakṛti*, is not the owner, then it does not act independently because it is subordinated to the possessor. If *puruṣa* is passive and has no intentionality, that is, It does not have mental states projected into the mind (that is, thoughts, beliefs, desires, or hopes), thence, It can't be the owner of actions and mental content and yet It is perceived as the owner of everything that happens in the mind. However, It would then also be the owner of actions in the mind that operates in the world of mental and physical phenomena, *prakṛti*, because it is impossible to perceive or experience them without *puruṣa* as the unintentionally projected awareness, which illuminates the contents of the mind reflected in it. These states of affairs are not entirely clear, for how can it be that *prakṛti* is the performer of actions but is not their owner? How can we understand this and undo the tension it represents?

To do this, we return to the metaphor of the sun, the mirror, and the world of objects. The static sun is a constant source of light and heat independent of what is happening in our world. It is likened to *puruṣa*. The light and heat radiating from it are likened to pure primordial awareness, which radiate (*citi-śakti) without* any dependence on what is happening in our inner and outer world, *prakṛti*. The sun warms and illuminates, and is an active essential principle, without any intentionality. By its very nature, the sun could be understood to own an infinity of processes that take place in our world that would not happen without it, including daylight, solar energy, and the process of photosynthesis. Like the sun, pure primordial awareness is the owner of everything in the world of phenomena. It 'experiences' these occurrences, It embodies and underlies them even though they do not affect It at all.

A reading of kārikās 19 and 20[16] reveals that *puruṣa* is an isolated, indifferent, inactive witness, meaning It is not subject to causality – It is pure awareness. This motif of purity (*śuddhi*) appears in sūtra 3.56, which teaches that when the *sattva* quality is completely dominant, and the intellect (*buddhi*) and *puruṣa* are equal in their purity, liberation will occur.[17] That is, with the absolute overcoming of the causes of distress and pain (*kleśa*s), the discerning wisdom and the intellect's *sattvic* quality dominates the mind. There is then transparency, serenity, and purity in the intellect, in a way that is similar to the absolute purity of *puruṣa*.[18] This resemblance between the pure primordial awareness and the *sattvic* intellect allows for the closest intimacy between them so that a person can 'see one's Self', one's essence as a *puruṣa*, as a pure primordial awareness utterly distinct from the psycho-physical components of their mind. However, although there may be this similarity between the true Self as pure primordial awareness and the *sattvic* intellect, they are not entirely identical. A skilled yogi may distinguish between them. Here, the difference is that the *sattvic buddhi* is a component of the phenomenal mind which, even its purified state, is still subjected to the activity of the *guṇa*s insofar as *sattva* is actively dominant, while *puruṣa* is neither active nor changing. That said, the similarity can definitely be employed to enable liberation.

The purity of the two is similar but not identical. *Puruṣa* is purified of any routine ordinary activity, of any object or individual subject, of anything that might interrupt Its eternal silence. According to Vācaspati Miśra,[19] purity is freedom from the cycle of birth and death (*saṃsāra*), meaning freedom from day-to-day existence, and any transmigrating or wandering within it. According to Vyāsa,[20] purity is also the absence of experiences of pain or pleasure. A pure mind is not dominated at all by the causes of affliction, nor by their active and actual expression on a daily basis. Furthermore, it does not exhibit the quality of *rajas* (attraction to an object of pleasure) or the quality of *tamas* (rejection or avoidance of an object for fear of experiencing pain).

Under the influence of Sāṃkhyan meditation – being a philosophy of negation in action that consumes itself to a state of absence – and under the influence of training in deep yogic meditative absorption which consumes itself until the mind comes to a halt – the mind is 'cleansed' of any activity caused by the two *guṇas*, *tamas* and *rajas*. The mind then is dominated and occupied by a state in which the *buddhi* is *sattvic* – that is, calm and transparent. *Rajas*, the craving for knowledge, and *tamas*, as lethargy, are no longer dominating it. Consequently, the yogi comes to know the Self as their true nature and the meaning of abiding in a pure primordial awareness that is entirely different from existence as a psycho-physical entity. The yogi thereby comes to realise something that was previously unknown to them or hidden from their eyes, and thereby gains the insight – 'this is who I am'.

However, as soon as such a statement or the like arises in the mind of the yogi, the thirst for existential certainty becomes evident. Such a sentence in itself violates the dominance of the *sattvic* quality of the *buddhi* through the intrusion of the *rajasic* quality, the desire for certainty or identity, and with this intrusion the silence of the *sattvic buddhi* is stirred into a mental process. One can realise the eternal silence or inactivity of the Self, the pure primordial awareness, only in the absence of any such verbal activity as 'this is who I am', in the presence of a deep and abiding stillness that pervades the yogi's purified mind. Although this state of consciousness dominated by the *sattva* constituent is supreme, the yogi seeking liberation is required to abandon it and remain in their true Self, a state in which the *guṇas* have no role. The Self has never been bound and, therefore, has not been liberated. Only the mind is bound and liberated.[21]

In this state of liberation, the mind is entirely pure. It is a mind endowed with potentiality that does not come into action or manifestation. It is not dominated by the *guṇas*, even the most refined one (the *sattvic* constituent of deep and peaceful clarity of mind).

The multiplicity of *puruṣas*

I would like now to discuss another theme related to *puruṣa* – the multiplicity of *puruṣas*. This multiplicity is implied in sūtra 2.22 and in Vyāsa's commentary upon it: 'Even though "she" (prakṛti, the seen) ceases to exist in respect of "him" (a certain puruṣa) for whose sake "her" purpose has been achieved, "she" continues to exist for others (for other puruṣa-s who are still afflicted by avidyā), being as "she" is of a common nature.'[22] With the attainment of a completely still mind and with it liberation, *prakṛti* and the mind – being the central component of *prakṛti* – cease to actively exist for one who has been liberated and settled in their true nature, their true Self, *puruṣa*. *Prakṛti* and the mind continue to exist only for those others who are still trapped in the tangled and confusing weave between *puruṣa* and *prakṛti*, a weave that, as mentioned earlier, produces ignorance, an erroneous worldview, and suffering. Raveh sees 'others' (*anya*) as meaning all those who exist in *avidyā*, in the tangled and confusing fabric between *puruṣa* and *prakṛti*. Bryant, like Raveh, also sees them as unliberated *puruṣas*.[23] In his interpretation, Vyāsa clearly indicates two types of *puruṣas*: the skilled (*kuśala*) that is free, and the unskilled that has not yet been liberated and continues to experience the world of phenomena and remains bound to it.[24] In addition to these two, there is another type of *puruṣa*, and it is the sublime, sovereign god (*Īśvara*) that is associated with the theistic dimension of yoga. These form of *puruṣa* will be discussed in more detail in what follows.

The existence of a multiplicity of *puruṣas* is even more clearly stated in kārikā 18: 'As a result of different patterns of birth, death and different abilities and the lack of continuity between the various activities [these] constitute the multiplicity of *puruṣas*; also because of the prevailing counter opposed forces between the three *guṇas*.'[25] Obviously, human beings are born at different times and have different traits and qualities; they act differently and die at different times. From this we learn that each of them is a centre of Selfhood or awareness, which is unique to each person. This idea of the multiplicity of *puruṣas*, however, does not reconcile with what follows in kārikā 19, according to which *puruṣa* is an awareness, an aloof and inactive witness.[26] Likewise, the classical Upaniṣadic view of the true Self also sees a core singular Selfhood in all individuals.

How can these two positions on multiplicity and singularity of *puruṣa* be settled, if at all? The multiplicity of subjects entails that they all have differing objective content from one another. However, since all of these contents are abandoned, dismantled, or fade away, what remains is a mind in a state of absence, that has been emptied of all the attachments and aversions that could potentially cause someone to act conditionally, and thereby becomes a vacuity in which nothing exists. If no object exists as mental content, then there is no perceiver subject in that vacuity. There may then be a singular awareness that cannot be the same as multiple subjects. Sāṃkhya philosophers see the infinite activity within the world of phenomena, *prakṛti*, as an objective reality that manifests within the minds of the multiplicity of subjects.

In his works on Sāṃkhya, Gerald Larson, a well-known Indologist, clarifies that pure awareness, true Selfhood, is not personal but individual.[27] That is, it is not the ego as a functional component of the mind but something intrinsic, which is reflected in an individual mind, and enables perception and experience of objective reality. This awareness, the true Self, is utterly different from any feeling, emotion, or knowledge, from any action or desire, and is likened to an isolated, indifferent, and inactive witness. Without it, an actual experience of reality is not possible as a unique experience that is unrelated to personal tendencies, impulses, and emotions. If so, this awareness is not personal, but is intrinsic, reflected in the individual mind, enabling liberation precisely realising the radical difference between the Self and the world of phenomena.

Burley, a philosopher, sees the Sāṃkhya as a philosophical doctrine. However, he does not fully accept the explanations that seek to reconcile the tension between the singularity and multiplicity of *puruṣa*s. In his view, the ability of Sāṃkhyan and yogic methods to bring about a state of pure awareness depends upon the psychological or psycho-physical experience of those methods.[28] That is, to resolve the tension between the multiplicity and singularity of *puruṣa*s one must examine the direct experience of the yogi or of the Sāṃkhyan philosopher. That is, the resolution of the tension between the multiplicity and singularity of *puruṣa*s depends upon the direct experience of the yogi or of the Sāṃkhyan philosopher.

Although the question of the multiplicity *of puruṣa*s in Sāṃkhya and Yoga remains open, I too, like Burley, believe that this tension does not reflect a weakness in the adequacy and consistency of Yoga and Sāṃkhya philosophy, and therefore does not disrupt the soteriological principle of these practices. At this point, I prefer to cautiously adopt Larson's approach, which sees the multiplicity of *puruṣa*s as an immanent reflection of *puruṣa* as pure primordial awareness in the individual mind, without affecting the ontological status of *puruṣa* as an eternal witness, as a constant pure and unconditioned awareness. This process is likened to the sun, which is one but can be reflected in countless mirrors.

The said tension may challenge the practitioner's or the reader's understanding, a provocation that causes them to 'come out of themself', from their familiar and comfortable positions towards an experience that is entirely non-conceptualised. The discourse of negation is a formative idea, a force underlying the philosophical view of Sāṃkhya, which is capable of dismantling or unravelling the ordinary and familiar perceptions of the individual, connecting the philosopher with unfamiliar realms of empty space of mind, a connection that is free from ignorance and suffering. Moreover, the discourse of negation makes it possible to turn a theoretical reading into a spiritual practice.[29]

Furthermore, there is another 'type' of *puruṣa* that needs to be understood; and, without examining it, an understanding of the philosophy of yoga would be incomplete. In this type of *puruṣa*, it is a god or a deity (*Īśvara*). God is not mentioned at all in *Sāṃkhyakārikā*, not even implicitly. It is, however, mentioned in the *Yogasūtra* and is a clear expression of the theistic component of yoga as an optional practice.

Īśvara is not the Creator in the Judeo-Christian tradition, and it is not the first cause of creation, preservation, or destruction. Nor is it the *Brahman* presented in the Upaniṣads – an infinite, uniform, and absolute essence beyond time and causation. It is not even the Buddhist *Bodhisattva* – an enlightened entity which postpones the final realisation of his Buddha's nature for the well-being of sentient beings, similar to *Avalokiteśvara*, the *Bodhisattva* of compassion. Patañjali sees it as a unique Self that is not 'infected' with the causes of afflictions, actions, and their consequences, nor with any mental imprints.[30]

Larson presents an intriguing observation regarding *Īśvara* as the theistic component of yoga: on the one hand, the philosophy of yoga follows Sāṃkhya's orientation that, given the metaphysical system of *puruṣa* and *prakṛti*, God is not a creator but is one among the plurality of *puruṣa*s; on the other hand, the philosophy of yoga corresponds with the Buddhist notion that there is no God as creator, at the same time placing *Īśvara* as the Guru or the one who primordially possess Self-knowledge on the same plateau as the enlightened ones, those who have realised Buddha nature.[31] In other words, *Īśvara* has never been associated with the world of phenomena, hence its uniqueness. All the other *puruṣa*s were connected to and involved with *prakṛti* at some point, mistakenly identifying themselves with it, compelled by the ignorance existing in *prakṛti* and enclosed within vicious circles of karma. *Īśvara*, in contrast, is liberated from such cycles from the beginning, rooted in pure transcendental awareness. Patañjali[32] sees *Īśvara* as an entity that contains the core of knowing everything. It is the eternal Guru of all yogis throughout the ages, and the sound that emerges from it is the syllable 'aum'. Upon recitation of this sound over and over again, one can get to know *Īśvara*.

All of these characteristics are closely related to the practice and application of mantra recitation and devotion to *Īśvara* (*Īśvara praṇidhāna*). In this practice of devotion to *Īśvara*, devotees feel *Īśvara*'s presence in the depths of their being, dedicating to it the fruits of their deeds. According to Vyāsa, *Īśvara* 'bends' toward devotees, bestowing grace and fulfilling their wishes. Devotees approach the long-awaited liberation with such devotion because *Īśvara* enables them to achieve supra-cognitive concentration, or enstacy, and the capacity to implement and sustain it for prolonged durations.[33] With the contemplation of *Īśvara*, a liberated 'entity', the mind becomes peaceful and concentrated in the knowledge that emerges from this clarity. The spiritual needs of the devotee are fulfilled. With the recitation of the 'aum' or some other mantra related to *Īśvara*, the mind becomes calm and concentrated because a complete, silent, or inner pronunciation of a mantra entails practising breath control (*prāṇāyāma*), which enhances clear concentration. Breathing is a psycho–physical junction as is demonstrated by the experience of shock or anxiety which can cause one's breath to freeze. Likewise, fatigue and exhaustion can cause heavy, slow, and flat breathing, while nervousness can cause fast and shallow breathing. Peace, on the other hand, can bring about quiet and optimal breathing. Clearly then, sensations and feelings affect the rate and quality of breathing. Similarly, the manner or patterns of breathing affect feelings and states of mind. When we have a cold or a stuffy nose, or suffer from sinus congestion, the body will be in a state of stress and the mind will be foggy. Hence, there is a connection between mantra recitation, breathing, and states of mind.

Some references to Tamil poetry from the seventh and eighth centuries CE may help us to imagine how *Īśvara praṇidhāna* could be performed. I would like to emphasise the notion of imagination as pointing to a possible resemblance between the poem's focused meditation accompanied by the visualisation of *Īśvara*, and yoga's devoted meditation or concentration on *Īśvara*. Although there is no obvious connection between the Tamil poem and the practice indicated in the *Yogasūtra*, the meditative processes described in the poem are still worthy of exploration.

The essence of this poetry is focused meditation accompanied by the visualisation of *Īśvara*, in an attempt to give it – the object of meditation – a real and vivid presence. David Shulman presents a Tamil poem which was written by a devotee of Śiva in the seventh century CE, which is directed to the deity *Īśvara*. The deity is created by means of a poem or mantra recitation and the imagination. That is, the form and entire iconography of the deity that is the object of meditation is vividly constructed in the imagination. A poem from the eighth century CE suggests that the reader identify with Śiva as 'honey flowing through the minds of those who imagine him'. Through this identification, it is possible to see *bhāvanā* as a situation that creates or constructs an inner mental picture of the deity as the object of meditation that inhabits the imagining mind. Because the concept of deity is usually mysterious and inaccessible, one attempts to give it presence through the act of imagining. At the same time, the act of meditative imagining seeks to nullify the objectification of the deity and strip the imagining devotee of their sense of subjectivity in order to allow the wisdom of the deity to flow as honey in the mind that imagines it.[34]

A twelfth-century CE poem is dedicated to the tantric ritual of the deity Saundarya Laharī. In the poem, the purpose of the *bhāvanā* is to imagine the deity as one's true Self. The poem mentions visualisation exercises and mantra recitations aimed at establishing focused attention to evoke the deity as an active presence. These exercises and mantra recitations represent one of the types of yoga of the imagination. They result in the awakening of the *kuṇḍalinī*, a force that enables the yogi to enter an ecstatic state of awakening and become acquainted with their true Self.[35]

British–Hungarian Indologist Csaba Kiss also translates *bhāvanā* as imagining; a meaning, he claims, has a central significance in his philological study of *Matsyendrasaṃhitā*, a thirteenth-century CE Sanskrit text of the Shaivite sect of yogis from Southern India.[36] For him, *bhāvanā* as imagining is a meditative process focused on visualising a deity, a process aimed at creating an identity or union between the meditating person and the object of meditation. Imagining involves intense emotion, which Kiss refers to as 'empathy'.[37] He concedes that the use of the term empathy is not entirely precise, but he uses it mainly to emphasise that the meditative process is not a mechanical one. That is to say, *bhāvanā* is not only an intense, vivid construction of the object of meditation as an imagined mental picture, but is also accompanied by a strong emotional gesture. I would argue that this gesture is an expression of the intense yearning to merge with the object of meditation – whether a god or otherwise – and become freed from pain and suffering.

From the concise description of *Īśvara* and the practice of adhering to it, a relevant question arises regarding the distinction between *puruṣa* and *prakṛti*. How does *Īśvara* – being a special *puruṣa*, of a transcendental kind – intervene in the world of phenomena? If indeed *Īśvara* has never been associated with the world of phenomena, how can it interact with all the other *puruṣas*? For they exist in the world of phenomena and are influenced by ignorance, mistakenly identifying their pure innate awareness with their ego. How can it 'prefer' or 'favour' one of the *puruṣas* and 'bend' toward them? If it were to concretely exist in the world of phenomena and 'wear' a psycho-physical figure, then its existence would lead to desires and needs and, with them, the production of a particular kind of karma. How can *Īśvara* prefer a certain devout yogi without giving up its status as not being involved in any activity? On the other hand, if *Īśvara* cannot interact with the other *puruṣas* that exist in the world of phenomena, how can the practice of devotion be effective, and what is the point of it?

What do the classical commentators have to say in regard to these difficult questions? Vyāsa points out that *Īśvara* is a 'pure being' and uses the term *sattva*. Vācaspati Miśra believes that *Īśvara* 'bends' toward its devotees by 'touching' the purity of the *sattvic* quality and clarity of the mind, beyond the activity of the other qualities of passion (*rajas*) and exhaustion (*tamas*). *Īśvara* is pure awareness, a special *puruṣa*, which 'touches' the pure aspect of the mind and becomes its sovereign without being involved in the world of phenomena.[38] That is, the yogi's mind can be open to such a 'touch', and the very occurrence of the 'touch' indicates that the yogi has experienced unparalleled clarity. In the context of the *guṇa*s, Vyāsa emphasises that despite the *sattvic* state, representing a tangent point between *Īśvara* and a yogi's mind in which the *sattva* quality is dominant, *Īśvara* is not subject to the world of phenomena nor to existence in *avidyā*. He points out that *Īśvara* does this to help devotees on their pathway to liberation and that proof for this is to be found in the scriptures. In his view, the scriptures express the sublime wisdom that comes from *Īśvara*'s wisdom and manifest its perfect *sattva*.[39] Liberation, being a state of purity, is never subject to any *sattvic* quality, however pure. It seems that these interpretations are inconsistent with the status of *puruṣa* since the very act of *Īśvara* 'bending' toward the yogis on their way to liberation ontologically deviates from its characteristics. Nevertheless, I believe that such commentaries are beneficial since the 'encounter' between *Īśvara* and devout yogis is a shared experience for them, a central component in the yogic religious culture, similar to that described in the *Bhagavad Gītā*. Even interpretations by contemporary scholars such as Whicher,[40] Feuerstein and Eliade, who portray *Īśvara* as a metaphorical guru, an archetypal yogi or the teacher of all yogis, being a 'pure entity', are not entirely satisfactory because *Īśvara* is seen to exhibit empathy or metaphysical compassion, thereby attributing to it an activity that does not correspond with *puruṣa*.

Larson, in his article, 'Yoga's "A-Theistic"-Theism: A New Way of Thinking About God',[41] states that in order to understand the unique status of *Īśvara* in the philosophy of yoga, one is required to 'deconstruct' one's belief system and the usual ways one perceives God along four possible pathways. Such 'deconstruction' entails: (1) an act of de-personalisation that may lead to the realisation that *Īśvara* is never personal; (2) an act of de-anthropomorphism which may lead to the realisation that *Īśvara* is not a creator in the way causality is understood by us as active agents; (3) an act of de-mythologisation that may lead to the understanding that even a mythical language[42] does not have the capacity to adequately explain the unique status of *Īśvara* in the philosophy of yoga; and (4) an act of de-conceptualisation that may lead to the understanding that *Īśvara* is ineffable.[43] That is, that only by abiding in absence, or a contentless mind, that the understanding and realisation of *Īśvara* may occur.

Thus, until we are able to abide in absence or contentless mind, philosophically the question of *Īśvara*'s activity in the world of phenomena remains open. There seems to be a tension between *puruṣa*'s characteristics and its 'activity' in the world of phenomena, as *Īśvara* vis-à-vis the yogis that are *puruṣa*s on the path to liberation. However, I do not think these tensions significantly weaken the adequacy and consistency of yoga and Sāṃkhya philosophy in a way that might contest their practice. This is because even from the phenomenal point of view, the mind, which is subjected to the three qualities (*guṇas*) and interacts with the world of phenomena, turns inward from its habitual tendency to objectify. It does so in the process of meditative convergence and absorption, focusing on *Īśvara*, on what represents the true Self, the pure primordial awareness. This is what it means to achieve discerning wisdom, the distinction between the mind in its *sattvic* intellectual component and *puruṣa.*

Notes

1 Henceforth, the true Self will at times be referred to as the Self (with a capital S).

2 G. Feuerstein, *The Philosophy of Classical Yoga* (Rochester, VT: Inner Traditions, 1996), 19.

3 See sūtras 1.2; 2.17; 4.23.

4 See sūtra 2.6.

5 See sūtra 2.25.

6 See sūtra 2.20.

7 In Vyāsa's commentary to sūtra 1.3: "Then (upon the dissolution of the vṛttis) the seer rests in his nature". He expands on this and adds that the seer is a pure potential force of consciousness (*citi- śakti*) that rests in its nature when all mental processes are restrained and stopped. See in U. Arya, *Yoga-Sutras of Patanjali with the Exposition of Vyasa: A Translation and Commentary: Volume I Samādhi-pāda* (Honesdale, PA: Himalayan Institute Press, 1986), 114.

Vyāsa uses the term "*citi-śakti*", inspired by Patañjali, who indicates in sūtra 4.34 that it refers to the power of pure consciousness gathered or collected within oneself: "kaivalya is the turning back of the guṇa-s to their source, once (their work) for the sake of puruṣa is accomplished;

or, it is the power of pure consciousness (citi-śakti) abiding in its own essence." D. Raveh, *Exploring the Yogasutra: Philosophy and Translation*, annotated edition (London: Continuum, 2012), 139.

8 Raveh, *Exploring the Yogasutra*, 141.

9 Larson et al., eds., *The Encyclopaedia of Indian Philosophies*, 162.

10 Kārikā 64 in Larson et al., eds., *The Encyclopaedia of Indian Philosophies*, 162.

11 Ian Whicher, *The Integrity of the Yoga Darśana: A Reconsideration of Classical Yoga* (New York: State Unversity of New York Press, 1998), 139–141.

12 The seer (*draṣṭṛ*) is pure seeing (*dṛśi-mātra*). Although pure (that is, contentless), the seer "sees" mental activity. Raveh, *Exploring the Yogasutra*, 131.

13 Kārikā 66 in Larson et al., eds., *The Encyclopaedia of Indian Philosophies*, 162.

14 Raveh, *Exploring the Yogasutra*, 131.

15 See verse 19 in the entry on "Bereshit - Genesis - Chapter 14," in Avroham Yoseif Rosenberg, ed., *The Complete Jewish Bible, with Rashi Commentary*, https://www.chabad.org/library/bible_cdo/aid/8209/jewish/Chapter-14.htm, retrieved10 October 2022.

16 M. Burley, *Classical Samkhya and Yoga: An Indian Metaphysics of Experience (Routledge Hindu Studies Series)* (London: Routledge, 2012), 168.

17 In Raveh's translation: "When *sattva* and *puruṣa* are of equal purity, this is *kaivalya*." Raveh, *Exploring the Yogasutra*, 136.

18 H. Āraṇya, *Yoga Philosophy of Patanjali: Containing His Yoga Aphorisms with Vyasa's Commentary in Original Sanskrit and Annotations Thereon with Copious Hints on the Practice of Yoga* (Calcutta: Calcutta University Press, 1981), 344.

19 E. Bryant, *The Yoga Sutras of Patañjali: A New Edition, Translation and Commentary* (New York: North Point Press, 2009), 117.

20 Āraṇya, *Yoga Philosophy of Patanjali*, 344.

21 Kārikā 62 in Burley, *Classical Samkhya and Yoga*, 177

22 Raveh, *Exploring the Yogasutra*, 131.

23 Bryant, *The Yoga Sutras of Patañjali*, 226.

24 Āraṇya, *Yoga Philosophy of Patanjali*, 185.

25 Burley, *Classical Samkhya and Yoga*, 147.

26 Burley, *Classical Samkhya and Yoga*, 168. Burley makes the observation: "And thus, due to [its being] the opposite [of *prakṛti*] the witnessing, aloneness, equanimity, awareness and inactivity of *puruṣa* is established."

27 G.J. Larson, *Classical Samkhya: An Interpretation of Its History and Meaning* (New Delhi: Motilal Banarsidass, 2014), 170.

28 Burley, *Classical Samkhya and Yoga*, 53.

29 G. Ifergan, *The Man from Samye: Longchenpa on Praxis, Its Negation and Liberation* (New Delhi: Aditya Prakashan, 2014), 93–97.

30 See sūtra 1.24, Raveh, *Exploring the Yogasutra*, 128, which states that "īśvara is a special puruṣa untouched by the kleśa-s ('causes of affliction'), by action and its fruits, and by 'long-term karmic imprints' (āśaya)."

31 G.J. Larson, "Classical Yoga as Neo-Sāṃkhya," *Asiatische Studien – Études Asiatiques*, 52(3) (1999), 729–730.

32 Sūtras 1.25–28, Raveh, *Exploring the Yogasutra*, 128.

33 Āraṇya, *Yoga Philosophy of Patanjali*, 36.

34 D. Shulman, *More than Real: A History of the Imagination in South India* (Cambridge, MA: Harvard University Press, 2012), 118–119.

35 Shulman, *More than Real*, 120.

36 C. Kiss, "The Matsyendrasaṃhitā: A Yoginī-Centered 13th-Century Yoga Text of the South Indian Śāmbhava Cult," in D. Lorenzen and A. Muñoz, eds., *Yogi Heroes and Poets: Histories and Legends of the Nāths* (Albany, NY: SUNY Press, 2011), 160.

37 Kiss, "The Matsyendrasaṃhitā", 160.

38 Whicher, *The Integrity of the Yoga Darśana*, 84.

39 Āraṇya, *Yoga Philosophy of Patanjali*, 58.

40 Whicher, *The Integrity of the Yoga Darśana*, 85.

41 G.J. Larson, "Yoga's 'A-Theistic'-Theism: A New Way of Thinking About God," *Journal of Hindu Christian Studies*, 25 (2012), Article 6.

42 For an example of this kind of mythical language, see my earlier discussion in chapter 2 of the the Sāṃkhyan worldview, which employs a mythical language for the creation of the cosmos.

43 Larson, "Yoga's 'A-Theistic'-Theism," 4.

4 The Discerning Clear Gaze *Viveka-Khyāti*

In previous chapters I discussed the *saṃskāras*, both in the context of binding and subjugating dormant mental imprints (in which the *guṇas* of *rajas* and *tamas* are dominant) and in the context of stilling the mind (in which the *guṇa* of *sattva* is dominant). The yoga practitioner engages in prayer and ritual, physical and mental training, and cultivating virtues in order to erode and dilute these binding *saṃskāras*. It is through these actions, a cultivation of their own goodness and worthiness through good deeds, that the yogi comes to pacify their *saṃskāras*. However, these efforts alone are insufficient to free the practitioner from the binding *saṃskāras*, since the ego's identity is involved in these efforts and their consequences. The practitioner remains dependent upon actions and their results, whether they are actions that bring pleasure, gain or achievement, or those that produce pain or loss. The obvious question is what kind of knowledge or insight can reveal the striving of the ego to the practitioner and expose the investments made in various actions and their consequences? After all, through such exposure the ego is seen in its proper place, as something belonging to the world of phenomena, *prakṛti*. Through this kind of deconstruction of the ego's solidified identifications, the practitioner is able to face the true Self, *puruṣa*. How can this knowledge be cultivated, practiced, and held; how can we come to abide in it?

Samādhi is a deep, fullsome, and intense form of concentration that relies and leans on an object for its sustenance, whether this be tangible or subtle (*ālambana*) object. As we saw in the last chapter, this can include a subtle object in the form of *Īśvara*, who may also be the object of concentration. The *samādhi* that leans on an object in order to be established is known as *saṃprajñāta samādhi*, cognitive meditative absorption. As this form of concentration pervades the mind, it opens up a mental space within which insights may arise about the target object. According to interpretations of sūtra 1.17, in that mental space may arise the kind of insight that can discern between the ego, being a product of *prakṛti*, and the true Self. For the religious yogi, such insight may be a discernment between the sense of subjectivity (I-am-ness) and *Īśvara* as a 'special *puruṣa*'. Insight may arise through a meditation in which *Īśvara* is the 'object', through which a mental image of *Īśvara* is vividly constructed step by step. When its construction is complete, a deep meditative absorption is established which evokes the deity as an active presence. The yogi is thereby stripped of the sense of subjectivity, reduces their identification with the ego, and suspends this until a merging is achieved with *Īśvara*, for example, in the form of Śiva. Whichever the particular path this kind of meditation takes, it is a *samādhi* of wisdom, a process in which the true nature of the object of meditation is realised. In the words of the sūtra: 'Cognitive (saṃprajñāta) samādhi (or cognitive yogic meditation) consists of vitarka (absorption in sthūla or tangible objects), vicāra (absorption in sūkṣma or subtle objects), ānanda (feeling of joy), and asmitā ("I-sense")'.[1]

This category of *samādhi* is considered to be cognitive because it relies on language and processes involving perception and memory. It is accompanied by an awareness of the act of reflection itself, and the way such reflection seeks to know a given object. It is characterised by four stages or scenarios which culminate in the dawning of an insight that can discern the true Self from the world of phenomena, where the intellect is the primary component. The work of the mind makes it possible to reveal the true Self, which only through a mistaken identification has become seemingly associated with the ego, which is an integral part of the world of phenomena.

This first form of *samādhi* relies on a tangible object and is characterised by conceptual thinking, which is known as *vitarka samādhi*. In this form, the yogi uses thought to conceive an object of meditation and then examines it in great detail. The focus of the meditation is on one of the components of the world of phenomena, such as the five elements (ether, air, fire, water, and earth), the human body or one of its five organs (mouth, hands, feet, anus, and sex organs), the five senses, or one of the three subsystems of the mind. Let us take the example of *manas*, which receives sensory data, translates it, and classifies it into concepts. Such a meditation focuses on one selected object with the intention of remaining free of distractions. Such an object may also be a particular deity, such as Śiva, drawing on the rich visual symbolism (iconography) that characterises it, and its latent and manifest meanings. Other objects could be a cow, a vase, a colour, or even the solar system. This would entail a sustained act of conceptual thinking that is centred on the chosen object, its label or name, and its etymological meaning, its components, how it changes over time, and its physical and mental proximity to the yogi, including its latent and manifest qualities and characteristics. Thus, such a meditation could be directed at the earth element, and thereby explore how it is expressed in the yogi's psycho-physical system, in their body and mind, which may lead to an insight that culminates in the understanding that the true Self is differentiated from the earth element identified with the skeleton of the human body, for instance.

In a meditation that first focuses on one tangible object, all distracting thoughts that are foreign to the object are literally blocked, thereby allowing silence to gradually pervade the mind. However, distracting thoughts, those that go from one thing to the next without any restraint like a wild horse, are not actually eliminated. Such thoughts are not allowed to intrude into the mental space between the yogi and the object created by the meditation; they are blocked by the focus of the meditation but they are not eliminated as such. According to Usharbudh Arya (1933–2015), an Indian scholar and academic, such meditation is first accompanied by conceptual thinking directed at the object, and consists of a plan that focuses on each of the details and components of the object one by one.[2] Whicher sees in this conceptual thinking a spontaneous thought process, which arises from observing the object, a process which culminates in a merging of the object, its perception, and that which perceives it.[3] Both Usharbudh and Whicher agree that at the end of such a meditative process, the object is not only perceived from a process of conceptual thinking that lingers over its every detail and all of its components but, in one instance, as an act of cognition that grasps the entire object in a single act of conjuring. When foreign thoughts about an object are not allowed to intrude, questions about the object will arise out of the silent mind. I tend to agree with Whicher's approach, which suggests that the ego as the agent of perception or the act of concentration is less involved in the act of cognition after such a meditative process. Whicher's interpretation points to an enduring space of serenity and clarity, out of which a wondering curiosity and reasoning may arise, a unique mental state that is different, for example, from the activity of an investigation that is willed and planned.

In any case, a one-point meditation that focuses on a tangible object and the union that is achieved through it, between the subject, the object, and its perception, is not yet perfect enough. This is the case because the various layers that obscure the object, its name and our accumulated knowledge about it, have not yet been discerned. Whenever we come in contact with an object, the name of the object, the memories and ideas we have about it, are all projected onto it immediately, such that they automatically occur in our mind. That is, the name, the concept, and the knowledge we have associated with a particular object all depend upon each other. Thus, for example, when we see a flower, its name, and various conceptualisations and memories associated with it, along with feelings related to it such as attraction, immediately come to mind. We do not separate the flower itself from its name and from the ideas and feelings we project onto it. All of these things – the object, its name or label, and the related ideas we have about it – can be used to instigate a one-point meditation that recognises the union between the subject and the object, and the subject's perception of the object. But even these cognitive acts in the end are nothing but a form of mental activity that remains as a transparent wall between the yogi and the object. Such activity detracts from the yogi's ability to see the object as it is, in its entirety. That is, as soon as the thought arises in our mind, 'Here is a beautiful daffodil, and how intoxicating it smells!', what we experience are thoughts that are imposed on the flower and which mediate the relationship between us and the flower. We do not see it directly, as it is, but through the specific thoughts we have about it, and these thoughts also include our prior knowledge, memories, and psychological tendencies relating to the particular object.

Consequently, when we have the intention to advance in the practice of yogic meditation, it is appropriate to dismantle the conditioned connections we have formed between the object, its name and label, and the knowledge and ideas we have about it. This is required in order to purify the mind from the memories we have associated with it and the information we know about it, which are stored in the reservoir of memory. Upon dismantling these conditional relationships, we undo all the projections we direct at the object. The object will thereby rise in the mind denuded of all of these layers of projection, and thus exposed the mind can reflect it as it is, without any influence from the way it has been shaped in our memory, the circumstances of its various previous encounters, the time and place it was experienced, and freed of any influence from our acts of imagination or conceptualisation. At this point of culmination, cognitive *samādhi* is devoid of any conceptual thinking and no longer depends on the memories and linguistic understandings we have associated with the object of meditation. According to Vyāsa, the object of meditation 'colours' the mind and pervades it exclusively, without any conceptualisation and judgment, and without the habitual tendencies that have been conditioned into us by its identity and name.[4] In this respect, it becomes similar to a clear crystal that has been placed on a red tablecloth and which takes on the colour of the cloth and therefore appears to be red. Such cognitive *samādhi* is known as *nirvitarka samādhi* – the mind is still fixed in concentration on a tangible object. Although it is the object of meditation, meditation is no longer accompanied by exploratory conceptual thinking but by non-verbal and non-conceptual observation that abstains from formulating any statement that could get between the subject and the object. The perception of the object is direct, consistent, and corresponds with its concreteness. Such a perception is similar to an object that is fully reflected in a polished and clear mirror, such that as long as the objects sits in front of the mirror it seems that the reflection of the object (whether it is stationary or mobile) and the surface of the mirror are completely integrated. The mirror is the entire reflection, and the whole reflection is the mirror.

Patañjali emphasises that a cognitive *samādhi* without conceptual thinking depends on the purification of memory.[5] In essence, memory is psychological, as it allows experiences related to an individual's past to continue to exist, even though the experience itself has long since ceased to exist. These experiences are stored in the memory of the individual's mind. When certain stimuli we perceive appear reminiscent of the object, events and the experiences associated with it are recalled in memories which ignite and stimulate mental processes. These processes will obscure the clarity of our perception of the object and our ability to see it as it is, free from all the psychological influences and the beliefs we have stored in our memory. Thus, the precondition for the realisation of meditation devoid of conceptualisations, a process known as *nirvitarka samādhi*, is the purification of memory.

When the purification of memory is achieved, a yogi's meditative ability is greatly improved and has grown more skilful; as a consequence, the yogi may undergo profound inner transformations. However, we must remember that establishing a non-conceptual *samādhi* is still conditioned by a tangible object. Such an object is itself absorbed into a continuous mental wave of intentional concentration that pervades the yogi's mind and is accompanied by insights about the object. This state of mind is still involved with some kind of mental effort. Such a state is contrived, 'staged', and is part of a plan in which the mind is identified with the object, even though the object has been denuded of any conceptualisation. In contrast, the true Self is free from effort and does not depend on these states of mind, nor on any 'directing instructions'. It is impossible to identify the true Self with these deep mental states of meditative absorption and wisdom, whether it is a *samādhi* accompanied by conceptual thinking or a *samādhi* that lacks any conceptual thinking about the object.

The next *samādhi* mentioned in sūtra 1.17 is *savicāra samādhi,* a meditative immersion consisting of reflection and contemplation that is a refinement of the kind of cognitive *samādhi* that we have just discussed, which as we just saw was either accompanied by conceptual thinking about an object, or an absence of such thinking about an object. *Savicāra samādhi* is instead directed at a subtle object, such as one of the *cakras* of the subtle body. The *cakras* are central intersections or branches of meta-physiological channels, an invisible metaphysical nervous system through which flows *prāṇa*, the vital force. The *cakra*s are therefore not identified with the physiological nervous system. The central *cakra*s are located in a central channel, the *suṣumṇā*, which runs through the body's spine, from the sacrum to the apex. Each *cakra* has a system of symbols and sounds, representing psycho–spiritual states and potential forces stored in the mind. Meditation on a subtle object leads to deeper insights into the nature of the object and the development of further skills, and the capacity for the next category of *samādhi*, which is *asaṃprajñāta samādhi.* This category of *samādhi* is an objectless meditative absorption that indicates that the mind is empty of any content and mental activity, but it is still considered a 'cognitive' meditation because it still bears *saṃskāra*s though in a different, more subtle manner. However, the critical principle of this kind of meditation is the absence of an object. If there is no object, there is also no subject that will seek to conceptualise desire or avoid it. That is, because there is no object there will be no circumstances that will present stimuli that stir the *saṃskāra*s and that will cause someone to act them out. As the *saṃskāras* are dormant by nature, we can say that 'cognition' here is only in a state of potentiality. Concentration on a subtle object is made possible by the perfection of yogic skills of meditation, since the more subtle the object, the more difficult it is to concentrate upon. Thus, for example, a meditation on a mystical chart such as a complex Tibetan *maṇḍala*, must be constructed through a process of internal visualisation and then held as a single image in a uniform and continuous concentration without any decrease of effort. This requires a very significant kind of effort compared to the kind of meditation in *savitarka samādhi* which is directed, for example, at a statue of Śiva. In this respect, the physical statue is a tangible anchor for meditation, as it is something that the eyes can easily focus upon and that can easily absorb the mind's concentration.

In *savicāra samādhi*, in contrast, we could choose, for example, the components of the first *cakra* of the subtle body as a subtle object for meditation and concentrate on it. Meditative concentration on the first *cakra* means constructing it in our mind as a mental image through a process of visualisation. By 'construction', what is meant is focusing on each component, one after the other, contemplating the function of each as a symbol, and attempting to understand what it represents about our mental or physical state according to the meaning concealed within it.

One can decide to focus on one element from the first *cakra*, for example, the yellow square. It symbolises the earth and represents a vast body of meanings and knowledge, including the world of phenomena and of people as psycho-physical entities. Psychologically, for instance, this symbol could signify to the person meditating that they are driven by a distorted excess of the earth element, which could possibly be expressed as a form of arrogance. Expressions of such excess could be the aspiration to conquer, control, use and exploit the earth and its treasures to fulfil one's selfish desires, or some form of pride that has no regard for the earth. This symbol could also disclose to the person meditating that they have a tendency to avoid all of the abundance that the earth offers because they do not feel worthy of its goodness. Such denial may result from a heavy sense of guilt, which may characterise people who have survived tragic events in which their loved ones have perished. In the context of the psychology of yoga, arrogance and avoidance are nothing but causes of affliction, *kleśa*s.

Savicāra samādhi as a category of meditation may also include reflection on concepts and perceptions. Concentrated thinking about the earth element in the subtle body, for example, can bring about insights that emerge from serenity, clarity, and reflection. These insights may bring the person meditating toward an equilibrium where they enjoy what the earth offers to them and become open to a fulfilment of their needs without denial. At the same time, such a person may also come to thereby cherish the earth, see it as an essential part of an ecosystem, and strive to maintain its balance. In a balanced state of mind, composed of contentment and profound humility, the person meditating is less and less distracted by thoughts and activities arising from intense desires or passive fatigue. The dominant forces in the mind find peace, clarity, and harmony. This enables the awakening of liberating wisdom, by grasping the grip that the *kleśa*s have on them. It allows a state of mind that settles into a deep humility that becomes acquainted with knowledge relating to the soil – from minerals to herbs to plant foods. However, the direct realisation of the nature of this object of meditation in our example, the yellow square of the first *cakra*, is dependent upon and related to its specific location in the subtle body. Such a realisation entails different insights emerging from that concentration that relate to different states of body and mind and depends on the circumstances. These insights may change during the repetitious course of meditative practice depending on the changing circumstances of body and mind. As such, these insights are limited and specific to the meditation object itself and the circumstances of the meditation.

This kind of meditation involving conceptual thinking that is directed at a subtle object has two main goals. The first is knowing the object itself, which is made possible through insights. The dominant qualities of the mind are *sattvic*, transparency and clarity, which enable the awakening of wisdom. For me, wisdom is the ability to see things as they are, or the ability to identify new aspects of an object or situation we have not seen before. As a meditative practice, cognitive *samādhi* consists of wondering, thinking, reflecting, and contemplating. Wisdom and knowledge in this regard mean reaching an understanding that the object of meditation and the yogi are part of the same psycho-physical world, *prakṛti*, and therefore that these things have nothing to do with the true Self. The more the yogi knows the elements of *prakṛti*, the closer they will get to undoing the tangled and confusing weave between the world of phenomena and the true Self. The second goal is that through this knowledge of the object and the wisdom that arises from it there is a reduction in the yogi's suffering, since they are able to see the object as it is, nakedly without any projections of desire or aversion. The object ceases to evoke prejudices or limiting beliefs for the yogi.

Usually, any injury or harm done to an object with which we have a relationship or that is important to us may cause some distress or pain. However, in this meditative process, a peace is established that is not disturbed or distracted by thoughts and activities that originate in attraction or aversion. The meditative state is increasingly emptied of mental processes and causes of distress, and takes the form of a continuous intense concentration, which is accompanied by new insights about the object.

As their meditative ability continues to develop beyond this stage, the yogi undergoes further profound mental transformations and progresses to *nirvicāra samādhi*. Although this type of *samādhi* still leans on a subtle object, it is devoid of any discursive activity concerning the object. That is, in this process, there is no internal discourse about the object, as it is no longer being mediated through interpretation, language, conceptualisation, mental images, or through recollections of its name, function, size, and when and where it was previously encountered. In such one-pointed meditation, the object is perceived instantly or immediately as a whole in a non-conceptualised and non-verbal manner. This is *samādhi* as 'seeing' only, with the yogi's gaze 'resting' on the object. Here the yogi is in complete unity with the object of meditation through an intimate knowledge of it that is beyond the boundaries of language, time, and place. Here, too, the object is reflected as it is, as in a polished and clear mirror when the reflection of the object in the mirror and the mirror's surface are melded together, in the sense that the mirror is a complete reflection, and the whole reflection is the mirror. However, even this profound meditative absorption still requires an object as a point of reference, an anchor that must be in place in order for the meditation to settle and establish itself.

An example of this kind of meditation could be one that is focused on inner sounds, a subtle object of meditation that is mentioned in a fifteenth-century CE yogic text, the *Haṭhayogapradīpikā*, in a chapter dedicated to *samādhi*. In this meditation, the yogi fixates their concentration on the sounds that arise and are heard from within. These sounds emerge from the depths of the mind without us discerning an action that preceded or caused them, such as stroking, tapping, or plucking. These sounds, therefore, make an ideal subtle object for this kind of meditation. The ability to hear inner sounds through practice gradually intensifies such that they overwhelm outer sounds. The *Haṭhayogapradīpikā* enumerates a series of sounds: those that are reminiscent of the ocean, a drum, a seashell, a horn, a bell, flutes, strings, and bees. In this meditation, the yogi shifts their concentration from robust notes to subtle sounds and settles into them without being distracted, and sound becomes the only object that pervades their mind. Such concentration on the unstruck sound progresses until the mind unites with it, becoming absorbed in it and dissolving into its origin, like a fire that burns in a log which is consumed when burned to the end.[6] The text of the *Haṭhayogapradīpikā* mentions the 'dissolution of mind' within the sound. The sound captures the mind like a hunter catches a deer in their net, until the mind becomes still. Dissolution here is nothing but a 'forgetting'[7] of the name or label of the sound, its meaning, and the recollection of when and where it was heard. The other side of this 'forgetfulness' is the enabling of the knowledge of the object as it is and the way that it arises, and its cause even when such a cause might be invisible.

This forgetfulness is a mental space of openness. There is neither belief nor disbelief in it, but instead openness to the possibilities, situations, and circumstances of life. It is an openness that allows one to say 'yes' and 'no' as appropriate to given circumstances. This space is where all material and mental phenomena appear naturally, and extreme limitations or perceptions no longer define their essence. The mind ceases to impose any conceptual perception, fixed ideas, or beliefs on this space of openness. For it is clear that mental openness, which is concerned with curiosity, clarity, and consideration, cannot be linked to such superimposition. There is no hope or fear in this space of openness, for such feelings force a particular emotional or behavioural stance that is opposed to the freedom of openness.

As the mind dissolves into the object of meditation and the forgetfulness that accompanies it, the mind becomes lucid, and clear knowledge arises about the Self. Sūtra 1.47[8] denotes the Self by employing the concept of the '*ātman*', a Sanskrit term that usually means the pure, true Self. The question that arises is: how is that a meditation of this kind which involves intimate acquaintance with the true Self can occur even though the meditative gaze is directed towards an object that is external to the true Self, subtle as it may be?

One can understand the concept of the ātman not only in relation to the true Self but also in relation to the individual, who is in a meditative state and reaches into the depths of their mind, into its transparent and clear realm, into the intellect in its purity. Even the purest and most refined intellect cannot directly discern what is more pure and subtle than it, the true Self. Hence, it can be understood that in this state, the individual indirectly notices that there is a pure, true Self by means of insight along with an awakening to the spiritual identity reflected in this clear realm of mind, the intellect in its purity.

Alternatively, we could nevertheless adopt the ordinary interpretation of *ātman* as the true Self. What distinguishes it in the context of this sūtra is that it emerges in a particular moment of clarity. It is an insight that arises suddenly and momentarily, a window that opens for a moment and then closes immediately. In this clarity, the yogi gets a 'taste' of pure primordial awareness, their true Self, and realises that the sense of I-amness or individuality is not the ultimate Self. This can be likened to the sun which on a cloudy day is visible to us for a moment through the clouds that then cover it over again. The yogi then understands that what must be achieved to progress further is that they must be able to sustain this, and turn this 'tasting' into an enduring state, that is ongoing and abiding, through the development of their meditative skills. The two interpretations of the notion of Self in the context of sūtra 1.17, as pure awareness or the true Self, and as the individual, seem satisfactory in the sense that they teach a momentary discernment – indirect or direct – of the true Self. Meditation of this kind is beyond inquiry, but it also rests on an object that is external to the true Self, and it needs an object to establish itself.

As the mind dissolves into the object of meditation and the oblivion that accompanies it in *nirvicāra samādhi*, the mind becomes more transparent, and the inner individual (or Self) becomes clearer as well, and a state of mind which is 'truth-bearing' (*ṛtam bharā*) is established. This state of mind is truth-bearing because the essence of the object, its latent and manifest characteristics, is exposed and revealed to the naked mind. The object is reflected in the mind without the mediation of its name, free of any conceptual and linguistic associations, and without any of the habitual psychological tendencies and narratives that the subject projects onto the object. Moreover, this clarity of mind expands to permeate the yogi's psychological makeup, who thereby fulfils yoga's moral principles and enjoys the fruits of this fulfilment. Such complete and vivid clarity of mind may be accompanied, for example, by the complete absence of any habitual tendency to engage in violence (*ahimsā*). This state instils safety, confidence, and harmony in the yogi's immediate environment. That is, stilling the mind entails the cessation of mental processes that distort the perception of reality, and that dilute wearying and compulsive thoughts and behavioural patterns that can arise through the accumulation of karma.

Stilling the mind produces mental imprints of the *nirodha* type that can become insights or wisdom associated with the object of meditation. These imprints can arise from engaging in inquiry, reasoning, reflection, or contemplation in cognitive *samādhi*. They can impede the accumulation of the *vyutthāna* type of mental imprints, and thereby intensify stillness and clarity of mind, enabling the birth of an insight that is capable of discerning between the world of phenomena (including the phenomenal self), and the true Self. In this way, mental imprints of the *nirodha* type can intensify the restraint of mental fluctuations in a process of mind *sattvification*, a concept coined by Ian Whicher.[9] In this process, the *sattva* quality of clarity, transparency, and purity dominates and permeates the mind, deepening the shift of the focus of meditation from tangible objects to subtle ones, culminating in a *samādhi* which is beyond inquiry even while still leaning on an object. The yogi experiences a purification of their mind, no longer being subject to mental processes, causes of affliction, patterns of behaviour, and latent mental imprints.

The central theme of the last sūtras (1.42–51) of the first chapter of the *Yogasūtra* is cognitive *samādhi*, which can be one of two types: firstly, it can be a *samādhi* aimed at a tangible object (this itself has two forms, one accompanied by conceptualising thinking and the other not); secondly, it can be a *samādhi* aimed at a subtle object (this likewise has two forms, one accompanied by reflective observation and one that is beyond observation or inquiry). An objectless *samādhi*, which also appears in the first chapter of the *Yogasūtra*, is somewhat beyond ordinary cognition and is not aimed at any object, and does not need any reference point to be established.

Patañjali mentions cognitive *samādhi* earlier, in sūtra 1.17, namely the form accompanied by conceptual thinking (*savitarka*) and the form accompanied by observation or reflection (*savicāra*). Nevertheless, in the same sūtra he also adds two categories of cognitive *samādhi* that are aimed at an object: a sense of bliss or joy (*ānanda*) and the sense of I-amness (*asmitā*). The last two are not mentioned in the last sūtras of the first chapter, 1.42–51.

What are the *samādhi* of joy (*ānanda*) and the sense of I-am-ness (*asmitā*)? What is their place on the roadmap of yogic meditation? Their position does not seem to be entirely clear as Patañjali does not clarify the hierarchy between *ānanda* and *asmitā samādhi* on the one hand, and *nirvicāra samādhi* on the other (which is devoid of any discursive activity that mediates the object to the yogi). Also, classical and contemporary commentators disagree about their relative positions on the roadmap of yogic meditation leading to liberation. For example, Vācaspati Miśra[10] argues that the sense of joy arises when concentration shifts from the senses and their objects to the consciousness underlying the senses, which serves as a subtle object for meditation. The mind becomes aware of the mechanism of perception, the means of sensory perception, and the sorting and processing of information that is received through them. The quality of *sattva*, whose essence is peace, transparency, and wisdom, becomes dominant in the intellect, the *buddhi*, which leads to a sense of joy or ecstatic pleasure, *ānanda samādhi*.

In contrast, Vijñānabhikṣu, the fifteenth-century CE Vedāntin, argues that the ecstatic sense of pleasure appears already in the first stage of cognitive *samādhi*, accompanied by a conceptualised thinking and directed towards a tangible object (*savitarka*). He emphasises the instrumental functioning of the senses themselves rather than the consciousness underlying them. Vijñānabhikṣu sees the intensification of the *sattva guṇa* already present at this stage as being a cause of the ecstatic sense of pleasure.[11] For example, the eye is an instrument or a means, and it is devoid of consciousness. However, visual awareness is created between the eye and the object of sight in the mind's relevant faculty. Vācaspati Miśra thus emphasises the consciousness underlying the senses, that is, the visual awareness which is a space for the sense of joy to occur, while Vijñānabhikṣu regards meditation on the instrumental functioning of the senses themselves, of the eye itself, as a space for the sense of joy to arise. In either case, the experience is an arising sense of joy in a mental space where the *sattva* quality is dominant and pure.[12]

Feuerstein believes that the sense of joy and the sense of I-am-ness accompany any cognitive *samādhi* and do not occur as separate stages that stand apart on their own.[13] In contrast, Whicher regards the cognitive *samādhi* of joy and I-am-ness as stages in *nirvicāra samādhi*, beyond reflection (devoid of any discursive activity that mediates the object to the yogi), as stages in which joy and I-am-ness become objects for yogic meditation.[14] I agree somewhat with Feuerstein and believe that joy and I-am-ness can occur in the early stages of cognitive *samādhi*. However, when they dawn and arise largely depends on the yogi's meditative capacity, feelings, and wisdom. Cognitive *samādhi* progresses from conceptual thinking aimed at a tangible object to concentration beyond reflection aimed at a subtle object. Joy and I-am-ness may already arise during yogic meditation in its early stages as meditative experiences, which arise and permeate body and mind for a moment. This takes place during the establishment of *nirvicāra samādhi*, and here I agree with Whicher, which prepares the mental space for their emergence. In this preparation, the frequency of appearance of joy and I-am-ness increases, embracing body and mind for more extended periods, in the same way drops of water can eventually become a continuous uniform flow. Joy and I-am-ness then become objects for a yogic meditation that is beyond reflection. The two sensations spontaneously produce a new, subtle object for a meditation that is beyond reflection, *nirvicāra samādhi.*

I will now continue to focus on the sense of joy as the object of *nirvicāra samādhi*, by exploring it from a psycho–somatic perspective, related to *prāṇa*, which is vital energy or life force. I will then discuss the sense of I-am-ness in the context of *nirvicāra samādhi* and the capacity to discern between the sense of I-am-ness and the true Self.

As mentioned, the sense of joy may already arise in the early stages of cognitive *samādhi*, because it is already characterised by an intense form of concentration in which the circulation of *prāṇa* in the physical and subtle bodies decreases, and mental processes fade. Yogic meditation restrains mental processes, silences them, and thereby also enables control of *prāṇa*.[15] Because of the natural, inherent correlation between *prāṇa* and breath, *prāṇa* can be curbed through breathing exercises.

Prāṇā is the energetic basis of mental processes, latent mental imprints, behavioural patterns, and causes of distress that arise in response to circumstances, events, and objects. When the mind is unstable, distracted, or unfocused, *prāṇa* becomes inefficient and moves without restraint. For example, when an emotion arises and the mind has no control over it, *prāṇa* will actively express it psycho–somatically. To illustrate, when a person loses their composure and becomes agitated or angry, their body releases stress hormones, and their heart rate, blood pressure, body temperature, and respiration rate all increase. That is, the mental state elicits a somatic response, and in terms of yoga the main symptom indicating *prāṇa*'s inefficient condition is fast and flat breathing rate. In such situations, *prāṇa* is mainly dominated by the quality of *raja*s. Another example, this time from body to mind: when a person catches a cold, fluids accumulate in their lungs, making it difficult for them to breathe, thus preventing oxygen from reaching their bloodstream. The mind becomes fatigued, slow, drowsy, cloudy, and exposed to gloomy moods. In this situation, when the life force, *prāṇa*, is not flowing properly, the mind is mainly dominated by the quality of *tama*s. It is understandable, therefore, that *prāṇa* and mind are tightly related and interconnected. Thus, the yogi can influence their *prāṇa* through yogic meditation, and vice versa, the yogi can influence their mind through the practice of *prāṇāyāma*.

A sense of joy arises in the clear mental space in which the *sattva guṇa* is dominant and pure. In this state of mind, *prāṇā*'s activity settles to a level that is required to sustain the body. The occurrence of a sense of joy is associated with the subtle body. It is composed of meta-physiological channels (*nāḍīs*) and psycho–spiritual centres, *cakra*s, which are the major intersections of these channels, or the pathways through which *prāṇā* flows. The *cakra*s, as I have already stated earlier, are located in a central canal called *suṣumṇā*, which runs through the spine, from the perineum to the apex. In the root *cakra* is *kuṇḍalinī*, a dormant meta-physiological psycho-spiritual force, with enormous psycho–somatic and spiritual transformative potential, that is a potential for radical change. Its realisation in the highest degree can lead one to liberation. The ascent of this power from the base or root *cakra* to the crown *cakra* is accompanied by a sense of ecstatic pleasure that is made possible through a yoga practice that includes complex postures, breathing exercises, and concentration. The purpose of such practice is to powerfully concentrate and gather the *prāṇā* in a particular point within the subtle body in order to influence and stimulate *kuṇḍalinī*'s power, arousing it from its dormant state. It seems that the power of *kuṇḍalinī* is nothing but an extension of *prāṇā* into new configurations or manifestations, and highly-enhanced transformative qualities. Such a practice is described, for example, in the *Haṭhayogapradīpikā*, a yogic text from the fifteenth century CE.

Since *prāṇā* and the mind are tightly interconnected, an intense yogic meditation like *samādhi* may evoke *kuṇḍalinī*. Gopi Krishna (1903–1984), an Indian official who practiced meditation consistently for many years, testifies to this in his autobiography:

> One morning during the Christmas of 1937 [...] I was meditating, breathing slowly and rhythmically, my attention drawn towards the crown of my head, contemplating an imaginary lotus in full bloom, radiating light. I sat steadily, unmoving and erect, my thoughts uninterruptedly centred on the shining lotus, intent on keeping my attention from wandering and bringing it back again and again whenever it moved in any other direction. The intensity of concentration interrupted my breathing; gradually it slowed down to such an extent that at times it was barely perceptible. My whole being was so engrossed in the contemplation of the lotus that for several minutes at a time I lost touch with my body and surroundings. During such intervals I used to feel as if I were poised in mid-air, without any feeling of a body around me. The only object of which I was aware was a lotus of brilliant colour, emitting rays of light. This experience has happened to many people who practise meditation in any form regularly for a sufficient length of time, but what followed on that fateful morning in my case, changing the whole course of my life and outlook, has happened to few. During one such spell of intense concentration I suddenly felt a strange sensation below the base of the spine, at the place touching the seat, while I sat cross-legged on a folded blanket spread on the floor. The sensation was so extraordinary and so pleasing that my attention was forcibly drawn towards it. The moment my attention was thus unexpectedly withdrawn from the point on which it was focused, the sensation ceased. Thinking it to be a trick played by my imagination to relax the tension, I dismissed the matter from my mind and brought my attention back to the point

> from which it had wandered. Again I fixed it on the lotus, and as the image grew clear and distinct at the top of my head, again the sensation occurred. This time I tried to maintain the fixity of my attention and succeeded for a few seconds, but the sensation extending upwards grew so intense and was so extraordinary, as compared to anything I had experienced before, that in spite of myself my mind went towards it, and at that very moment it again disappeared.[16]

This testimony indicates the emergence of a cognitive *samādhi* aimed at an 'inner' subtle object – the visualisation of the lotus and the reflecting observation of it. As the concentration intensifies, the frequency of distracting thoughts decreases, and the internal discourse weakens and dissipates. Simultaneously, the breathing slows down and with it, the movement of *prāṇā* weakens until it becomes almost unnoticeable. Krishna becomes more immersed in the meditation directed toward the lotus, a meditation that is beyond reflecting observation, internal discourse, and the sense of time and place. At its peak, he experiences the rise of *kuṇḍalinī* and with it the sense of pleasure. He tries to focus on this feeling, and this evokes in him an inner discourse. At times, he loses the feeling and returns to the object of meditation, the lotus. A sense of pleasure again involuntarily captures his attention. When he tries to focus on it, it eludes him. That is, in such moments he cannot remain present and in equilibrium, and instead returns to the discursive cycles of mental processes and causes of affliction. This meditative experience demonstrates that the feeling of joy arose in the mental space created at the height of the yogic meditation on the shimmering lotus, which was a meditation beyond reflection.

This concise review of the connections between *samādhi*, *prāṇā* and breath reveals the possibilities for feeling ecstatic pleasure, a feeling similar to a wave of emotion that embraces the body and mind. It draws on the perspective of phenomenology that views the yogi as a laboratory. This is the case with Gopi Krishna's experience, or with any yogi who experiences a state of suspended breath. Such a state occurs suddenly, by itself, in accordance with intense meditative concentration, *samādhi*, which serves as a mental space where the feeling of pleasure arises and floats. However, the yogi may suddenly experience a wave of pleasurable emotion, not necessarily during the practice (whether it be physical or meditative), but after it, as a side effect of the practice.

In any case, this sense of pleasure is not the sublime bliss associated with *Brahman*, a central concept in the Upaniṣads. In the context of cognitive *samādhi*, the sense of pleasure is a temporary and conditional phenomenon deriving from the dominance of *sattva* during meditative absorption. As the yogi gains control and skill in a yogic meditation that is beyond reflection, the reliance or dependence on the subtle object that is used to instigate the meditation becomes weaker. Consequently, so does the applied effort that is required to anchor the meditation in the object. Simultaneously, the sense of ecstatic pleasure becomes more dominant and replaces the object of meditation, hence the transition to *ānanda samādhi*, a meditation on joy, in which the object of concentration becomes joy itself. Joy can serve as a subtle object for yogic meditation, through which one becomes capable of 'forgetting' its name or label, any interpretation about it, and the recollection of the time and place of its occurrence. A feeling of joy accompanies such meditation: 'I am happy', where joy becomes the object of meditation, and it embraces the yogi's body and mind in waves of emotion. Thus, unlike Feuerstein's position, the *samādhi* of joy is not only a by-product of cognitive *samādhi* but a cognitive *samādhi* that stands apart on its own.

This feeling of pleasure threatens to drown the yogi in waves of joy, and to prevent this they must 'keep their head above water' through a stable yogic meditation that is beyond reflection. One of the streams of Tantra is aimed at transformation through sexual intercourse. This culminates in abiding in the clear presence of awareness while engaging in sexual intercourse without drowning in the pleasurable sexual feeling. An intense sense of pleasure may distract the yogi's focus of concentration against their will. Thus, instead of restraining, controlling, or simply being present, abiding in the sense of pleasure, the yogi becomes governed by it. Being immersed in the experience of pleasure, the yogi can marvel, and it is precisely this euphoria that can fixate and control them, and make them conditioned by the sense of ecstatic pleasure such that it will be challenging to ever give it up. The only thought that might come to mind then is: 'I am all pleasure and happiness'. This thought carries with it residues of the causes of affliction that are expressed in the identification of the ego with an attraction to pleasure that at times can become an obsession. Hence, the ecstatic pleasure is not attributed to the true Self and, as such, is not the ultimate goal of yoga. Accordingly, the yogi must continue to concentrate on it until they know its true nature. The closer the yogi gets to knowing its true nature, the closer they get to dissolving the attachment to the sense of pleasure, and thereby undo the confusing entanglement between the ego and true Self.

Hence, the yogi continues to focus on the feeling of pleasure and learns to abide in it without drowning in it, not getting drunk from it, or 'adding oil to its fire'. Although joy is the only object that the yogi concentrates upon, such that it completely 'colours' their mind, there remains a mental space where the grip of joy over the yogi loosens, stemming from the understanding that joy is not the ultimate goal of yoga. The mind then becomes still and free from mental processes and causes of distress, almost completely. Once the yogi knows the nature of joy, has become aware of it and free of its grip, they progress to *asmitā samādhi*, in relation to the sense of I-am-ness, where they become aware of the one who experiences the pleasure, that is, the ego, or the phenomenal 'I'. The *buddhi*, intellect, is so pure at this stage that it can reflect to itself the true Self, the pure primordial awareness. In terms of the mirror analogy, the mirror is the mind with its three constituents (the intellect, the cognitive processes, and the sense of I-am-ness), and the sun is the true Self. As a consequence of the previous stages of *samādhi*, the mirror is pure and polished, and is now rotated away from the world of objects towards the sun, which it reflects to itself. Although the yogi becomes aware of the true Self, this occurs only through the Self's reflection in the *buddhi*. This awareness is indirect, therefore, since the *buddhi* mediates it.[17] The yogi becomes aware of the sense of self as the phenomenal 'I' or 'here I am'.

The emergence of *asmitā samādhi* naturally begins with a meditation on the one who experiences joy – the ego or phenomenal self (as the axis or centre of physical and cognitive actions, control, ownership, and self-importance). It culminates in the insight that the source of I-am-ness is the true Self and that the phenomenal self – 'I am I' – has been purified of any identifications or content. That is, the status of I-am-ness as a cause of affliction has been transformed and has become pure. As indicated earlier, I-am-ness is nothing but a product of misidentification, a state in which the seer and the seen are mistakenly perceived as one undivided entity. Patañjali presents the seer as a synonym for the true Self – *puruṣa*, the primordial presence of awareness, otherness – while the power of sight is the mind, an apparatus of dynamic perception. It is not only the principle of awareness or the true Self that arises in the mind and enables it with the power of perception, but also the sense of I-am-ness that is formed as a constituent of the mind. The mind is certain that it is more than just an instrument of dynamic perception, that it is also the source of pure primordial awareness. This wrongful perception which conflates these two principles as an inseparable unit produces *asmitā* – I-am-ness.[18] In a *samādhi* that is directed at the sense of I-am-ness, which in itself is a cause of affliction that has been purified, there arises the (indirect) realisation that the source of I-am-ness as self-awareness is the pure primordial awareness. The yogi then understands the proper place, function, and role of the ego in the domain of the world of phenomena, *prakṛti*.

A concrete realisation of the true nature of the ego emerges in *asmitā samādhi*, in which there is a growing understanding that the ego is not the source of awareness. It is the understanding that the ego, although being an evolute, was originally pure, free from the tendency to objectify and act, not conditioned, dependent, and related to actions and their results (whether gain or loss, pleasure or pain); it is indifferent to these influences.

This being the case, how does the yogi act and behave when they emerge from this intense *samādhi* back into the world of phenomena? How do they perform their daily activities, such as eating, communicating with those around them, and resume studying, debating, or writing? It seems that at this stage of *sattvification*, the world of phenomena is gradually being perceived as it is, and the effect of the mental processes and causes of affliction that distort how the world of phenomena is experienced is diminishing considerably. As the sense of I-am-ness becomes pure, the intensity of the causes of affliction decreases. However, the potency of *avidyā* (ignorance) remains unchanged because a direct and complete knowledge of the true Self has not yet been realised, and consequently specific mental contents may still arise due to habitual tendencies and mental imprints.[19]

As the stabilisation of the mind intensifies, the yogi involved with the world of phenomena communicates and acts without selfishness, according to what is reflected in a mind that has now become pure and clear. They tend to respond appropriately to given circumstances without being conditioned by them. At the same time, they also operate under the mental imprints generated by insights, and the cultivated virtues and moral behaviour of yoga, the *yamas* and *niyamas*. These dormant mental imprints countenance against the possibility of violating moral rules and falling back into a cycle of actions and results, resulting in the accumulation of karma.

Viveka-khyāti emerges, and it stems from the realisation of the true nature of the ego, as it is, distinct from the true Self. This is the insight the ego is not the source of pure primordial awareness but the true Self. Such insight occurs as the manifestation of the *sattvic* quality dominating the intellect, which at its culmination embraces and entirely permeates the mind. Vyāsa argues that in this state, the *buddhi* realises the difference that exists between itself and the true Self, and nothing more. Although such insight about the nature of things and their properties is available to the yogi, it is still not the situation described in sūtra 1.3, in which the entanglement between the true Self and the world of phenomena has disintegrated, and the true Self resides in its Self, isolated, in its true nature. It is, therefore, appropriate to abandon this discerning insight as well. The yogi must strive and progress from it to supreme states of uninvolved awareness (*para-vairāgya*) that abandon even this state of mind of yogic insight, towards meditation that does not rely on an object in order to be realised. This is because in this state of awareness *viveka-khyāti* still lacks complete knowledge of the dynamics and formation of the entanglement between the true Self and the world of phenomena, or the cycle of *saṃsāra*. Also, the state of *viveka-khyāti* is an insight that embraces and permeates the mind and does not allow the true Self's radiance to shine fully in the mind. This renders *viveka-khyāti* nothing more than an experience that takes place in the *buddhi*, serving only as a springboard to the next, objectless *samādhi*, one that is not conditioned by any object – the *asaṃprajñāta samādhi*.

One can describe the discerning insight that emerges in cognitive *samādhi* that is dependent on an object through the following question: what happens to the mental processes and causes of affliction that yoga is interested in bringing to a cessation? Through its four principal types, cognitive *samādhi* brings about concentration which becomes increasingly intense, uniform, and stable. These forms of *samādhi* evoke insights about the objective world through the knowledge gained of the objects of meditation and the components of the mind involved in the processes of this knowing. During this effort, there is a growing intelligence forming that exchanges one truth for another, thereby reflecting reality in a more reliable manner. However, this intelligence is nothing but a change of states of mind that leads to the formation of mental imprints of wisdom, of the *nirodha* type. Under certain circumstances, such mental imprints will become the seedbed for the formation of mental processes of further restraint and stillness, processes that will obstruct mental imprints that produce the causes of affliction and mental fluctuations. This will create a mental space that is purified of them, enabling and generating mental imprints of wisdom, which in their germination will bear fruit of further wisdom and in turn will become seeds that will germinate further insights and so forth. However, in order to bring the process of *sattvification* to completion, the yogi must say 'enough' to all these insights of wisdom, and to the supernatural forces that accompany states of mind during cognitive *samādhi*, and move instead towards a higher state, to an objectless *samādhi* that does not lean or depend on an object. In such a state, the mind is completely still and clear. The mental imprints are no longer producing causes of distress, and the true Self returns to dwell in its nature.

Discerning insight and time

The concept of discerning insight is also presented in the third chapter of the *Yogasūtra*, which is concerned with supernatural forces, the extraordinary abilities that are developed in a yoga practitioner due to their determined and consistent practice. As Raveh translates sūtra 3.53: 'Through saṃyama on moment (kṣaṇa) and sequence (krama), knowledge born of discernment (viveka-jaṃ jñānam) is obtained.'[20] Here the yogi is required to find out what time is, and of what it is composed. Āraṇya, in his translation of the same sūtra, uses the terms 'Self' and 'non-Self', although these words do not originally appear in the sūtra, and translates it as follows: 'Differentiating Knowledge Of The Self And The Non-Self Comes From Practising saṃyama On Moment And Its Sequence.'[21] Both translations are linked to an insight that discerns between the world of phenomena and the true Self.

The 'moment' (*kṣaṇa*) is the smallest and most minute unit of time, during which an 'atom' moves from one point in space to a point adjacent to it. A flow of moments is the sequence (*krama*) in question in the sūtra. A sequence of time, Vyāsa tells us, is a product of the concept of time, its literal expression, even though time itself is not real. However, for the yogi, the moment refers to an actual present object, and the time sequence is the ongoing moment, relating to a specific real object. It does not refer to objects that originate in the imagination or memory. Therefore, Vyāsa adds, the present is but one (continuous) moment. The previous one has passed long ago and the next one has not yet arrived, and both do not exist in the present, since it is impossible to be in two places simultaneously or to think two thoughts together.[22]

What is the ongoing and present moment? Suppose there is a bakery on the street where I live, and as I pass by, the aroma of the freshly-baked bread wafts into the air in the street. This aroma of freshly-baked bread captivates me and sends me back in time, to my childhood, to the days when my mother baked bread for the weekend. In my mind I can recall seeing her standing in the kitchen kneading the dough, and inadvertently I sink into heart-warming nostalgic thoughts and emotions. These thoughts so dominate my mind that I am no longer present on the street in my neighbourhood, and I no longer smell the bread baked in the bakery in my street, but have instead become absorbed by my memories. This is an example of a mental process that has taken over the mind. The *saṃskāra*, a latent mental imprint in the depths of memory formed in reaction to a childhood experience, was stimulated by the smell of bread. It is like a seed that, given the right conditions, sprouts and bears fruit.

Suppose I had remained aware of what was happening in the bakery and continued to smell the bread calmly without allowing conceptions to arise, without then pursuing the mental associations that developed and that branch out from these. In that case, one could say that I would have been present in an ongoing moment while just acknowledging the memory, without elaborating or extending it. Although this lingering moment folds into it the past as the sum of my memories, thoughts, and actions, and the future as the sum of possible results, neither past nor future can be allowed to dictate or condition my conduct in the present. I believe that concentration in the continuous moment is not static, frozen, and reduced only to the aroma of the bread, but expands to a 'panoramic' awareness, which includes the whole range of what takes place in the vicinity of the bakery. That is, I could, for example, go with a friend and talk to him about an event from the past and at the same time be aware of the aroma of bread without being distracted. This is similar to listening to music while driving. Although listening to music, I am not distracted from what is happening on the road. Moreover, if that were the case, it would have disastrous results.

Does being aware and present in the ongoing moment while being in the vicinity of the bakery or while driving mean that the discerning clear gaze, the *viveka-khyāti* state, has been reached? It is a situation in which the mind, or more precisely the *buddhi*, is dominated by the *guṇa* of *sattva*. The *sattva* quality of clarity, transparency, and purity increasingly dominates and permeates the mind such that the sense of I-am-ness experiences a dilution of its identifications with the temporal transformations associated with birth, existence, change, growth, decay and destruction. With the present moment as the object of meditation there is a deepening shift from tangible objects to subtle ones, culminating in a moment in which a window opens for the occurrence of discerning wisdom.

A modern analogy for this notion of a lingering moment and a sequence of moments would be, respectively, still photographs and a film as a sequence of still photographs. If contemplating mental processes that dominate the mind as a 'sequence', slowing down and stilling the mind can 'reduce' the sequence into one lingering moment, and in this way undoing our identifications with the phenomenal transformations associated with the passage of time. The sequence has a beginning and an end that is subjected to time, but for the yogi, the lingering moment is eternal and irreducible while still folding the past, present and future.

The most developed ability of the yogi – applying stillness in its entirety, and abiding in it in all sorts of varieties and shades of mental states – represents, for me, a true quality of freedom. This is the essence of being in a state of forgetfulness that also allows for recollection. In the lingering moment, the yogi can look with great pleasure at the summit of a mountain touching the sky or at a vivacious wise face without having the sense of being the observer. The yogi is calm, forgetting about the past and what the future might bring, and the sights and feelings they have experienced. Were they to be asked to describe to us from memory what they saw and felt, they would undoubtedly have been able to tell us about the sights and the great pleasure these brought, but they would have done so without the influence of psychological memory. Psychological memory is driven by the desire to recreate feelings of pleasure from memory, and this motive may have many reasons. People are attached to such feelings and identify with them.

Nevertheless, in the lingering moment, the yogi does not remember the sights and feelings of pleasure (and at the same time, they do not forget them). Achieving the goal of yoga, which is complete disengagement from the world of phenomena, requires the restraint of memory. It is made possible by the yogi's ability to generate silence as a mental space and abide in it in a variety of mental states. Through this the true Self is revealed, at which point pure awareness is fully present and untainted by mental processes.

Yogic meditation on this enduring moment discerned from the past and the future (from the materials of the phenomenal gaze), settling and abiding in the 'midst' of such a lingering present, enhances stillness and enables the rise of discerning insight. It is like a continuous stream of knowledge that discerns between the ordinary mind and pure primordial awareness denuded of any mental content. In other words, such yogic meditation discerns between the sense of I-am-ness and the true Self. The sense of I-am-ness tends to objectify and appropriates time for itself ('my past', 'this is what happened to me in the past', 'my childhood,' 'what will happen to me?', 'what will I do if this happens?'), and locates and places itself in a time 'sequence'. In contrast, a discerning mind reflects occurrences only in the continuous 'moment'. This meditation on time can be articulated in the following instruction: 'Do not follow to the past, do not wait for the future, and do not follow distracting thoughts in the present.'

Despite acquiring an understanding that discerns the moment from the sequence, as in the meditation proposed in sūtra 3.53, this understanding is still an intellectual knowledge, which only slowly permeates the mind. It takes time for the mind to assimilate and integrate this understanding until it has a concrete effect on the causes of affliction, behavioural patterns, and latent mental imprints. In practice, there is a gap between the intellectual knowledge that the true Self is folded in the continuous moment and is not subjected to time, and the way we live by such knowledge. I will seek to deal with the theoretical and practical implications of this gap, from the perspective of the psychology of yoga, in the next chapter.

Notes

1 D. Raveh, *Exploring the Yogasutra: Philosophy and Translation*, annotated edition (London: Continuum, 2012), 128.

2 U. Arya, *Yoga-Sutras of Patanjali with the Exposition of Vyasa: A Translation and Commentary: Volume I Samādhi-pāda* (Honesdale, PA: Himalayan Institute Press, 1986), 227.

3 I. Whicher, *The Integrity of the Yoga Darśana*: A Reconsideration of Classical Yoga (New York: State Unversity of New York Press, 1998), 223.

4 Arya, *Yoga-Sutras of Patanjali with the Exposition of Vyāsa*, 388.

5 In Raveh's translation: "nirvitarkā (samāpatti) ('meditation beyond contemplation') occurs when memory is purified (i.e., emptied of its contents), consciousness as if emptied of its (subjective) nature, and the object (of meditation) alone shines forth." Sūtra 1.43, Raveh, *Exploring the Yogasutra*, 129.

6 Svātmārāma, *The Hatha Yoga Pradipika: The Original Sanskrit and An English Translation*, trans. and ed. B. D. Akers (Woodstock, NY: YogaVidya.com, 2002), 101–109.

7 Svātmārāma, *The Hatha Yoga Pradipika* , 92.

8 In Raveh's translation: "When (the meditative state called) nirvicāra becomes lucid, clarity emanating from the inner-self occurs." Raveh, *Exploring the Yogasutra*, 129.

9 Whicher, *The Integrity of the Yoga Darśana*, 86.

10 E. Bryant, *The Yoga Sutras of Patañjali: A New Edition, Translation and Commentary* (New York: North Point Press, 2009), 64.

11 T.S. Rukmani, trans. and ed., *Yogavārttika of Vijñānabhikṣu: Samādhipāda*, third edition (Delhi: Munshiram Manoharlal Publishers, 2007), 107.

12 For a broader picture of disagreements among other classical commentators see in Arya, *Yoga-Sutras of Patanjali with the Exposition of Vyasa*, 233.

13 Feuerstein, *The Yoga-Sutra of Patañjali: A New Translation and Commentary* (Rochester, VT: Inner Traditions, 1989), 38.

14 Whicher, *The Integrity of the Yoga Darśana*, 86.

15 Svātmārāma, *The Hatha Yoga Pradipika*, 85, 89.

16 K. Gopi, *Kundalini: The Evolutionary Energy of Man* (Boston, MA: Shambhala, 1997), 11–12.

17 Bryant, *The Yoga Sutras of Patañjali*, 66.

18 G. Ifergan, *The Psychology of the Yogas* (Sheffield, UK: Equinox Publishing, 2021), 29–30.

19 In Raveh's translation: "In the interstices of this (as the consciousness approaches kaivalya), other mental content (may arise) from the saṃskāra-s." Sūtra 2.27, Raveh, *Exploring the Yogasutra*, 138.

20 Raveh, *Exploring the Yogasutra*, 136.

21 H. Āraṇya, *Yoga Philosophy of Patañjali: Containing His Yoga Aphorisms with Vyasa's Commentary in Original Sanskrit and Annotations Thereon with Copious Hints on the Practice of Yoga* (Calcutta: Calcutta University Press, 1981), 336.

22 Āraṇya, *Yoga Philosophy of Patañjali*, 336–7.

5 Meditation on the Sense of I-am-ness

So far we have mapped out the path leading to the rise of the insight that distinguishes the phenomenal self and the true Self from the yogic meditative absorption focused on the sense of I-am-ness, the phenomenal self. This meditation deepens to the point of assimilating the knowledge that I-am-ness is not the true Self. Patañjali outlines the procedure as stages in meditation, aimed at the dawn of discerning insight. It will rise spontaneously, in one leap, at the height of the cognitive *samādhi* that is beyond reflection which focuses on I-am-ness. Although, according to the yogic plan, meditation is focused on the phenomenal self, the discerning insight cannot be forced or imposed, and it arises through the maturation of meditative processes and in the maturity of the yogi.

The method I propose as a means of enabling the rise of the discerning insight between the ego and the true Self rests on the psychology of yoga and is fundamentally based on the view that in everyday life, our ego takes on and strips off various characters and roles, with which it identifies and becomes attached. This process usually occurs rapidly. Since we do not have a language that can describe the process, it is almost impossible to examine these characters' motives and reactions, and their interrelationships. Similarly, we can observe our thoughts and their content without realising that they arise from the dynamics of an internal discourse. The mind may contain several internal dialogues taking place at once. They exist through several languages, including the language of images, the language of feelings, or the language of words.

Richard Schwartz developed a therapeutic method that revolves around the multiplicity of the ego's characters. He was surprised to find that most of his patients pointed to some character or figure that characterised their personality. Thus, although the ego is mistakenly perceived as an indivisible unit, it is multifaceted and has diverse characters and roles. All of these characters are together engaged in the various activities associated with the complexities of modern life.[1]

We can name almost any character that our ego wears and the identities that it assumes, and see these as all being 'part' of our personality. Such characters are not just temporary emotional states or particular patterns of behaviour, but are instead latent autonomous mental systems that each have a range of emotions, expressions, abilities, desires, and worldviews. It seems that in each of us, there are several characters. They differ in age, skills, temperament, or desires, and there is an interaction between them. In people with schizophrenia, there is an extreme polarisation between the characters that occupy their mind, and there is no connection between them.

These characters have a variety of names: the 'ambitious', the 'appreciative', the 'argumentative lawyer', the 'pessimist', the 'caregiver', the 'abandoned child', the 'introverted protector' or the 'wise guide'. Here we must be careful in relation to their names, as we do not want to limit our understanding of each character by focusing only on their name. When we observe an 'angry' character, we do not want to miss the other emotions that the 'angry' part of us feels, such as pain and fear. In many cases, we are led to take on a character or role that we do not want, but we adopt it because of its vitality to our existence within family or society. According to Schwartz,[2] in families where alcoholism is a problem, you will find various characters such as the 'person in charge', the 'angry rebel', or the 'hero'. Children in such a family are led to taking on these roles due to the given circumstances of their lives. Once they manage to extricate themselves from the chains of the role to which they were bound by necessity, they manage to change and discover their authentic and mature individuality. Such changes and processes may also occur when the various other characters that 'clothe' the ego have been cast aside.

We will examine this idea, the cast of characters assumed by the ego, through the case study of Sandy, a client of Jay Earley. Having the intention to finish a creative video project, Sandy found difficulty making a start. She first cleaned her office at home, a task that took over most her day, after which she then spent some time running on the treadmill. On her way back to her office, she went through the kitchen and prepared a three-course meal. By the end of the day, it dawned on her that she was deliberately refraining from starting the project and that due to the delay, she felt tired and stagnant.

A 'part' of Sandy does not want to work on the project, and in her therapy she came to call it the 'busy part', meaning the part that employs her in other activities to avoid the project, even though the project is her top priority. Admittedly the busy part is unconscious, but it can deter her from approaching her creative work. While Sandy was unaware of this figure, she had no way of dealing with it. That is, a part or character may be very influential precisely because they are hidden and cannot be approached and dealt with. Sandy could have reflected on her personal history to deal with the 'busy part'. However, it is rare for profound change to occur due to intellectual knowledge alone. Trying to identify the characters within her who were interacting with the 'busy character', Sandy was led to recall situations in her childhood where her friends mocked her every time she did something that would make her stand out. Eventually, whenever she was required to complete a task that might cause her to stand out in the public domain, the 'shy girl' figure came up. This being the case, we may conclude that the 'busy part' was just attempting to protect the 'shy girl' part who feared she may be the subject of ridicule again if indeed Sandy managed to complete the work on the video project (and stand out).

Another character in Sandy's inner drama is the 'the producer', who criticises Sandy whenever she refrains from completing her work. The 'busy part' opposes the 'producer' and rebels against it because it does not want Sandy to feel criticism and judgment, which would be the risk entailed if she returned to the video project. Simultaneously, the 'busy part' cannot enjoy these tasks due to the criticism of the 'producer' in the background.[3] We can imagine these two characters within Sandy having verbal and non-verbal dialogues with each other, each with its own body language and unique feelings. In this situation, it can be seen that these characters conflict with each other, as if caught in a vicious circle. Sandy must bridge the differences between the characters and promote trust among them in order to feel good and complete her project. Sandy needs to connect to her mature, wise self in order to extricate from this state of affairs, to that which is a centre of compassion, curiosity, and openness, which is different from all the other characters in her mind.

In relation to Indian philosophy, Schwartz also believes that the true self is passive, a witness devoid of any judgment.[4] In his view, the true self has the clarity and other qualities required to successfully lead the other characters or 'parts' of the personality. Schwartz bases his remarks on a meditation exercise in which practitioners are asked to imagine that they are climbing a mountain and leaving behind all the various parts and figures of their egos. Almost everyone reported that they found themselves rooted in their mental centre. This made them feel peaceful and lightened their hearts, such as to make them open, free, self-assured, and connected to the world. Such a state, he argued, is similar to a deep meditative state, such as Buddhist mindfulness. According to Schwartz, people may be in this state of mind even when they are focused on a particular activity. Unlike Schwartz, I believe it would be wrong to identify the true self with Buddhist mindfulness, since one of the fundamental doctrines of classical Buddhism is that there is 'no Self'. That is, in classical Buddhism there is no independent singular essence that underlies the world of phenomena or reality. In contrast, according to this view, the ego is nothing but a fictitious identity, a subjective sense of a concrete and enduring reality, which is nothing but a collection of tendencies and impressions.

For Schwartz, the true self observes, feels, loves, communicates and interacts with the various characters that the ego wears, and knows what each character needs. In his view, it is the seat of consciousness, arguing that his concept of true self is similar to the concept of the Self in monistic spiritual philosophical systems, such as the Self (*ātman*) in the philosophy of the Indian Advaita Vedānta, or those non-dualistic systems, such as the presence of natural awareness (*rigpa*) in Dzogchen. He argues that such a true self interacts with the world of phenomena but at the same time transcends such a world.[5] Schwartz contends that this self is like the seat of consciousness, such that it does not need to be developed, but also is not at all damaged. It is a form of consciousness lacking boundaries and yet Schwartz identifies eight key characteristics for this self: serenity, clarity, curiosity, compassion, confidence, courage, creativity and connection. The identification of these characteristics seems to contradict the notion of this true self as a consciousness lacking boundaries. These characteristics are limiting, as they do not really allow the self to be truly an open consciousness without boundaries. According to Schwartz the true self participates in one's personality through the eight characteristics that he attributes to it.

I would like to examine Schwartz's understanding of this authentic natural awareness, *rigpa*, which is at the heart of the Tibetan Dzogchen, through the words of Longchenpa, the 14th-century Tibetan Buddhist teacher. According to Longchenpa, *rigpa* is empty of binding connections, discursive or compulsive thinking, and precedes the ordinary mind which is subjected to, and occupied with, mental and psychological processes.[6] However, as such, *rigpa* cannot be intentionally assimilated with any of the characteristics that Schwartz identifies with the true self, such as leadership, confidence, and courage.

Rigpa is not only empty but also a state of clarity and comes to expression in the world of phenomena in a spontaneous and unintentional manner. That is, even though *rigpa* is empty of any discourse, it is manifested spontaneously in the world not as a strategy or unconditioned reaction but as an appropriate response to given circumstances through a direct perception. This direct perception is experienced through unconditioned awareness, unmediated by one's beliefs and perceptions, without leaving any karmic traces. Spontaneity brings with it wisdom in certain moments like the pure awareness that flickers for a moment, like a ray of sunshine momentarily penetrating the clouds on a winter day. It could be that from the perspective of Dzogchen, the insights that arise during Schwartz's therapy sessions are moments of grace in which pure awareness momentarily breaks through the mental processes and psychological layers. Its arising in this setting could in fact unintentionally resolve internal conflict. But it is also possible that the insights arise from deep processes of the ordinary mind, such as intelligence and intuition, in which case, this self is just another figure that the ego takes on. The very question of whether the insights arise from the intelligent and intuitive ordinary mind or whether they arise from the presence of pure awareness has the potential to challenge Schwartz's definition of the true self.

Schwartz's understanding of the true self and its characteristics in relation to Self (*ātman*) in the philosophy of Indian Advaita Vedānta comes through the Advaitic concept of *adhyāsa*. Śaṅkara, the eighth-century Indian teacher and philosopher, explains this concept as '[t]he apparent presentation, in the form of remembrance, to consciousness of something previously observed, in some other thing'. That is, a mutual superimposition, each takes on the characteristics and attributes of the other. For example, when someone gets a fright by mistaking a rope for a snake at twilight, or when someone mistakes mother of pearl for silver they are pleased. These feelings that occupy one's mind fade way once one gets closer to the rope or the mother of pearl and realises their wrong perception. The rope or mother of pearl arouses a memory, whether of a snake or a piece of silver, of something the person has previously seen and which has left a residue in memory. Although these examples are one-way superimpositions they can be reworked to demonstrate the opposite-way of superimpositions – in which someone feels safe by mistaking a snake for a rope at twilight, or when someone mistakes silver for mother of pearl and is disappointed.

In the context of his philosophy, Śaṅkara speaks of the mutual superimposition of *ātman* and non-*ātman*, the latter being the body, senses, and the mind. These are opposed to each other as much as darkness and light. 'Extra-personal attributes are superimposed on the Self, if a man considers himself sound and complete, or the contrary, as long as his wife, children, and so on are sound and entire or not. Attributes of the body are superimposed on the Self, if a man thinks of himself (his Self) as stout, lean, fair, as standing, walking, or jumping. Attributes of the sense-organs, if he thinks "I am mute, or deaf, or one-eyed, or blind." Attributes of the internal organ when he considers himself subject to desire, intention, doubt, determination, and so on. Thus the producer of the notion of the Ego (i.e. the internal organ) is superimposed on the interior Self, which, in reality, is the witness of all the modifications of the internal organ, and vice versá the interior Self, which is the witness of everything, is superimposed on the internal organ, the senses, and so on.'[7]

The *ātman* is neither the agent nor an experiencer, but rather eternally exists, actionless, self-effulgent and simply a witness of all the modifications of the mind. Hence the eight characteristics, which are nothing but mental modifications, that Schwartz attributes to the true self – serenity, clarity, curiosity, compassion, confidence, courage, creativity and connection – are not identical with the *ātman*. As noble and refined as these attributes may be, they are but a superimposition on the *ātman*, the true Self of Advaita Vedānta.

Furthermore, Schwartz claims that the true self is passive and boundlessly open and active, compassionate, and a natural leader of all the other personality parts or characters; the true self is therefore both individual and aware. The true self, in this understanding, is capable of reflection on inner states, on the various parts of the personality and their interactions in various situations. This self is present in everyone, and the various parts of the personality are prepared to protect the true self at all costs, however, in a moment of trauma or pain, all the characters or parts separate the self and disconnect it from such feelings to block out the pain and suffering.

Nevertheless, Schwartz's perception of the true self is also fundamentally different from that of yoga. The true self, according to Schwartz, is nothing but another part or character that the ego takes on, the character of the 'mature and wise' or the 'healthy ego'. This character plans its actions wisely and is devoid of obsessions, compulsive behaviours, addictions, and anxiety; it has good self-esteem, empathy, long and satisfying personal relationships, and exhibits emotional balance when confronted with anger, love, or jealousy. Unlike the 'mature and wise' part, the real yogic Self, *puruṣa,* is an isolated witness, non-active, not subject to causality, a pure primordial awareness. It is the root of awareness that exists in everyone, precedes any mental activity and is free from the objective world; it is a primordial independent awareness, independent of the world of phenomena, transcending subjectivity and objectivity, internal and external. Simultaneously, it is not a pure absence or nothingness that can be perceived in discursive thought. In primordial awareness, no discourse exists, but it is also impossible to turn that awareness off. Hence, according to yoga, the true Self does not generate actions and is not active in the mental and psychological dimensions, which are components of the world of phenomena, *prakṛti.*

However, there is a certain resemblance between pure primordial awareness and one's mind, since even according to yoga, a person may overcome the causes of afflictions and dormant mental imprints so that their *buddhi* becomes transparent, peaceful, and pure, resembling the unconditioned purity of the true Self, *puruṣa*. This resemblance allows for the closest intimacy between the two to occur, through which *puruṣa* is revealed. In this intimacy, the yogi can 'see their true Self', their essence, as pure primordial awareness, which is fundamentally different from their psycho–physical makeup. The similarity between these two principles may therefore allow the yogi to 'come face to face with their Self', just like a window that opens momentarily, though for a skilled and highly trained yogi, for increasingly longer periods of time. And yet, *puruṣa* and *prakṛti* are not the same, for the *buddhi*, being a component of the phenomenal mind, is subject to the activity of the *guṇa*s, whereas *puruṣa* is not active at all and does not change. That is, from the point of view of the phenomenal mind, these two principles might seem similar, as they do to Schwartz, but from the point of view of the yogi present in the discerning insight, they are not identical at all.

Schwartz therefore relies on this resemblance and sees the true self as a product of the *prakṛtic* mind in its intelligent and healthy state. In contrast, from the point of view of the philosophy of yoga, such a product is nothing but another part or character that the ego takes on. This character observes the other characters, and merges with the others to create a harmonious and deep unity between them as an integrated mature individual. Of course, the question then arises: who observes the healthy character, the one that observes and recognises the other figures? This question implies an infinite regression. To start with, who observes the observer that observes the observer? Who is the observer of the yogi? Is the yogi nothing more than another figure amongst an array of other characters and parts of the personality? Or is the yogi a figure who strives to advance and achieve transcendent states of wisdom, clarity, and unification? Or maybe the yogi is a scholarly figure, with extensive knowledge of Indian and Western philosophy, who has practiced yoga and meditation with great teachers?

In this respect, Chögyam Trungpa argues that many who engage in spiritual practice including yoga 'collect' knowledge and life experience, and that these serve as a display of the ego, as nourishment for the ego's tendency to bolster and glorify itself. When they present these collections to the world, these practitioners seek to validate their existence and secure themselves as 'spiritual' people.[8]

In order to establish the discerning insight that distinguishes between the ego and the true Self, I propose a meditative method on the sense of I-am-ness, the phenomenal self, or the ego, which relies on the psychology of yoga and Schwartz's understanding of the multiplicity of ego figures. In the context of yoga, every character that the ego takes on is nothing but a collection of mental processes, whereas here, in the context of the psychology of yoga, every such character is a wide cluster of *saṃskāra*s, *vāsanā*s, and *kleśa*s. Dealing with a particular figure in this type of meditation is an opportunity to dismantle its latent mental imprints, habitual tendencies, and causes of distress, diminishing their power to compel, and restraining their thoughts, feelings, and emotions. Such a meditative approach makes it possible to perfect the discerning clear gaze of yoga and prepare it for the rise of the discerning insight that can distinguish between the ego and the true Self, stilling the mind, and bringing mental processes to cessation. In such meditation, the yogi, instead of restraining specific thoughts or particular emotions, can dismantle a character their ego takes on that has become dominant, and thereby pacify the cluster of *saṃskāra*s, *vāsanā*s and *kleśa*s associated with that character. Thus in dealing with one character, the yogi can restrain an array of *vṛtti*s and still the mind, while such dismantling can sometimes ensure that the *vṛtti*s associated with that character will no longer occur and intrude upon the mind.

I do not intend to discuss this method in relation to the psychotherapeutic process that Schwartz proposes, since this section of the book is not about Western psychotherapeutic processes. Instead, my aim is a discussion of the yogic meditative method aimed at I-am-ness, which can purify and prepare the mental space for the rise of the discerning insight, *viveka-khyāti*, as the realisation of the absolute difference between *prakṛti* and *puruṣa*. Meditation in this respect means identification of urges and habitual tendencies which motivate the individual to undertake acts of self-preservation, appropriation, pleasure-seeking, and avoidance of pain. Whenever a habitual tendency takes on a particular character that motivates internal conflict, judgment, or internal discussion, we do not reflect upon them and see them for what they are but instead experience them as mental activity and inner dialogues. Once these are established they can create an active mental sheath that prevents the stilling of the mind, thereby precluding the possibility of the discerning insight, *viveka-khyāti*. This dominance of a particular character and the inner dialogues that it generates creates a mental wall between the sense of I-am-ness and the true Self. The very identification of the characters that the ego takes on in various circumstances can lead to the dismantling of the afflictive power of *saṃskāra*s, *vāsanā*s, and *kleśa*s that are associated with any given character. This is the aim of yogic meditation, to reduce the oppressive mental burden and suffering caused by these afflictions. I will now turn my attention to how the various parts of the ego can be identified, acknowledged, and reconciled.

Identification of the figures that appear in our minds in daily life and through meditation, prevents the 'wise and mature adult' part from becoming entangled in their interactions, such that it can remain in the position of the sincere and open watcher. Sometimes, the very identification of a character, the recognition of its existence, may promote trust and reconciliation between the 'wise and mature adult' and the other character, and thereby reduce the intensity of the conflict between them, leading towards resolution of this conflict. Such a resolution is possible if the interrelationships between them are not too intense, such that the 'wise and mature adult' is not inextricably caught up in their web. Alternatively, suppose that the attachment between the 'wise and mature adult' and another character is very complicated and intense. In that case, the method of *imagining the opposite*, *pratipakṣa bhāvanā*,[9] may be sufficient as a means of reconciling the conflict, and promoting trust between the characters, rather than necessarily engaging in Schwartz's psychotherapeutic method. Identification of the various figures (including the yogic observer's figure) together with *pratipakṣa bhāvanā* (imagining the opposite) may be enough to evoke trust, closeness, and unity between all of them, thereby pacifying the mind and allowing the discerning insight to arise.

The process by which the ego takes on and strips off characters is rapid. In the absence of a language to describe it, how do we identify the characters? We must understand that the characters are not an enemy to be avoided. Some were shaped to protect us from pain and suffering; others were formed to make us feel good about ourselves. However, although their motives may be positive, they do not always work wisely for us. Extreme perceptions may drive them and, in some situations, they may even act in a confused way, awkwardly, or immaturely, and thereby distort our perception of reality. In any case, looking into the origins of these characters, we will find that they are driven by a desire to do what is best for us.

The first step, then, is connecting with the 'wise and mature adult', coming to an understanding of the various characters that the ego wears in different situations, and trying to cultivate trust, closeness, unity, and reconciliation between them.[10] In his model, Schwartz identifies three categories to which those characters belong. Firstly, there is the category called 'exiles'. These characters represent psychological trauma, often carried over from childhood, and they hold onto the pain and fear created by these traumas. They are so named because they may be in exile from the other parts, isolating themselves and thereby polarising the inner relationships between all of the other inner figures. The other two categories are the 'managers' and the 'firefighters', which are characters who try to protect someone by preventing the 'exiles' and their painful memories from resurfacing and dominating the mental space. 'Managers' have a role to play in protecting against the feeling of pain, and they influence the way one communicates and interacts with the outside world. 'Firefighters' are characters that emerge whenever 'exiles' have resurfaced and begin to dominate the mind. Their purpose is to divert attention from the harm and shame that arises with the resurfacing of the 'exiles'. 'Firefighters' are expressed as impulsive or inappropriate behaviours aiming to 'turn off' the pain and shame, through behaviours such as overeating, violence, or drug use. 'Firefighters' can also distract someone from their pain by over-focusing on various tasks related to work, hobbies, or cultivating an extensive social network.

Jay Earley[11] adds a few more sub-categories to those presented by Schwartz. The figure of judgment and criticism emerges from memory, and appears in response to particular situations. For example, when meditating, a person can settle into the 'wise and mature adult' character and their mind can thereby become calm and open. Then, a memory of an argument with their employer from the day before may suddenly resurface, an argument in which another part of them was dominant, the 'arrogant' part who knows better than the employer how to perform in the work environment. This person understands that the 'arrogant' part accompanies them in many situations in their life, causes them great sorrow, and bears responsibility for making them closed in both heart and mind. Such arrogance is projected onto the work environment, and becomes dominant in the person's relationships with their colleagues and their manager. Everyone around them senses this arrogance, and can see that it may harm their possibilities for promotion, professional abilities, and capacity to earn a living. In response to the damage and grief caused by the 'arrogant' part, another character emerges, the 'judge', who is irritated by the 'arrogant' part and critical of its tendencies. In such a situation, one must make sure that the 'wise and mature adult' part is distinguished, so that one's mind is calm, open, and curious. The 'wise and mature adult' part should be distinct from the other characters or parts, not allowing them to dominate and control the mental space, not through suppression or avoidance, but through understanding and empathy.

Another character of the ego identified by Earley is embodied in the 'avoidant'. Its purpose is to avoid dealing with the figures of the 'exiles' that the 'arrogant' part protects. That is, arrogance protects and covers up any vulnerability resulting from a painful early experience associated with the exiled parts. Once the 'wise and mature adult' is distinguished from the other characters, it can empathise with them and begin to establish an atmosphere of trust between the 'exiles', the 'arrogant', and the 'judge'. It is essential to pay attention to the 'atmosphere', as the mental climate indicates the degree of internal integration under the leadership of the mature, healthy part of the ego. When this is achieved, the other characters are not dominating or controlling the mental space, nor are they dictating a person's day-to-day conduct. These characters then vacate the mental space. Contemplating the various characters that the ego takes on in such a manner will encourage them to vacate the mental space without avoiding or suppressing them, leading to stillness, clarity, and an openness of mind.

Another character that the ego wears can be the 'intellectual'. It analyses the other characters the ego takes on instead of listening to them. Through its analyses it excuses certain states of dissonance that arise in the moment of encounter with mental pain from the past. The 'intellectual' is absolutely important, and it is desirable to engage it in dialogue. It is worthwhile thanking it for its helpful intellectual understandings and at the same time letting it know that it is diverting the process from directly dealing with the vulnerability, arrogance, avoidance, and judgment that the other characters represent, and then asking it to vacate the mental stage.

When we are identifying the parts that arise during meditation and that come to dominate the mental space, attempting to reconcile and moderate the conflicts between them, the figure of the 'impatient' might surface, a character who wants immediate results. For example, an attempt to appease the 'exiled' before the 'wise and mature adult' has talked to the 'arrogant' who protects them is an attempt to speed up the process associated with the 'impatient' part, and perhaps even other figures may be involved who likewise wish to inhibit the process of exposing the pain or fear held by the 'exiles'. Therefore, in meditation, the 'wise and mature adult' will make sure that the 'impatient' is distinguished from the others. The 'wise and mature adult' should have an internal dialogue with it, acknowledging its desire to heal the vulnerable exiled parts while asking it to vacate the mental space and move behind the scenes.

Another sub-category may express the meditator's lack of confidence in being able to settle into the 'wise and mature adult'. The absence of trust may produce another character that thinks 'I am not able' to identify and observe the other characters the ego takes on. It is advisable to focus on this character and stay with it, introduce an internal dialogue that acknowledges its role in protecting the meditator, and come to an understanding that it is only one part of the meditator's personality, and that surely they have other talented and enabling parts which can assist. Such a dialogue enables the 'wise and mature adult' to dominate the mental space, while 'I am not able' vacates the mental space and moves behind the scenes.

Schwartz has described his method[12] as being focused on healing the damaged characters (the parts) that the ego wears, and restoring mental balance and harmony between them by regulating their conflicts. This is made possible when the characters are released from performing the extreme roles that for whatever reasons they have taken on, building trust between them, and restoring the confidence of the 'wise and mature adult', thereby creating harmony between all the characters under its leadership.

As I noted earlier, the discussion of Schwartz's practical psychotherapeutic method goes beyond this book's purpose. My interest here is in the psychology of yoga and the process that enables the emergence of the discerning insight. In summary, there are three main reasons for this choice. Firstly, there is a difference in the perception of the true Self between Schwartz's theory and the psychology of yoga. The second concerns the context of the psychology of yoga that is at the centre of the discussion. The third concerns the point of view of yoga. According to the philosophy of yoga, any elaboration of a psychotherapeutic process does not move beyond being a mental discourse, and therefore is likened to a wall of mental activity that stands between the ego and the true Self, thereby preventing yogic stillness and coming face-to-face with *puruṣa*. However, this does not entirely negate the psychotherapeutic process and its effectiveness as, in some situations, this process may be beneficial and complementary to the psychology of yoga.[13]

The meditative process recognises the various characters that the ego wears, acknowledges their role, appeases them, and then coaxes them to vacate the mind's stage and to move behind the scenes, creating an open and transparent mental space. It is directed by the 'wise and mature adult', who separates and frees itself from the dominance of the other various characters and prevents their intrusion into the mind during meditation. At the culmination of the process, the 'wise and mature adult' may rise to the insight that it, too, is a part of the ego, albeit a part that is empathetic, intelligent, whole, and confident. And yet, it too and the bureaucracy it creates must be dismantled, for this 'intelligent adult', being the leader of a collection of characters that the ego takes on, is not competent enough to fulfil the primary purpose of meditation, stilling the mind. The 'wise and mature adult' becomes irrelevant, and having cleared the mental stage, it too settles behind the scenes. Subsequently, vast mental spaces of clarity and wisdom unfold, preparing the ground for the rise of the discerning wisdom, a ground of absence: without the mediation of beliefs, conceptualisation, causes of affliction, and behaviour patterns.

Sometimes the 'wise and mature adult' vacates the mind in a regressive process in which another 'wise' figure or 'yogi' observes, as yet another character is distinguished from the original 'wise and mature adult'. Then the 'wise' figure or 'yogi' themselves are distinguished by another observer, and so on until the mind is exhausted. Exhaustion is what makes it possible to stop giving in to the conceptualisations and judgments of mental activity, and it makes it possible to collapse, to give up the tense alertness of the psychological defence mechanisms and to settle into a state of indifferent openness.[14] Eventually, this situation may give rise to the insight: 'I am not (awareness), (awareness) does not belong to me, the "I" is not (awareness).'[15] Meaning, the mind understands that just as the mirror reflecting light is not a source of light, it is not the source of primordial awareness. This is the discerning insight that must be sustained and into which one must settle. Through the eyes of the true Self that reflect the mind's eyes, the mind recognises that this insight is complete and pure, absent from any perceptual error and uninvolved with any agency.

If so, what is the process that enables the rise of the discerning insight associated with the psychology of yoga? This process is a meditation aimed at a subtle object, the ego. It is first accompanied by a conceptualisation similar to the early stages of cognitive *samādhi*, which includes language, perceptual, and memory mechanisms, and an awareness of the act of thinking itself. The process culminates with the dawn of the discerning insight that distinguishes between the true Self and I-am-ness, the phenomenal 'I'. This exposes the erroneous cognition that identifies the true Self with the ego which is merely a component of the world of phenomena.

Identifying the parts

Direct and experiential identification of the various figures that the ego takes on can reduce oppressive mental burden and suffering. The description of Schwartz's three main categories (exiles, managers, firefighters), and of their various sub-categories (such as the avoidant, the sceptical or the arrogant) together with the language we can employ to communicate with them, may give us points of reference for identifying the characters that emerge within, and take over, our mental space.

During meditation, such a process of identification places the meditating yogi in the position of a watcher or observer of the various situations that arise in their mindstream, whether these are related to the activity of meditation itself or to other situations that occur in daily life. Actual observation slows down the mindstream, and allows us to place a magnifying glass over our experiences or difficulties. This gives us the opportunity to identify the various parts of the ego that may come to take over and dominate the meditative space, recognise what that part is doing, and form a trusting and conciliatory relationship with it. For example, a person sitting for a few minutes in meditation may notice that their mindstream is flooded with intrusive and distracting thoughts such as: what am I going to do after meditation?; where will I go?; where should I eat and with whom?; should I have just a snack here at home and then go out to a movie?; should I send the plans for the work that I need to complete tomorrow? The character that emerges from this stream of thoughts is the 'time manager', who effectively takes over the meditation, while the 'wise and mature adult' is almost drowned out. The 'wise and mature adult' observes, identifies and recognises the 'time manager', expresses appreciation for its typically efficient and essential services but points out the inappropriate timing, politely asks it to vacate the mental space with the promise that it will be given attention later on. In the vacant mental space that is created, it is now the 'wise and mature adult' who is watched and identified as the leader of all the other characters of the ego. This is an infinite regression into the depths of the mind: where the 'time manager' is observed by the 'wise and mature adult' who is observed by the 'yogi', who is observed by yet another observer, who in turn is also observed by another observer, and so on and so forth. This infinite regression is something that I will now discuss in the context of stilling the mind.

Some will say that each of these characters are just thoughts, or at most a wave of mental activity. Such a view would insist these characters must be silenced as they have nothing to do with the true Self, so there is no point engaging with them. Giving attention to an egoic figure may amplify it, so instead it is best to attend to the object of meditation, or proceed with an analytic mediation. For example, according to Ramana Maharshi, the first thought that enters the mind during meditation is the 'I', representing the ego or the sense of I-am-ness. Asking the question 'who am I?', and persisting with this question in a focused one-pointed manner, searching for the origin of the thought of the 'I', leads to a state in which all other discursive thoughts are blocked and dissipate until finally the thought of the 'I' also disappears.[16] Such an inquiry ends the false identification of the true Self with the mind, the ego, and the world of phenomena.

When asking 'who am I?', the first thing that may come to mind is the unity of the body's organs or the connection between mind and body. We perceive ourselves as one existential unit that cannot be divided. However, when we try to locate and find the ego in practice, we discover that it too is nothing but a collection of components that can be divided further. There is no single element that represents the ego, nor is the collection of elements really the ego. Thus, as we examine each of the components of the psycho-physical subject, we cannot actually find and point to the ego's place. After the investigation has been exhausted, we find nothing, and this prepares the ground for stillness of mind to arise.

Such a form of inquiry is valid not only for the individual subject, but also for other objects. A tree, for example, is a union of leaves, branches, trunk, and roots. As soon as we look at it and break it down into its interdependent components, the unified tree will 'disappear', and this disappearance will also prepare the ground for stillness of mind.

Yet in our daily realities, most of us remain subjected to the causes of affliction, the ego, and habitual tendencies despite the intellectual knowledge that these are nothing but mental processes that have nothing to do with the true Self. The causes of affliction repeatedly inflict pain and sorrow, and such intellectual knowledge takes time to assimilate effectively. Once this is achieved it can have a real impact in enabling us to dismantle the causes of affliction, behavioural patterns, and dormant mental imprints.

The testimonies of practitioners presented by Kornfield[17] also tell a similar story. In these testimonies, there is a recurring gap between: intellectual knowledge that the true Self is not our body, senses, mind, thoughts, memories, emotions, nor any of our immediate experiences of ourselves and others; and our immediate experience of ourselves, others, and our daily existence. Consequently, despite their ability to maintain steady states of stilled mind, skilled practitioners may continue to experience emotional crises, addiction, and tremendous regressions in self-esteem.[18] In contrast, in a specific meditation focused on the ego, a mental climate arises where recognition of the different characters can generate honesty, sensitivity, empathy, and closeness that can lead to an inner reconciliation between them. According to the psychology of yoga, it is precisely in this meditation, which is directed and focused on the ego, that the fuel supply that feeds the causes of affliction and habitual tendencies is diminished. Such a mental atmosphere is essential for clearing the mind as a mental space in which the discerning insight may emerge.

Self-deception

One of the critical characteristics Chögyam Trungpa identifies in the ego is the tendency to self-deception based on the need for self-esteem and the recourse to long-term memory. This is a tendency to retreat in time, into nostalgic states of mind, remembering things that evoke a positive feeling. In these moments, the presence of one's self-awareness fades and dissipates. Regressing to earlier, happier times prevents the rise of current emotions such as pain, loss, and depression. To protect against these feelings, the ego floods the mind with memories, such as compliments we have heard in the past, comforting us. And thus, the possibility of inspiration or breakthrough in the present is lost in favour of a nostalgic reliance on the past. Thus, the practitioner becomes spiritually self-deceived, suppressing their depression and preventing it from surfacing. They justify this by invoking their fortunate destiny, having been blessed with spiritual experiences and teachers who have transmitted their wisdom to them so that they have no room for depression.

Self-deception is associated with several characters that the ego wears: the 'nostalgic' whose purpose is to protect the 'depressed' from the feeling of pain by preventing painful or traumatic experiences from floating up into the mind.

Self-deception has another facet: the person feels that they are fulfilling a hope or a dream. It is a self-deception for a person to live their life under the sway of a dream rather than in accordance with reality. And a person who has already fulfilled a dream will want to recreate the feeling associated with its achievement. They will strive to do it again (out of nostalgia) without re-examining the condition of their present reality. Similarly, a practitioner may feel an unusual joy when they first become acquainted with a clarity of mind, but the attempt to recreate (out of nostalgia) these experiences (which are but one of many possible experiences), instead of remaining in their given reality, is also a form of self-deception.

The meditative process

As we sit in ego-focused meditation, the figures the ego takes on will rise one after the other. They will permeate and dominate the mind and determine the content occupying the mind. The 'wise and mature adult' may be caught up in them and unsettled. These contents may produce seeds of action according to each character. These seeds germinate under certain circumstances, and through the actions that these bring about, karma is accumulated.

Some of the figures that might be identified during meditation are, for example: the 'commentator', who offers a running commentary about what is happening during the meditation or expresses their interpretation about some narrative or event from the distant or recent past; the 'facilitator' who whispers instructions to us about meditative practice even though it is already clear to us; the 'arrogant' who refuses to follow instructions relating to the meditation because they know better how it should be conducted; the 'time manager' who incessantly plans what to do after the meditation with great efficiency; the 'nostalgic spiritual yogi' who tries to replicate wonderful spiritual experiences from the past without being aware of the present and what is actually happening in the meditation; the 'thought catcher' who tries to suppress specific thoughts and encourages positive thoughts to arise and proliferate; the 'judge' who evaluates their steps in the meditative activity (what is excellent, what is wrong) and exercises judgment towards events and people, even if they were not necessarily directly involved with them; the 'spiritual bypasser' that clings to spiritual meditative activity so that they do not need to confront their pain, frustration, or jealousy.

It is essential to focus on such figures one by one while slowing down the mindstream through concentration, observing the mental activities and pictures one by one. The term 'mindstream' usually refers to the stream of consciousness or flow of thoughts that constantly arises, goes from one thing to the next without restraint and passes away in the mind. It is a concept that is often used in various Buddhist traditions,[19] where it is viewed as a continuum of mental events or states that occur in one's mind. The mindstream is believed to be a repository of one's accumulated karma and experiences, and the ultimate goal is to purify the mindstream and attain liberation from the cycle of rebirth. The concept of mindstream is not explicitly mentioned in the *Yogasūtra*. However, the idea of the mindstream can be related to the mind as being constantly active and subject to fluctuations or modifications (*vṛttis*), interacting with the external world. Stilling these mental activities in order to realise one's true Self is the goal of yoga. While the concept of mindstream can be seen as being related to this process of stilling the mind. In Buddhist terms, the mindstream is seen as being purified through the practice of mindfulness and meditation, which helps to reduce the influence of negative mental states and cultivate positive qualities such as compassion and wisdom. Similarly, in yoga, the practice of meditation and other techniques such as pranayama (breath control) and asana (physical postures) are seen as helping to still the mind and cultivate inner awareness.

Thus, there may be a vast range of figures that may arise in one's midstream and come up in meditation, and some may be linked to memories and events from different times. So it is just as possible to encounter an injured or vulnerable young child as it is to find a protective figure fully dressed in a knight's armour. When I shared this idea of meditation focused on the ego with my colleagues, I was surprised to find that most of the students with whom I applied this meditation, managed to be intuitively aware of their inner figures. Encouraged, I have found it appropriate to suggest four scenarios of meditation that are tailored to different levels of meditator skills and mental temperaments and in relation to the states of mind they experience during meditation, from being calm to being agitated or stuck. Here are four main scenarios that include examples of figures such as the 'time manager' and the 'meditation manager,' but each person may encounter different figures depending on their psychological makeup.

First meditative scenario

This scenario refers to a specific state of meditation in which calm and peace are accessible and easily implemented, almost effortlessly. During such a meditation we observe our mindstream and identify a specific figure without getting mixed-up with the proliferating thoughts associated with it. Let us take, for example, the 'time manager'. Upon identifying and recognising the 'time manager', they immediately vacate the mental space and fade away. For the most part, once we identify a thought or feeling in which we may be trapped, that thought or feeling is released by the very act of identification. Such an uninvolved gaze projected without any mental effort, without trying to force or persuade the figure, should be sufficient to enable the 'time manager' to walk away, vacate the mental space and go behind the scenes, leaving the mind still. This is similar to the feeling of annoyance. Just by recognising our condition of annoyance, such a feeling immediately upon arising begins to fade and no longer activates us or distorts how we relate to the given circumstances and the persons involved. It is like a snake that uncoils itself, by itself, without any external intervention. The absence of such external intervention is similar to the uninvolved gaze.

However, there is a part of us that has identified the 'time manager', which is the 'wise and mature adult' who is itself an 'egoic' figure. And now, upon identifying and recognising it, it too vacates the mental stage and moves behind the scenes. Nevertheless, there now remains another part of us, the observer who has identified and recognised the 'wise and mature adult', who is itself nothing but an egoic figure. Let's call this observer that remains, the 'meditation manager'. When the 'meditation manager' departs due to being identified and recognised there is yet another figure who has observed the 'meditation manager' who has recently identified and recognised the 'wise and mature adult'. Further, there is another figure that remains – let's call it the 'seeker after liberation' – who has identified and recognised the 'meditation manager' that implies an ongoing regressive observation process involved with egoic figures, expressions of the sense of I-am-ness, the phenomenal 'I'.

In the process, the mind, exhausted and clear of all those figure, arrives at a dead end in the sense that the mind becomes completely pacified. The regressive observation process is no longer relevant, and the observer or watcher as an identity does not dominate the mental space. At that moment in which the mind arrives at a dead end, there will be nothing left then that we can point to and call 'I'. We reach a point where there is no answer to the question of identity. At this stage, the question of identifying the phenomenal 'I' becomes irrelevant since both the question and the answer fade away spontaneously.

Longchenpa, the fourteenth-century CE Tibetan Buddhist scholar and teacher of Dzogchen explains this state of mind with the following words: 'There is no reference point – no, "How is it?" "What is it?" "It is this!" What can any of you do? Where is the "I"? What can anyone do about what was so before but now is not?'[20] In that state of mind devoid of ingrained fixations, plans, and actions, what is left there for us to do? The internal reference point of the sense of I-am-ness, which rigidly reifies things and its seeming continuity of what is reified as the 'I', or self-identity, has been released. There is no place to which we can refer, about which we can say, 'This is the place to which I have been brought, the place I have reached.'

It is a place in which stillness remains, a quietude that is not accompanied by beliefs, conceptions, education, and conclusions. This silence is not nihilistic but is transparent and clear due to the radiating true Self, being a pure primordial awareness reflected in a transparent mind. This silence is the mental space in which discerning insight may arise with the pure intellect purified from the sense of I-am-ness, which wholly understands that it is not the source of pure primordial awareness, just like the mirror that reflects light even though it is not its source.

This clear, bright, and discerning gaze is the culmination of meditation on the ego or sense of I-am-ness, the discerning insight. Continual abiding in this clear discerning gaze becomes in itself a means of attaining the supreme insight.[21] Yoga thus becomes a means as well as a goal. Vyāsa indicates that there are seven kinds of insight or results that can be derived from the discerning clear gaze: (1) confidence that suffering can be alleviated; (2) *avidyā* is attenuated (3); a profound understanding that liberation from *saṃsāra* is realised through *samādhi*; (4) that yogic discerning wisdom can be applied as a means of liberation from conditioned existence; (5) that the *buddhi* has fulfilled its function; (6) that the tension between the *guṇa*s in the *buddhi* lose their interaction as opposing forces and converge into a pure state of potentiality; (7) that *puruṣa*, abiding in its nature, is a light to itself and isolated from the world of phenomena, *prakṛti*.[22]

Second meditative scenario

During meditation, when our mind is at peace, we observe the mindstream, identify a particular figure and focus on it. This character takes over the mental space and becomes dominant, such that we are almost captivated by its narratives. This time mere identification is not sufficient for that figure to vacate the mental space and move behind the scenes as this character, the 'time manager', is anxious and demands attention. Observing the character, its appearance, age and body language, we conduct an internal dialogue with the 'time manager' in which we validate its role. Such dialogue is a mental effort. That is, in this discourse, we recognise the 'time manager', empathise with it, warmly thank it for its excellent skills in managing our time effectively, and express appreciation for its concern for meeting tasks and goals. At the same time, we make it clear to it that, at the moment, there is no need for its services, and we ask it to leave the mental space and move behind the scenes. We promise it that we will attend to it at the end of the meditation session and consult it on any urgent matters that need attention. Since aggressive–compulsive motives do not drive this character, such a discourse is usually enough to appease it, calm it down, and thereby allow the 'wise and mature adult' to unblend and part company with it so that the 'time manager' goes behind the scenes.

This is also the place to practice a friendly attitude towards the other, as Patañjali recommends in sūtra 1.33: 'Through the practice of friendliness (*maitrī*), compassion (*karuṇā*), joy (*muditā*), and equanimity (*upekṣā*) toward the happy, the suffering, the virtuous, and the unvirtuous (respectively), consciousness is clarified.'[23] The reason is that the other, towards whom Patañjali recommends practicing a friendly attitude, is no different from a specific character that the sense of I-am-ness or the phenomenal 'I' takes on.

At this point in the meditative process, the 'wise and mature adult' gradually unblends and separates from the 'time manager' and extricates itself from the latter's dominance. But then another character emerges, the 'meditation manager', who distinguishes itself from the 'wise and mature adult', and which being an egoic figure in itself, indeed the figure who has just recognised the 'time manager', now leaves the mental space and moves behind the scenes. Now the 'meditation manager' remains, but it too is nothing but an egoic figure. And yet, even then, there is still someone else – lets' call it the 'yogi' – another figure or character, watching the 'meditation manager' who just a few moments earlier observed the 'wise and mature adult'. Is it not the case that this observer, the 'yogi', is simply another egoic figure, an expression of the sense of 'I am-ness'?

Here, the meditator continues to abide in this state, wondering about the 'observer' in question. Due to engaging with the ongoing regressive observation process, the mind at this stage is exhausted, and observation becomes no longer relevant, understanding that there is no button that the 'observer' can press to produce discerning insight and come to know *puruṣa* directly. Gradually the 'last observer' in that regressive observation process, becomes hopeless, collapses and disappears. The mind becomes still! From this stillness, the discerning insight may emerge: 'I am not (awareness), (awareness) does not belong to me, the "I" is not (awareness).' The phenomenal 'I' is not the source of pure primordial awareness, just as the mirror that reflects light is not the source of light.

Third meditative scenario

We sit for meditation, observe our mindstream, identify a particular figure and focus on it. Unlike the previous meditative scenario, this character, let's call it, for example, the 'time manager', is very intense and dominant, it takes over, and we are overwhelmed by it and the circumstances of its sudden dominance. On this occasion, identification and observation of its characteristics, and the use of a conciliatory and empathetic inner dialogue, are insufficient to bring appeasement and to encourage it to leave the mental scene. The 'time manager' may refuse to respond to the pleas of the 'wise and mature adult' due to its total compulsive commitment to the fulfilment of its role, a commitment that is most important at this given moment of meditation. It is also possible that this character does not have faith in the 'wise and mature adult'.

Let us now return to the character of the 'time manager', who is about 27 years old, stubborn, anxious, restless and compulsive. Its discourse fills the mind and takes it over, and it repeats its words, incessantly offering further possibilities to schedule, restlessly moving from one thing to another without restraint. When the 'wise and mature adult' is momentarily able to recognise this state of affairs it turns to the 'time manager' to appease it, but the latter refuses to enter into a dialogue with the 'wise and mature adult'.

To overcome the overwhelming dominance of the 'time manager' and vacate it from the mental scene, two options are suggested. The first option involves the 'wise and mature adult' identifying and recognising the 'time manager', and then attempting to maintain its position for as long as possible without pressing it. By patiently observing and settling in, the 'wise and mature adult' can gradually encourage the 'time manager' to drop its defences and become more open to dialogue. Once this occurs, the meditative process can continue according to the previous scenario.

The second option, inspired by Patañjali and Vyāsa, involves the practice *imagining the opposite*, that relies on sūtra 2.34: 'To cultivate the opposite is (to reflect upon the fact) that thoughts which contradict the yama-s, such as violent thoughts and so on, whether executed, planned to be executed, or even approved, whether driven by greed, anger, or delusion, whether mild, moderate, or intense, result in endless suffering (duḥkha) and ignorance (ajñāna).'[24] Vyāsa points out that if a person feels negative emotions such as hatred, and they are engulfed in a tangle of causes of affliction and acts under their influence, then they must cultivate opposite thoughts. For him, to cultivate opposite is to initiate a meditative inquiry and reflect about the consequences of such negative emotions, thoughts and actions that inflict pain. Such reflection enables them to open a gap between ideas and negative actions, and their results.[25] In the present example, this gap would take place between the 'wise and mature adult' and the 'compulsive time manager', separating and unblending them.

Here, as the inner dialogue continues to take place, we observe the 'compulsive time manager' with empathy, recognising its stress and pressure. We, as the 'wise and mature adult' invite it to consider the consequences of its present state and actions on our coexistence. Once the 'compulsive time manager' becomes open, and remorsefully realises how it affects the coexistence between the egoic figures, we thank it for its skills and the concern it has for our schedule and tell it that, at this point, its presence is not required, asking it to leave the mental space and move behind the scenes.

Similar to previous scenarios, the 'wise and mature adult' separates from the 'time manager', followed by the emergence of the 'meditation manager'. The 'meditation manager' then leaves the mental space and moves behind the scenes, leaving behind the 'yogi' as another egoic figure. The 'yogi' is an observer, an expression of the sense of 'I am-ness'.

Now, an 'observer' remains and identifies the 'yogi' as an egoic part whose intervention in the mediation has been very efficient, leading to a vacated mental space that has enhanced the restraint of cognitive processes. Then, this 'observer' acknowledges the 'yogi' and asks it to leave the mental space and also move behind the scenes. Yet, still, there is a 'presence' who observes the 'observer' who has watched and identified the 'yogi'. Isn't it true that they are all but egoic figures, an expression of the phenomenal 'I'?

That 'presence' continues to abide in that vacated and still mental space. Gradually even that 'presence' falls away, dissipates, and disappears, along with all labelling, effort, and avoidance. The mind becomes stillness, the ground from which the clear discerning gaze can emerge: 'I am not (awareness), (awareness) does not belong to me, the "I" is not (awareness).' The phenomenal 'I' is not the source of pure primordial awareness, just as the mirror that reflects light is not the source of light.

Fourth meditative scenario

There may be a situation where we would need to invest enormous mental effort and patience compared to the previous cases, attending to a 'difficult' character that takes over. That character is particularly intense. It refuses to participate in any inner dialogue because of its role in protecting another character who is lurking in the mind's outskirts.

That problematic character, for example, is the 'stubborn compulsive time manager'. It overtakes our meditative mental space and, as we observe it, we can see that it is taking an aggressively defensive stance, that it is anxious and compulsive, and does not respond to our attempt to enter into a discourse with it. We continue to watch it with great patience without pressing it. When we ask it why it is not responding to us, it points to another character, a little distant, vague but clear enough, this is a 16-year-old child, ashamed, embarrassed, its shoulders drooping, 'dead ashamed'. A floating memory: the child was supposed to participate in an international exchange of youth delegations. It had planned to fly with its classmates and stay with families in the destination country, but it realised that it had forgotten its passport and has consequently missed its flight due to arriving late at the airport. Shame is a strong emotion that arises as an unpleasant feeling when a person thinks they have done something that they should not have done, something unacceptable or stupid, and they feel humiliated and exposed to judgment.

We reflect upon the 'dead ashamed' character. In our imagination, we look at its face, body language, its fragile and exposed presence, feeling its pain and wonder about what it is feeling and what it is going through. We then understand the magnitude of the shame, disappointment, and frustration it felt when it missed the flight. We emphatically comfort, listening to its version of events about the missing flight, the shame, and its consequences, but ask it to consider its effects on our coexistence. We tell it that it is important for us to understand the oppressiveness of the mental burden it feels because it is a part of us, a figure of our own. We invite it to look at us as the 'wise and mature adult'.

The 'dead ashamed' child then develops trust in the 'wise and mature adult', feeling safe in its proximity. Its body straightens, and the fog that surrounds it dissipates. Even the 'stubborn compulsive time manager' who protected the child from triggering a painful memory, relaxes and its charged compulsion subsides.

There may be situations where a multiplicity of characters may flood and overwhelm the mind at once. Such situations result from unresolved and particularly charged mental matters such as trauma. It is also possible that the characters in these cases will be detached or prone to addiction. I suggest exploration of these characters is not undertaken on your own, and perhaps if needed it would be worthwhile seeking a suitable and supportive professional framework that may assist in dealing with these characters as a complementary option to yoga.

Let us return to the characters in our discussion. After pacifying the 'dead ashamed' child we as the 'wise and mature adult' address the 'stubborn compulsive time manager', and acknowledge and thank it for protecting the 'dead ashamed' child and ask it to vacate the mental space. As with previous scenarios, the 'wise and mature adult' separates from the 'time manager', followed by the emergence of the 'meditation manager'. The 'meditation manager' then leaves the mental space and moves behind the scenes, leaving behind the 'yogi' as another egoic figure. The 'yogi' is an observer, and egoic part, an expression of the sense of 'I am-ness'. An 'observer' remains and identifies the 'yogi' as being an egoic part and asks it to leave the mental space and move behind the scenes. Yet, still, a 'presence' observes the 'observer' who has watched and identified the 'yogi'.

That 'presence' continues to abide in that vacated and still mental space. Gradually even that 'presence' falls away, dissipates and disappears, along with all labelling, effort, and avoidance. The mind becomes stillness as the ground from which the clear discerning gaze can emerge: 'I am not (awareness), (awareness) does not belong to me, the "I" is not (awareness).' The phenomenal 'I' is not the source of pure primordial awareness. This discerning insight was the purpose of the cognitive *samādhi* that relies on an object (in our case the ego), and once achieved becomes a means to the objectless *samādhi*.

There are other yoga practices within the framework of yoga psychology that can help address egoic identification, such as the *yama*s and *niyama*s, which are the primary ethical guidelines or rules of yoga. However, because these ethical and moral rules were developed in a distant culture in ancient times, their meaning can vary between different societies and the siddhis or achievements associated with them; understanding them requires a thorough exploration of the historical, social, and cultural context in which they were formed. This study is beyond the scope of this discussion. Nevertheless, since the *yama*s and *niyama*s reflect universal values[26] that refine human drives of survival and those learned through socialisation, cultivating these ethical guidelines can reduce egoic identification. This can help practitioners on their path towards cultivating the discerning and clear gaze of yoga.

The *yama*s, which are the five primary ethical guidelines of yoga, include *ahiṃsā* (non-harming), *satya* (truthfulness and radical honesty), *asteya* (non-stealing), *brahmacarya* (celibacy), and *aparigraha* (non-possessiveness). The *niyama*s, which are observances of ethical guidelines, include five practices: *śauca* (internal and external yogic cleansing), contentment (*saṃtoṣa*), austerities or practices involved with inner heat (*tapas*), *svādhyāya* (self-study and mantra recitation), and devotion to the lord or deity (*Īśvara praṇidhāna*).[27]

Ego identification arises when individuals mistake the temporary and changing aspects of their experience for their true Self. This confusion creates a sense of attachment to one's own thoughts, emotions, and desires, leading to the addition of 'I' to statements reflecting such experiences, decisions, discernment, perceptions, or actions. Attachment is a strong connection to someone or something, a habitual tendency that provides us with a sense of safety, certainty and comfort. Attachment can develop in various relationships, such as parent–child, romantic, or friendship, and it can also extend to objects, places, or ideas.

The cultivation of *yama*s and *niyama*s can help reduce egoic identification by promoting a sense of detachment from one's thoughts, emotions, and actions. This involves developing a mental capacity to observe these egoic identifications without getting caught up in them or identifying them as part of one's core Self. The *yama*s encourage us to refrain from harmful behaviour towards ourselves and others, such as violence, lying, stealing, or greed. The *niyama*s encourage us to cultivate positive qualities, such as cleanliness, contentment, self-discipline, self-study, and surrender to a higher power or lord.

In the context of the regressive meditative process, this means unblending and separating from the habitual patterns of thought, emotion, and behaviour that are driven by specific parts or figures that the ego takes on. It involves retreating from various characters the ego assumes and accessing a more objective perspective by which it supports the model of the regressive meditative process on the sense of I-am-ness that is capable of inducing the state of 'absence', a mind devoid of mental processes, and facilitating a mental openness for the discerning insight to arise.

Notes

1 R. C. Schwartz, *Internal Family Systems Therapy* (New York: Guilford Publications, 1994), 33.

2 Schwartz, *Internal Family Systems Therapy*, 35.

3 J. Earley, *Self-Therapy: A Step-By-Step Guide to Creating Wholeness and Healing Your Inner Child Using IFS, Cutting-Edge Psychotherapy*, second edition (Larkspur, CA: Pattern System Books, 2009), 4–6.

4 Schwartz, *Internal Family Systems Therapy*, 37.

5 R. C. Schwartz and M. Sweezy, *Internal Family Systems Therapy,* second edition (New York: The Guilford Press, 2020), 139–140.

6 In G. Ifergan, *The Man from Samye: Longchenpa on Praxis, Its Negation and Liberation* (New Delhi: Aditya Prakashan, 2014), 157.

7 G. Thibaut, trans., *The Vedānta-Sūtras with the Commentary by Śankarācārya, Sacred Books of the East, Volume 1*, 2005, https://www.gutenberg.org/files/16295/16295-h/16295-h.htm#chap-1-1, retrieved 10 October 2022.

8 C. Trungpa, *Cutting through Spiritual Materialism* (Boston: Shambhala, 1987), 15.

9 See chapters 2 and 3 dedicated to *pratipakṣa bhāvanā* in Ifergan, *The Psychology of the* Yogas, 45–86.

10 R. C. Schwartz and M. Sweezy, *Internal Family Systems Therapy,* second edition (New York: The Guilford Press, 2020), 46–52.

11 Earley, *Self-Therapy*, 157–165.

12 Richard C. Schwartz and Martha Sweezy, *Internal Family Systems Therapy*, Second Edition, New York: The Guilford Press, 2020, 34.

13 See G. Ifergan, *The Psychology of the Yogas* (Sheffield, UK: Equinox Publishing, 2021), 87–109, chapter 5 "Western Psychology as a Temporary Complement to Yoga".

14 J. William, *The Varieties of Religious Experience: A study in Human nature*, trans. (Ya'akov Kopilevitch, Jerusalem: Bialik Institute, 1995), 140 (in Hebrew).

15 Kārikā 64 in G. J. Larson, R. S. Bhattacharya and K. Potter, eds., *The Encyclopaedia of Indian Philosophies, Volume 4: Samkhya, A Dualist Tradition in Indian Philosophy* (Princeton, NJ: Princeton University Press, 1987), 162.

16 R. Maharshi, *The spiritual teachings of Ramana Maharshi* (Boulder, CO: Shambhala Publications, 1972), 3–14.

17 J. Kornfield, *After the Ecstasy, The Laundry: How the Heart Grows Wise on the Spiritual Path* (New York: Bantam, 2001), see for example 155, 158–9 and 206–7.

18 Ifergan, *The Psychology of the Yogas*, 89–90.

19 The Sanskrit term 'citta-*saṃtāna*' is used to denote the mindstream, composed of 'Citta' which means 'mind,' and 'santana' which means 'continuity' or 'stream.' Buswell, Robert E. and Donald E. Lopez. *The Princeton Dictionary of Buddhism*. Princeton: Princeton University Press, 2013, 196.

20 L. Rabjam, *A Treasure Trove of Scriptural Transmission: A Commentary on the Precious Basic Space of Phenomena*, trans. T.R. Chagdud and R. Barron (Junction City, CA: Padma Publications, 2001), 341.

21 Sūtra 2.27, H. Āraṇya, *Yoga Philosophy of Patañjali: Containing His Yoga Aphorisms with Vyasa's Commentary in Original Sanskrit and Annotations Thereon with Copious Hints on the Practice of Yoga* (Calcutta: Calcutta University Press, 1981), 200–202.

22 Āraṇya, *Yoga Philosophy of Patanjali*, 201; Raveh, *Exploring the Yogasutra*, 141.

23 Raveh, *Exploring the Yogasutra*, 129.

24 Sūtra 2.34, Raveh, *Exploring the Yogasutra*, 132

25 For a detailed discussion, see chapters 2 and 3 dedicated to *pratipakṣa bhāvanā* in Ifergan, *The Psychology of the Yogas*, 45–86,

26 See sūtra 2.31in E. Bryant, *The Yoga Sutras of Patañjali*, 248–252

27 See sūtras 2.30 and 2.32 in E. Bryant, *The Yoga Sutras of Patañjali*, 243–254

6 Concluding Observations

Retracing our steps, it was established that the (artificial and confusing) weave between the world of phenomena and the true Self in which the different states of mind of the ego are mistakenly perceived as attributed and belonging to this principle of awareness or the true Self is the cause of suffering. For example if one experiences joy, peace, passion or boredom it will be attributed to the real Self where in reality there is no connection between such states of mind and the true Self as nothing can be imposed on the true Self. For the yogi, such identifications constitute a fundamental and profound misunderstanding, and they are the reason that existence is filled with suffering, sorrow, and pain. Hence dismantling and undoing of the weave means the undoing of suffering, which is what occurs with the rise of discerning insight. The discerning gaze is assimilated into the mind and leads to its transparent revelation of the true Self. On the way to clarify the notion of discerning insight and the window from which it arises it was necessary to consider and thoroughly explore the categories that constitute the weave between the world of phenomena and the true Self and the map that Patañjali plots on the way to the discerning insight.

To clarify the notion of discerning insight and the window of mental openness from which it arises, it was necessary to consider and thoroughly explore the categories that constitute the weave between the world of phenomena, the sense of I-am-ness, the true Self and the map that Patañjali plots on the way to discerning insight. Such explanations, however profound, might be but ink on paper. Nevertheless, in themselves, they are essential to the process, as they attest to a real attempt, even if only a mental one, to divert the gaze from the world of objects to the interiority of mind. This is an initial step in turning the gaze towards discerning insight, which could be accompanied and supported by various kinds of practice within the framework of yoga psychology such as the cultivation of moral principles mentioned at the end of Chapter 5.

The map to discerning insight that Patañjali unfolds is complex, demanding, lengthy, and not necessarily linear, as one is sometimes forced to go back to one of the yogic limbs to stabilise an earlier stage and progress to the next. This culminates as the last phase of cognitive *samādhi*.

The notion of *viveka-khyāti* has been pivotal to the *Sāmkhya*, one of the earliest schools of philosophy in India, which provides yoga with a metaphysical framework. Essentially, it is the systematic enumeration and rational examination of each of the elements and components of the world of phenomena. When the essence of these components of the world of phenomena become known, the philosopher understands that the world of phenomena and its components are not true Self, the pure principle of awareness. For the *Sāmkhya* philosopher, such an inquiry is demanding and lengthy, and it ends only after the discerning insight has been realised and assimilated.

The actual sūtras concerning the map that Patañjali plots on the way to discerning insight state that it occurs linearly in the final stage of cognitive *samādhi*. The departure point is the everyday gaze being shifted inwardly (*pratiprasava*), away from external objects and towards the interiority of the mind, which is external to the true Self and fundamentally different from it. This is an inverse process of evolution, a return to origins, that involves relinquishing the habitual tendency of the mind to objectify, including positive attitudes and beliefs necessary for the realisation of yoga that are attachments of the ego and must be abandoned. Instead, the mind must converge towards its source and become still.

The cognitive *samādhi* takes place once the phenomenal gaze has shifted inward and stabilised, turning into a uniform, stable, and continuous concentration on a particular object as described in sūtras 1.42–47. In these sūtras Patañjali elaborates on the notion of cognitive *samādhi* and its four classifications. The first stage is *savitarka*, a cognitive *samādhi* accompanied with thought processes related to a tangible object the yogi chooses to focus on with the intention of integrating with it. When conditioned connections between the object itself, the label for the object, and the meaning associated with it disintegrates, the yogi advances to the next one, *nirvitarka*. In this type of *samādhi*, the yogi merges with the tangible object into a state of integration that is devoid of thought and the conceptualising activity that characterised the previous stage, reflecting the object more purely, the only thing that occupies the mind, as if seen freshly, for the first time without any conceptualisation, attraction, rejection, or identification.

The third, *savicāra samādhi*, concerns the practice of *samādhi by* intensely concentrating on a subtle object, for example, by visualising a mystical diagram such as a *maṇḍala* or a component of the subtle body such as a *cakra*. The mental visualisation of the subtle object is constructed and maintained until it simply merges within the meditator. The mind then reflects the object as it actually is. The fourth, the *nirvicāra samādhi* concerns a meditation devoid of contemplative observation and conceptualisation, without the processes that characterised the previous three stages described above. It reflects a meditative capability to 'behold' the object, the mystical diagram that was mentally 'constructed' in the preceding *samādhi* in their mind. In the yogi's mind, a complete picture of the object is reflected instantly, at once.

The culmination of the integration between the subject and the object and the process of perception, *nirvicāra samādhi* can be visualised as being like a reflection of an object in a polished, clear, and limpid mirror. The mirror and the reflection have become identical – they are inseparable, and they are made of one 'mirror' material. Time and space no longer exist between the reflection of the object and the mirror itself. Like a mirror cleared of all dust and oil stains, so too the mind is empty of mental processes, and only the object is reflected in it. Just as the reflection cannot affect the mirror, so the integration of the object with the mind is not affected by potential distortions in perception associated with imprints of time and place left on the object.

Sūtra 1.17 mentions the two other types of *samādhi* that belong to this category of cognitive *samādhi*, the object-oriented intense concentration. These two are an extension of the fourth stage (*nir-savicāra)* of the cognitive *samādhi, which involves the integration of the meditating subject and the subtle object* devoid of conceptualisation, maintained continuously. One type involves the sense of happiness or bliss (*ānanda*) and the other involves the sense of I-am-ness (*asmitā*). Up to the fourth stage of cognitive *samādhi*, the meditator chooses either tangible or subtle objects for concentration as per their inclinations or the stream of yoga or sect they follow. However, in the case of the sense of happiness and I-am-ness, these objects are not consciously or intentionally chosen by the meditator. Rather, they arise spontaneously and become the object of meditation without any conscious effort on the meditator's part. In other words, the meditator does not actively select these objects but rather observes and experiences them as they naturally emerge in the mind.

During the highest stage of cognitive *samādhi*, the meditator achieves integration with the object of meditation, which triggers a wave of pleasurable feelings. These feelings can be physically and mentally intense, and the meditator may become fixated on them, locked within the attempt to recreate them repeatedly. To extricate oneself from this fixation, the fascination with the blissful experience, the meditator should cultivate an uninvolved inner gaze and abide in a meditation devoid of conceptualisations. By doing so, they can contemplate the intoxicating feeling without being consumed by it.

As the meditator continues to concentrate, and realises that the sense of I-am-ness arises as the experiencer the blissful feeling, the sense of I-am-ness becomes the new object of meditation. Abiding in a meditation focusing on the sense of I-am-ness, devoid of conceptualisations and free from attachment to blissful feelings, the meditator can internalise the insight that 'I am not who I think I am; I am not the source of awareness.' This discerning insight leads to a realisation of the true nature of the sense of I-am-ness and an understanding that it is distinct from the true Self.

In my opinion, the traditional approach to cognitive *samādhi* as represented by modern scholars like Rose and Bryant is static in nature. By 'static,' I mean that cognitive *samādhi* is achieved by fixating on a stationary object, whether tangible or abstract, and relying on it to sustain concentration. In contrast, I consider a dynamic approach to be one that seeks to uncover latent meanings in the various stages of cognitive *samādhi* and extract from these meanings a practice such as the regressive meditative process directed towards the sense of I-am-ness or ego as an ongoing, dynamic, and reflective process. This practice is the main theme of the fifth chapter of this study.

The practice of cognitive *samādhi*, including its types of objects, gradual stages, and achievements, is complex, demanding, and lengthy, and it may not follow a linear path. However, it is possible to apply the regressive meditative process already in the early stages of yogic meditation and progressively cultivate an unselfish attitude. By doing so, one can restrain the dominance of egoic attitudes, enhance the calm and clarity of the mind ultimately leading towards a state of 'absence', devoid of mental processes in which the discerning insight can arise. Like any yogic practice, the regressive meditative process is based on the two principles of yoga practice: repetitive activity (*abhyāsa*) and dispassion or uninvolved awareness (*vairāgya*). These two elements with the context of the regressive meditative process, an action resulting from an effort of meditative and repetitive reflection and concentration, and an uninvolved awareness cultivated by the regressive meditative process of separating from the egoic characters the ego takes on, seemingly oppose each other. Although these two principles may appear contradictory, in practice they are complementary, as they are two forces acting simultaneously. And as I showed in the fifth chapter of this study, these two forces are at the core of meditation on the phenomenal 'I'.

I propose such a dynamic approach that opens up a new possibility for the twenty-first-century practitioner for inner harmony and integration of all the psychological and spiritual aspects alongside cultivating the discerning and clear gaze. The culmination of this gaze is the emergence of discerning insight between the sense of I-am-ness and the true Self, the ordinary mind and pure, primordial awareness respectively.

Critics might argue that this model of the regressive meditative process on the sense of I-am-ness departs too far from the traditional understanding of the gradual progress of yoga meditation. However, I believe that the density and terseness of the sūtras allow for creative deciphering that extract new possibilities of understanding and effective practice from the text. The model of the regressive meditative process on the sense of I-am-ness is a result of such a creative reading, enabling a shaping of the meditative process capable of inducing the state of 'absence' and facilitating a mental openness for the discerning insight to arise. As previously described, this entails four possible methods of applying the regressive meditative process. The regressive meditative process offers further significant advantages as, from a psychological perspective, each egoic figure or character reflected upon in this meditation is constituted of a bundle of dormant mental imprints (*saṃskāras*), habitual tendencies or patterns of behaviour (*vāsanās*), and the causes of affliction (*kleśas*). Therefore, addressing a figure or egoic part that is comprised of multiple *saṃskāras*, *vāsanās*, and *kleśas*, employing the regressive meditative process enables access to the psychological states caused by these habitual tendencies towards their release. For example, when addressing an angry part or figure, we have the opportunity to address and release other emotions and patterns of behaviour that drive the anger, such as fear, inferiority, and a developed individual sense of justice that motivates protest and suppression of anger.

Supported by the *yama*s and *niyama*s, two ethical frameworks that provide guidance for practitioners on how to interact with others and cultivate moral principles, the regressive meditative process on the sense of I-am-ness reduces egoic identifications. By reducing egoic identifications and selfishness, this meditative process can improve relationships, increase happiness, enhance mental health, and promote spiritual growth, which makes the regressive meditative process a significant device for enhancing calmness and clarity, leading to the dawn of discerning insight. Its culmination is the steadfast discerning wisdom that continually distinguishes between the sense of I-am-ness and the true Self, which ends up dissolving into the source of mind

The special status of discerning insight, as a clearing of the confusion between the true Self and the world of phenomena, demands that we once again dwell on the meaning of yoga as a union or unification. It is not exactly a union between the pure subject, the true Self, and the world of sense objects, or the union of the true Self as the principle of awareness and the body, but rather it starts with the realisation of their radical difference. Understanding the separateness or duality of these two principles – of pure awareness and matter – resolves one's confusion and consequently alleviates one's suffering. Although radically different in terms of epistemology, the true Self is not divorced from the natural processes that take place within the world of phenomena, those processes that reflect the Self and sense objects as the different animate and inanimate forms of communication.

The notion of yoga as a union is clearly expressed in its ontology in the sense that *puruṣa* as a principle of pure awareness, or true Self, ineffable and unknowable even to itself, is realised by means of meditation that stills and empties the mind of its contents and mental processes. Then, the true Self dawns and returns to abiding in its true nature, and unites with the aggregate, all-embracing Selfhood.

The notion of yoga as a union manifests within the practice of yoga in which its peak is the state of *samādhi* – being absorbed in meditative concentration in which the object of meditation alone emerges in the mind, which is stripped of all other contents. When the object of meditation does not ignite mental processes of conceptualisation or judgment, a union between the pure subject and the object of meditation can occur. The mind, stilled of mental processes except for awareness of the object itself, reflects the object of meditation just as a clear, polished mirror reflects an object, whether the object is static or on the move. The surface of the mirror is unified with the object's reflection. Yet there is a higher form of *samādhi* which is objectless; that is, it does not depend on any object in order to establish itself. The mind then, emptied of all content, forms a union in the sense that the true Self becomes rooted in the all-encompassing aggregate Selfhood. This is yoga!

Appendix: *Yogasūtra*: Authors, Texts and Readers

Nothing is known about Patañjali, the legendary iconic figure, the historical author of the *Yogasūtra*, as he did not write anything about himself, nor did others write any biographical details about him. It seems characteristic of iconic figures in Indian history such as the Buddha, Śaṅkara and the authors of the Sanskrit epics that almost nothing is known about them biographically. Although some of the composers of the Vedic hymns included their names in the hymns as a marker of authorship, later Hindu tradition disregarded these textual ownerships, declaring the Vedas to be of non-human origin (*apauruṣeya*) and authorless. Signe Cohen concludes in his work *Text and Authority in the Older Upaniṣads* that most famous Hindu texts are anonymous. He adds that even texts ascribed to known authors (Manu, Vālmiki, Yājñavalkya) are often oral or mnemonic texts with a long compilation history adorned with the name of a mythological author to grant the text greater authority. Composing texts and ascribing them to a famous figure appears to have been a common and widely accepted practice.[1] What is known about such figures is mostly through their hagiographies; for example, Śaṅkara's eight principal hagiographies, including the *Śaṅkaradigvijaya*,[2] usually depict them and their course of life in a mythical, symbolic or legendary language, implying a clear hierarchy that places the sacred or ultimate meaning as liberation over the phenomenal realm of existence.

A similar, more specific contention can be found in Raveh's conversation with Mukund Lath, who writes that the notion of anonymity 'is complex, almost metaphysical in its ramifications.'[3] Such metaphysical anonymity in the context of Patañjali's philosophy more than likely stems from the radical difference between one's inherent real Self and the phenomenal world, which includes the phenomenal self. Release from being entangled in mundane existence does not leave any karmic traces behind hence not even one's signature, which may explain the absence of biographical details. Such 'absence' may imply the absence of the author as being the 'death' of his phenomenal self, his sense of *I-am-ness* (*asmitā*), thereby realising one's inherent real Self (*puruṣa*).

In the overall context of Hinduism, the relevance of the Upaniṣads and sūtras (with the exception of the *Nyāyasūtra*, which are notable for their focus on knowledge and logic) as texts capable of revealing truths that can lead to liberation from *saṃsāra*, has nothing to do with the identity of the composers of these texts. The emphasis in Indian religious literature is always on the message rather than the messenger. The Upaniṣads and sūtras are tapestries interweaving a multitude of voices, and this requires study of the history of how these texts were woven, and understanding how they have come to be what they are today, restricted to the one possible interpretation revolving around liberation.[4] Thus, it can be concluded that the motivation underpinning the absence of authors or their anonymity in the context of ancient Indian history and culture is metaphysical in nature and focuses on the notion of liberation.

The *Yogasūtra*, together with its classical commentaries, reflects debates, polemics and mutual influences between Sāṃkhya-Yoga and Buddhist schools that could enhance an understanding of the complex interrelation between Hinduism and Buddhism in India. However, it also reflects controversial discussions with the philosophical school of the grammarians, with Mīmāṃsā, Nyāya and Vaiśeṣika. Such studies of the text and its commentaries will also be fruitful for our knowledge of the general history of Indian philosophy. Therefore, the different contentions and arguments regarding the question of authorship of *Yogasūtra* should be looked at through the approach that emphasises the text's messages and contents over the messenger.

Philipp A. Maas, tracing references to the *Patañjalayogaśāstra* in the period between 650 CE to 1340 CE,[5] contends on the basis of a reading and comparison of the first pāda, that the so-called Yogabhāṣya or Vyāsbhāṣya, considered to be the oldest commentary to Patañjali's *Yogasūtra*, is not an independent work but an auto-commentary, since in ancient manuscripts, sūtras and bhāṣya are always found together. Therefore, Maas convincingly argues that both texts should be thought of as a unified work and called *Patañjalayogaśāstra sāṃkhyapravacana* (being the full title of the work written in the colophon in the manuscripts of the text), which can be translated as 'the exposition of the yoga of Patañjali, the doctrine of Sāṃkhya.'[6] That is to say, the *Yogasūtra* should be read together with a root Sāṃkhyan text.

We hardly know anything about Vyāsa as well, the author of the *Yogasūtra-bhāṣya*. Vyāsa is a name that appears in Indian history as the great author who compiled or composed the Vedas, the *Mahābhārata*, and the Purāṇas, three monumental works. However, these works, which are traditionally attributed to someone called 'Vyāsa', were written or compiled over a period of thousands of years, pointing to the possibility that the author of the *Yogasūtra-bhāṣya* called himself (or was called by readers) Vyāsa, as a synonym or a name standing for an author, editor, compiler or collator of texts.

Regarding the question of authorship of the *Yogasūtra*, Mikel Burley has explored a series of sūtras (4.14–22) in the Kaivalyapāda, the fourth and last chapter of the *Yogasūtra*. In these sūtras Patañjali's *puruṣa* is presented as being the quintessential real Self. These primarily contain an implied debate with a theory attributed to the vijñānavāda, the idealistic school of Mahāyāna Buddhism. Burley argues that the actual group of sūtras are neither realist nor anti-idealist, and are not intended as an attack on the vijñānavāda or any other form of Buddhism, but the traditional commentators of this group of sūtras, such as Vyāsa and Vācaspati, were eager to attack and tarnish the vijñānavāda, defending the realism they attribute to that series of sūtras.[7] That is, it was not Patañjali who was critical of vijñanavāda but rather Vyāsa and Vācaspati, which clearly implies that Patañjali and Vyāsa are two different authors, not one as has been suggested by Maas.

Such a conclusion is validated further by David Gordon White, who argues that the language of the sūtras is often closer to what he has termed 'Buddhist Hybrid Sanskrit', rather than to the classical Sanskrit that was the norm in Hindu scripture and commentary. The Buddhists of the period, quick to contest viewpoints that conflicted with their own, remained entirely silent concerning the *Yogasūtra*. According to White, a possible reason for this is that the Buddhists found the *Yogasūtra* to match their own philosophical principles; that is, they considered the *Yogasūtra* to represent a Buddhist work.[8] White's characterisation of Patañjali's *Yogasūtra* as a Buddhist text, and Burley's pointing to Patañjali as being neither realist nor anti-Buddhist, and his characterisation of Vyāsa as being hostile to Buddhism, give further credence to the contention that Patañjali and Vyāsa are not one but two different authors.

Also, Johannes Bronkhorst, who has examined two dozen sūtras, points to divergences between the *Yogasūtra* and Vyāsbhāṣya. For example, Vyāsbhāṣya 1.21 discusses a nine-fold classification of yogins while *Yogasūtra* 1.21, at best, presupposes a three-fold classification of yogins. Tracing the classification of yogins further in sūtras 1.22–23, Bronkhorst notes that Vyāsbhāṣya ends up with an eleven-old classification where the *Yogasūtra* can (at best) be made to yield a nine-fold classification. However, for Bronkhorst, as much as the divergences demonstrate that Patañjali and Vyāsa are two different authors, such divergence can also yield the hypothesis that 'the author of the Yogabhāṣya himself collected the sūtras on which he was to write his commentary, perhaps from different quarters, and that he sometimes gave them an interpretation that suited his purposes, even while knowing the original interpretation of those sūtras.'[9]

This hypothesis makes Patañjali an editor–compiler–commentator, not a founder of a different philosophical system. Thus, for Bronkhorst, as much as the divergences demonstrate that Patañjali and Vyāsa are two different authors, it can also yield the hypothesis that they were the same person writing with two different names. That is, possibly two authors; possibly one.

Jason Birch points to the fourteenth-century *Sarvadarśanasaṅgraha*, which is the first source that he identifies as clearly indicating the separate authorship of Patañjali and Vyāsa; and that, since then, the claim that the sūtra was composed by Patañjali and the bhāṣya by Vyāsa became the predominant view. As Birch observes, 'Nearly all yoga compendiums of the 16th–18th centuries, which we consulted, mention Vyāsa as the author of the Bhāṣya. A possible exception is the seventeenth-century Yuktabhavadeva (1.297–300), which quotes a passage from both the Sūtra and the Bhāṣya as the work of Patañjali.'[10] Given the time gap between the texts that Birch mentions and the time of the *Yogasūtra* and *Yogabhāṣya*'s composition, Patañjali and Vyāsa appear to be two different authors rather than the same person writing under different names.

A more clear-cut distinction demonstrating the separate authorship of Patañjali and Vyāsa can be seen in bhāṣya 3.44, where Vyāsa states in the context of the notion of inherent nature (*svarūpa*) of the elements (*bhūtas*) that 'Patañjali says …'[11] that an object is a collection of the different parts of which do not exist separately. This has been called the essential attribute or the inherent nature (*svarūpa*) of the elements (*bhūtas*).[12] The point here is that Vyāsa, the author of the bhāṣya directly refers to the actual content of sūtra 3.44 concerning the inherent nature of the elements as composed by someone different from himself, someone called Patañjali.

Based on these findings, it can be concluded that Patañjali and Vyāsa, the author(s) of the *Yogasūtra* and the author of its first commentary, could not have been the same author writing under two different names. Alternatively, at the very least, it can be said that the question of authorship of *Yogasūtra* remains unresolved. Perhaps the exact identification of authors, in this case, may not be that important. Not only because the Hindu tradition disregarded claims relating to textual ownership, and instead regarded texts such as the *Upaniṣads* as authorless, reflecting an emphasis on a liberation from phenomenal existence that does not leave any traces behind, but because of the concrete difficulty in identifying them given the conflicting hypotheses and conclusions presented so far.

Such conflicting and different views naturally produce tension since they are insoluble, thus risking an indefinite perpetuation of sterile scholarly debate. A way of coming to terms with such 'inconsistencies' is to reorganise those inconsistencies into a pattern that might clarify the development of ideas. Such an endeavour is undoubtedly useful and can offer a closer look not only into the history of ideas but also a clearer view of social and cultural trends and processes. However, is it not often true that research into the history of ideas, intended to clarify a contradiction, just perpetuates it, offering new angles and perspectives into the matter without any final resolution? As long as the contradictions under inquiry represent a significant problem, the research will be perpetuated because contradictions naturally produce tension and as such attract endless attempts to clarify them. In this state of affairs, critical scholars would go on endlessly analysing and dissecting the *Yogasūtra* and its commentaries, along with their respective research methodologies.

Given what has been said so far on the *Yogasūtra* in the context of authors–texts–readers, I have chosen to align myself with a group of contemporary researchers, such as Christopher Chapple, Mikel Burley, Ana Laura Funes Maderey, Stephen Phillips, Arindam Chakrabarti, Stephanie Corigliano, and the contemporary commentators mentioned earlier. Along with them, I approach the *Yogasūtra* in a thematic way, that emphasises the text's messages and contents over the messenger, exploring notions of body, imagination, death, idealism, realism, and the science of meditation, themes that have not yet been fully explored.

Notes

1 S. Cohen, *Text and Authority in the Older Upaniṣads* (Leiden: Brill, 2008), 293.

2 See J. Bader's most impressive work *Conquest of the Four Quarters: Traditional Accounts of the Life of Śaṅkara* (New Delhi: Aditya Prakashan, 2000).

3 D. Raveh, *Exploring the Yogasutra: Philosophy and Translation*, annotated edition (London: Continuum, 2012), 4.

4 Cohen, *Text and Authority in the Older Upaniṣads*, 293–94.

5 Maas is referring here to Madhava's doxagraphical work, *Sarvadarśanasaṅgraha*, "Compendium of all philosophical systems".

6 P. A. Maas, "A Concise Historiography of Classical Yoga Philosophy", in E. Franco, ed., *Periodization and Historiography of Indian Philosophy* (Vienna: The De Nobili Research Library, 2013), 79–80.

7 M. Burley, *Classical Samkhya and Yoga: An Indian Metaphysics of Experience* (*Routledge Hindu Studies Series*) (London: Routledge, 2012), 82–90

8 D. G. White, *The Yoga Sutra of Patañjali: A Biography*, Princeton University Press (Princeton, NJ: Princeton University Press, 2014), 230.

9 J. Bronkhorst, "Patañjali and the Yoga Sūtras." *Studien zur Indologie und Iranistik*, 10 (1984 [1985]): 3–4.

10 J. Birch and J. Hargreaves, "Patanjali and Vyasa," *The Luminscent* (2017), https://www.theluminescent.org/2017/06/patanjali-and-vyasa.html, retrieved 22 October 2022.

11 My emphasis.

12 H. Āraṇya, *Yoga Philosophy of Patanjali: Containing His Yoga Aphorisms with Vyasa's Commentary in Original Sanskrit and Annotations Thereon with Copious Hints on the Practice of Yoga* (Calcutta: Calcutta University Press, 1981), 322.

Glossary

abhimāna: self-importance associated with the ego, the phenomenal ordinary self (*ahaṃkāra*), which is self-conscious, the 'I' who wills, acts, and determines.

abhiniveśa: clinging to life or fear of death; one of the five **kleśas**.

abhyāsa: repetitive practice; cultivating a discipline of practice. Yoga practice consists of two foundational components implemented simultaneously: **abhyāsa** and **vairāgya**, repetitiveness and dispassion.

adhyāsa: superimposition of an attribute, quality, or characteristic of one entity or object in the form of remembrance onto another entity. For example, to think in the darkness of night that a rope near your door is a snake or to believe that one, being but a psychophysical entity, is eternal like the real Self.

Advaita-Vedānta: a philosophical school mostly associated with the great eighth-century Indian philosopher and teacher Śaṅkara. Its core tenet is that of a singularity as a unitary metaphysical essence (the Brahman) that underlies and precedes multplicity, the world of phenomena and that of the real Self (*atman*), and that essences are identical.

Advaitin: a follower of **Advaita-Vedānta**.

ahaṃkāra: 'I-maker', egoity.

ahiṃsā: non-harming; non-violence. One of the **yamas**.

ānanda: feeling of joy.

ānanda samādhi: cognitive *samādhi* that is aimed at the sense of bliss or joy (**ānanda**) as the object to be concentrated upon.

antaḥkaraṇa: the mind as the internal apparatus consisting of **buddhi**, **ahaṃkāra** and **manas**.

asaṃprajñāta samādhi: yogic meditation or innate concentration independent of mental process of cognition associated with any given object.

asmitā: 'sense of I-am-ness,' that in its initial form, **asmitā**, stands for sentience of pure awareness reflected in the mind. It stands as the agent's power of seeing or perceiving involved in the world distinct from the principle of inactive and uninvolved pure awareness (**puruṣa**). **Asmitā** is the agent, the empirical or phenomenal self that depends on the senses to perceive and cognize. It solidifies further when in contact with sense objects – tangible or intangible – grasps them, and refers to them with a sense of identification and ownership. Everything the ego knows, feels, and acts is known to itself as his own ('my pleasure') or identified with ('I am angry'). This sense of ownership or identification differentiates the individual as a separate unique being, defined by personal boundaries. As such, **asmitā** is one of the five **kleśas**.

asmitā samādhi: cognitive *samādhi* that is aimed at the sense of I-am-ness (*asmitā*) as the object to be concentrated upon.

aṣṭāṅga-yoga: the eight limbs of yoga, consisting of **yama, niyama, āsana, prāṇāyāma, pratyāhāra, dhāraṇā, dhyāna, and samādhi**.

avidyā: fundamental ignorance of one's inherent true Self that consists of a mundane phenomenal perspective through which one is involved in the world. Such perspective conceals the principle of pure awareness and 'covers' it by establishing a false identity, the sense of the ego that distorts perceptions of reality. As such, it is one of the five **kleśas** and the base for the other four.

Bhagavad Gītā: The poem of the Lord, a 700-verse Hindu scripture that dates from the fifth century to the second century BCE, and is set in a narrative framework of a dialogue between Pandava prince Arjuna and his guide and charioteer lord. It significantly covers various branches of yoga and ideas from **Sāṃkhya** philosophy.

bhāṣya: commentary; primary commentary based on the root text.

buddhi: the faculty or seat of intelligence; the intellect dominated by **sattva.**

cakra: wheel, centre of subtle energy or psycho–spiritual focal point within the subtle body associated with specific characteristics and functions presented in colours, shapes, sounds, deities and other iconographical details.

citta: complex structure of all of the mental and physical functions of the mind. It is the axis around which the **Yogasūtra** revolves.

citta-vṛtti: mental activity or mental processes. For Patañjali, yoga is the cessation of mental processes; stillness of mind.

citi: pure mind, empty (not in the sense of nihilism) of content or object, tangible or intangible.

citi-śakti: the power of pure mind as potentiality.

dhāraṇā: the very beginning of meditation where one concentrates and places attention on a single point. One of the eight limbs of yoga.

dhyāna: an advanced stage of meditation in which one is able to concentrate and to maintain one single train of thought for long durations without being distracted. One of the eight limbs of yoga.

duḥkha: suffering; pain; a condition in which one is confronted by thoughts, feelings, sensations and situations one would prefer not to experience, or a condition where one is confronted by separation from one's loved ones, and from pleasant and joyful experiences which one would prefer not to experience.

guṇa: a quality or dynamic force (as opposed to a potential one). There are three qualities that describe the manner in which activity is generated and takes place in **prakṛti** or in the world of phenomena. The three *guṇa*s are **sattva**, **rajas,** and **tamas,** and yoga is about their cessation or stoppage.

haṭha-yoga: force or power; a branch of yoga which is primarily concerned with postures and breath. The **haṭha-yoga** literature consists of the *Haṭhayogapradīpikā* (dated fourteenth or fifteenth century AD).

kaivalya: aloneness; aloofness; freedom; a state in which the mental processes are brought to complete cessation and pure awareness, and **puruṣa**, the real Self or one's metaphysical core Selfhood, is isolated and disengaged from its confusing entanglement with **prakṛti**, the world of phenomena.

Keśin: the archetypal yogic figure of Vedic culture; the long-haired ascetic wanderer with mystical powers who lives in the forest, far from any social framework.

kevala-kumbhaka: a suspended breathing that occurs abruptly, by itself, and in accordance with an intense meditative concentration (**samādhi**) enabling the dawn of discerning insight (**vivekakhyāti**) and supernatural powers.

kleśa: 'cause of affliction'; psychological dispositions through which one interacts and reacts to the world of phenomena causing himself and others harm, pain, or stress. The five **kleśas** are **avidyā**, **asmitā**, **rāga** (attraction), **dveṣa** (aversion), and **abhiniveśa**.

karma: literally denotes action and refers to results of given actions. Such results leave 'traces' that will be the seed beds that later will germinate and shape one's future circumstances. It is a vicious cycle of causes and their effects, from which a yogi attempts to extricate themself.

krama: sequence consisting of moments. A sequence of time, which is a product of conceptualising time, expressed in terms of past, present, future etc., that are but mental constructs.

kṣaṇa: the 'moment' as the smallest and most minute unit of time, during which an 'atom' moves from one point in space to a point adjacent in which the time sequence is but an ongoing moment, relating to a specific object. The present is such a (continuous) moment in which timelessness is to be found, usually unnoticed within the sequences of the phenomenal existence. The yogin's aim is to abide in the moment, the eternal moment while in the time-bound sequence.

kuṇḍalinī: a dormant meta-physiological psycho-spiritual force, with enormous psycho–somatic and spiritual transformative potential, that is a potential for radical change. Its realisation in the highest degree can lead one to liberation.

Longchenpa: the fourteenth-century CE Tibetan Buddhist scholar and teacher of Dzogchen.

mahā-vratam: the ultimate vow to observe the ethical principles of yoga independently of place, time, and circumstances.

manas: the faculty of mind that receives and sorts sense data from the world of phenomena and emits reaction to them.

nāḍīs: meta-physiological channels of the subtle body through which prāṇā flows.

nirvicāra samādhi: yogic meditative absorption concentrated upon subtle, imperceptible or intangible objects as contemplation devoid of subtle thoughts.

nirvitarka samādhi: non-conceptualising yogic meditative absorption concentrated upon a tangible, perceptible or gross object.

nirodha: cessation, stoppage, or suspension, referring to the mental processes.

nirodha saṃskāras: types of mental imprints that, when activated, intensify the control of mental processes and make them still.

nirvāṇa: literally 'blown out,' or the shutting down or extinction of all burning desires that perpetuate one's accumulation of karma, which represents the ultimate state of liberation from **saṃsāra**, or freedom.

niyama: observances of ethical guidelines. There are five **niyama:** śauca (internal and external yogic cleansing), contentment (saṃtoṣa), austerities or practices involved with inner heat (**tapas**), **svādhyāya**, and devotion to the lord or deity.

pariṇāma: transformations or evolutionary processes that occur in the world of phenomena as the constant changes that characterise relative reality.

prajñā: yogic insight or wisdom that occurs when in meditative absorption, bypassing perception, reasoning, and reliable testimony. Yogic insight means knowing something new about a certain object we did not know before, toward seeing the object 'as it is.'

prakṛti: the perceptible and imperceptible dimensions of the world of phenomena, events, and conditioned existence. *Prakṛti* and **puruṣa** (one's metaphysical core Selfhood) are radically different. Against our intuition, our mind, and its mental processes, our psychological makeup and its feelings and emotions, as well as our yoga practice, all are considered components of *prakṛti*.

prāṇa: the vital force of life.

prāṇāyāma: breath control or, more precisely, control of one's **prāṇā** (vital energy). As the mind is linked and bound with breath, practicing breath retention enhances mental pacification.

pratipakṣa bhāvanā: 'meditation on the opposite'; or 'cultivation of the opposite'; but also 'imagining the opposite.' When a yoga practitioner feels negative emotions or is overwhelmed by desires that cause pain and acts under their influence, he must cultivate opposite thoughts. He is required to focus his attention on the consequences of such thoughts and actions and to seek spiritual refuge in the moral principles of yoga. That is, he is to initiate a meditative inquiry about the consequences of thoughts and actions that inflict pain. The thought that violating the moral principles of yoga brings about endless pain and ignorance is in fact the opposite thinking!

pratyāhāra: withdrawal of the senses. It is concerned with the disengagement from sense objects, because contact with sense objects can trigger or ignite mental processes as reactions to the object. For me, it is the disengagement from the mental processes that are triggered or ignited when coming in contact with a sense object, not from the sense object in itself.

pratyāhāra: the fifth of the eight limbs of yoga.

puruṣa: core of Selfhood or the principle of pure inherent awareness; completely different from one's physical existence, including one's biological, mental, and psychological components of **prakṛti**. According to Patañjali, there is a multiplicity of *puruṣa*s.

rajas: one of the three **guṇas**, or dynamic forces (as opposed to a potential one) that generate activity in **prakṛti,** the world of phenomena, that is responsible for activities generated by vigour, heat, and passion.

rigpa (Tib)**:** seminal concept in Tibetan Dzoghcen to mean authentic natural awareness, empty of binding connections, discursive or compulsive thinking, and precedes the ordinary mind which is subjected to, and occupied with, mental and psychological processes.

sādhana: practice applied on the path to liberation from ignorance (**avidyā**) and suffering (**duḥkha**).

śakti: power; energy; capacity; potency.

samādhi: concentration; steadfast meditative absorption as an ecstasy in which the yogi withdraws from mental activity. It is first established when the object of meditation alone shines forth as if the mind is empty of its subjective essence or any other content (except the object of meditation itself). It continues being established until it is completely steady and independent of any object of meditation, which means that the yogi is liberated.

Samāpatti: the completion of a merge of meditating mind with the object concentrated upon in which only the object occupies the mind.

saṃprajñāta samādhi: yogic meditation involved with mental processes of cognition of a given object.

saṃsāra: wandering or transmigration referring to the cycle of death and rebirth or reincarnation, and to the aimless wandering in mundane existence caused by karma from which yogis aspire to extricate themselves and to become liberated. It is a fundamental belief of most Indian schools of philosophy, including Buddhism.

saṃskāra: dormant mental imprint etched in one's mind in reaction to events, conditions, and sense objects that construct psychological content, including self-perception, that determines the manner in which one interacts with the world. Such dormant mental imprints in certain circumstances have the potential to instigate and generate mental and physical actions.

saṃyama: yogic meditation in which **dhāraṇā**, **dhyāna**, and **samādhi** are applied together.

Sāṃkhya: probably the earliest school of thought of Indian philosophy which discerns between **puruṣa** and **prakṛti**, the metaphysical core Selfhood and the world of phenomena, respectively, and describes the latter as an evolutionary process from the subtlest realms of the mind to the concrete reality of objects, events, and activities, based on the elements earth, water, fire, air and space.

sattva: one of the three **guṇas**, dynamic forces that generate states of mind characterised by clarity, lucidity, purity, transparency, and peace.

siddhi: yogic accomplishment; special forces beyond ordinary capacities the yogi obtains as a result of a meditation directed to specific objects either related with one's body, one's subtle body, or yogic ethics. The achievement of such 'miraculous' forces that can generate wisdom and enable the yogi to assist others it is a mark of a liberated yogi. The yogi can be fascinated, entangled, and consumed by such powers.

sthūla: tangible, perceptible or gross object.

svādhyāya: recitation of mantras and study of texts by oneself, leading to purification or to liberation. Such a study implies self-reflection as well.

svarūpa: original independent essence as **puruṣa,** inherent in people.

sūkṣma: subtle, imperceptible or intangible.

suṣumṇā: The central meta-physiological channel on which the central *cakra*s are located, and which runs through the body's spine, from the sacrum to the apex.

tamas: darkness; heaviness; one of the three **guṇas**, characterised by inertia, fatigue, and passivity.

tapas: austerities or yogic practice that generate heat that burns the yogi's impurities.

vitarka samādhi: yogic meditative absorption accompanied by conceptualisation of a tangible, perceptible or gross object concentrated upon.

Upaniṣads: the ancient Sanskrit texts of spiritual teaching and ideas of Hinduism that deal with meditation, philosophy, and spiritual knowledge that revolve around the identity; composed from 800 to 300 BCE. **Advaita-Vedānta** traces its roots to the **Upaniṣads**.

vāsanā: a pattern of thinking and behaving, which together with **kleśas** and **saṃskāras**, consist of one's psychological framework that dictates one's existence.

Vedas: literally, knowledge; a large body of religious Sanskrit texts originating in ancient India. They are considered revelations heard by ancient sages after intense meditation, consisting of hymns dedicated to deities that entail rituals, mantras, ceremonies, and sacrifices.

vairāgya: dispassion toward or uninvolved awareness of the objective world. Yoga practice consists of two foundational components implemented simultaneously, of **abhyāsa** and **vairāgya**, repetitiveness and dispassion respectively. For example, in performing a posture, the practitioner performs it for the sake of it without being envious of how another practitioner in the studio performs that posture, without competing with him. Here envy implies that the practitioner lacks something that he desires which enhances distractive mental activity.

vicāra samādhi: yogic meditative absorption accompanied by an inquiry contemplating subtle objects.

vikalpa: verbal construction; a conceptualisation, as mental activity is unable to describe precisely and inform of subtle states of mind, particularly to portray **puruṣa**.

viveka-khyāti: yogic discernment between **prakṛti** and **puruṣa** that occurs in the culmination of cognitive object-based **samādhi**. In that steadfast meditative absorption, the object of meditation, 'sense of I-am-ness' (**asmitā**) alone shines forth as if the mind is empty of its subjective essence or any other content (except the object of meditation itself). The yogi then understands that the sense of I-am-ness, a component of **prakṛti**, as his personality is not **puruṣa**, the real Self. **Viveka-khyāti** is the key to liberation of entanglement with the world of phenomena.

vṛtti: process; activity; fluctuation.

vyutthāna saṃskāras: a type of mental imprint; when activated they force the mind to direct the gaze outward at sensory objects, like a magnet attracted by metal objects. They perpetuate a distorted perception of reality and cause the pain and suffering that perpetuates conditioned existence.

yama: principal yogic ethical guideline; restraint. There are five *yamas*: **ahiṃsā**, *satya* (truthfulness, radical honesty), *asteya* (non-stealing), *brahmacarya* (celibacy), and *aparigraha* (non-possessiveness).

Yoga: Patañjali is very clear and firm in his definition of yoga as the cessation of mental activity, which is different from the widespread view of yoga as union of body and mind. But the mind and body belong to the domain of **prakṛti**, already inseparably connected. In addition, it is not exactly a union between the pure subject, the real Self, and the world of sense objects, **prakṛti** or the union of the true Self as the principle of awareness and the body, but rather, yoga starts with the realisation of their radical difference. Yoga as a union occurs when the principle of pure awareness, or true Self, is realised by means of meditation that stills and empties the mind of mental processes. Then the true Self dawns and goes back to abide in its true nature and unites with the aggregated, all-embracing Selfhood.

Yoga Sūtras: the aphorisms or the verses of yoga.

Bibliography

Āraṇya, H. *Yoga Philosophy of Patanjali: Containing his Yoga Aphorisms with Vyasa's Commentary in Original Sanskrit and Annotations Thereon with Copious Hints on the Practice of Yoga*. Calcutta: Calcutta University Press, 1981.

Arya, U. *Yoga-Sutras of Patanjali with the Exposition of Vyasa: A Translation and Commentary: Volume I—Samādhi-pāda*. Honesdale, PA: Himalayan Institute Press, 1986.

Bader, J. *Conquest of the Four Quarters: Traditional Accounts of the Life of Śaṅkara*. New Delhi: Aditya Prakashan, 2000.

Barthes, R. "La Mort De L'Auteur." Webpage on *Les Chroniques de Marcel*, (originally published in French 1968), https://leschroniquesdemarcel.blogspot.com/2019/08/roulez-moins-vite-vous-pourriez-roland.html.

Bhattacharyya, K. C. *Studies in Philosophy*, 2 vols. Delhi: Motilal Banarsidass, 1983.

Birch, J. and J. Hargreaves. 'Patanjali and Vyasa.' *The Luminscent*, 2017. https://www.theluminescent.org/2017/06/patanjali-and-vyasa.html.

Bronkhorst, J. 'Patañjali and the Yoga Sūtras.' *Studien zur Indologie und Iranistik*, 10 (1984 [1985]): 191–212.

———. *Greater Magadha: Studies in the culture of early India*. Leiden: Brill, 2007.

Bryant, E. F. *The Yoga Sutras of Patañjali: A New Edition, Translation and Commentary*. New York: North Point Press, 2009.

Burley, M. *Classical Samkhya and Yoga: An Indian Metaphysics of Experience* (Routledge Hindu Studies Series). London: Routledge, 2012.

Chapple, C. K. and A. L. Funes Maderey, eds. *Thinking with the Yoga Sutra of Patañjali: Translation and Interpretation*. London: Lexington Books, 2019.

Cohen, S. *Text and Authority in the Older Upaniṣads*. Leiden: Brill, 2008.

Dickens, C. *A Christmas Carol and Other Christmas Writings*. London: Penguin Classics, 2003 [1843].

Earley, J. *Self-Therapy: A Step-By-Step Guide to Creating Wholeness and Healing Your Inner Child Using IFS, Cutting-Edge Psychotherapy*, second edition. Larkspur, CA: Pattern System Books, 2009.

Feuerstein, G. *The Yoga-Sutra of Patañjali: A New Translation and Commentary*. Rochester, VT: Inner Traditions, 1989.

———. *Encyclopedic Dictionary of Yoga*. New York: Paragon House, 1990.

——— *The Philosophy of Classical Yoga*. Rochester, VT: Inner Traditions, 1996.

Godrej, F. "The Neoliberal Yogi and the Politics of Yoga." *Political Theory*, 45(6) (2016): 772–800.

Grinshpon, Y. *Silence Unheard: Deathly Otherness in Patanjala-Yoga*. Albany, NY: State University of New York Press, 2001.

———. *Silence and Liberation in Classical Yoga*. Tel Aviv: Ministry of Defense, Israel, 2002.

———. *Crisis and Knowledge: The Upanishadic Experience and Storytelling*. New Delhi: Oxford University Press, 2003.

Halbfass, W. *Tradition and Reflection: Explorations in Indian Thought*. Albany, NY: State University of New York Press, 1991.

Heaven, D. "Location of the Mind Remains a Mystery." *New Scientist*, 22 August 2012, https://www.newscientist.com/article/dn22205-location-of-the-mind-remains-a-mystery/#ixzz5xf8iUeuv.

Horney, K. *Our Inner Conflicts: A Constructive Theory of Neurosis*. New York: W.W. Norton, 1992 [1945].

Ifergan, G. *The Man from Samye: Longchenpa on Praxis, Its Negation and Liberation*. New Delhi: Aditya Prakashan, Aditya Prakashan, 2014.

———. *The Psychology of the Yogas*. Sheffield, UK: Equinox Publishing, 2021.

Jain, A. R. *Selling Yoga: From Counterculture to Pop Culture*. New York: Oxford University Press, 2014.

Jakubczak, M. 'Ego-Making Principle in Samkhya metaphysics and Cosmology.' *Analecta Husserliana: The Yearbook of Phenomenological Research*, 89 (2006): 185–195.

———. 'The Sense of Ego-maker in Classical Sāṃkhya and Yoga: Reconsideration of Ahaṃkāra.' *Cracow Indological Studies*, 10 (2008): 235–253.

———. 'The Collision of Language and Metaphysics in the Search for Self-Identity: on "Ahamkara" and "Asmita" in Samkhya-Yoga.' *Argument: Biannual Philosophical Journal*, 1(1) (2011): 37–48.

Kiss, C. 'The Matsyendrasaṃhitā: A Yoginī-Centered 13th-Century Yoga Text of the South Indian Śāmbhava Cult.' In: D. Lorenzen and A. Muñoz, eds., *Yogi Heroes and Poets: Histories and Legends of the Nāths*. Albany, NY: SUNY Press, 2011.

Klein, M. *Envy and Gratitude, and Other Works, 1946–1963*. New York: Free Press, 1984.

Kornfield, J. *After the Ecstasy, The Laundry: How the Heart Grows Wise on the Spiritual Path*. New York: Bantam, 2001.

Gopi, K. *Kundalini: The Evolutionary Energy of Man*. Boston, MA: Shambhala, 1997.

Harper, D. R., comp. 'Theory.' Entry in *Online Etymology Dictionary*. https://www.etymonline.com/search?q=theory.

Krishnamurti, J. *Freedom from the Known*. San Francisco, CA: Harper, 2009.

Larson, G. J. 'Classical Yoga as Neo-Sāṃkhya.' *Asiatische Studien – Études Asiatiques*, 52(3) (1999): 723–732.

———. 'Yoga's "A-Theistic"-Theism: A New Way of Thinking About God.' *Journal of Hindu Christian Studies*, 25 (2012): Article 6.

———. *Classical Samkhya: An Interpretation of Its History and Meaning*. New Delhi: Motilal Banarsidass, 2014.

Larson, G. J., R. S. Bhattacharya and K. Potter, eds. *The Encyclopaedia of Indian Philosophies, Volume 4: Samkhya, A Dualist Tradition in Indian Philosophy*. Princeton, NJ: Princeton University Press, 1987.

Maas, P. A. 'A Concise Historiography of Classical Yoga Philosophy.' In E. Franco, ed., *Periodization and Historiography of Indian Philosophy*. Vienna: The De Nobili Research Library, 2013.

Maharshi, R. *The Spiritual Teaching of Ramana Maharshi*. Boulder, CO: Shambhala Publications, 1972.

———. *Eternal Consciousness: Conversation with Ramana Maharshi 1935–1939*, translated by Lily Benatav. Tel Aviv: Gal, 1994.

Mascaró, J., trans. *The Bhagavad Gita*, revised edition. Delhi: Penguin Classics, 2009.

Mehta, R. *Yoga: The Art of Integration: A Commentary on the Yoga Sutras of Patanjali*. Adyar, India: Theosophical Publishing House, 1990.

Mishra, N. 'Saṁskāras in Yoga Philosophy and Western Psychology.' *Philosophy East and West*, 2(4) (1953): 308–316.

Olivelle, P., trans. *The Early Upaniṣads*. Delhi: Oxford University Press, 1998.

Perrett, R. W. *Hindu ethics: A philosophical study*. Honolulu: University of Hawaii Press, 1998.

Rabjam, L. *A Treasure Trove of Scriptural Transmission: A Commentary on the Precious Basic Space of Phenomena*, translated by T. R. Chagdud and R. Barron. Junction City, CA: Padma Publications, 2001.

Raveh, D. *Philosophical Threads in Patanjali's Yoga*. Tel Aviv: Hakibutz Hameuchad, 2010.

———. *Exploring the Yogasutra: Philosophy and Translation*, annotated edition. London: Continuum, 2012.

Ricoeur, P. *History and Truth*. Evanston, IL: Northwestern University Press, 2007.

Rose, K. *Yoga, Meditation, and Mysticism: Contemplative Universals and Meditative Landmarks*. London: Bloomsbury Academic, 2016.

Rosenberg, A. Y., ed. 'Bereshit – Genesis – Chapter 14.' In *The Complete Jewish Bible, with Rashi Commentary*. https://www.chabad.org/library/bible_cdo/aid/8209/jewish/Chapter-14.htm.

Rukmani, T. S., trans. and ed. *Yogavārttika of Vijñānabhikṣu: Samādhipāda*, third edition. Delhi: Munshiram Manoharlal Publishers, 2007.

Schwartz, R. C. *Internal Family Systems Therapy*. New York: Guilford Publications, 1994.

Schwartz, R. C. and M. Sweezy. *Internal Family Systems Therapy*, second edition. New York: Guilford Press, 2020.

Shulman, D. *More than Real: A History of the Imagination in South India*. Cambridge, MA: Harvard University Press, 2012.

Stack, G. J. and R. W. Plant. 'The Phenomenon of the Look.' *Philosophy and Phenomenological Research*, 42(3) (1982): 359–373.

Svātmārāma. *The Hatha Yoga Pradipika: The Original Sanskrit and An English Translation*, translated and edited by B. D. Akers. Woodstock, NY: YogaVidya.com, 2002.

Thibaut, G., trans. *The Vedānta-Sūtras with the Commentary by Śankarācārya, Sacred Books of the East, Volume 1*. 2005. https://www.gutenberg.org/files/16295/16295-h/16295-h.htm.

Trivedi, H. P. 'Sense of Agency: The Mind in Samkhya and Yoga.' MA thesis, State University of New Jersey, New Brunswick, NJ, 2017.

Trungpa, C. *Cutting through Spiritual Materialism*. Boston, MA: Shambhala, 1987.

Tubb, G. A. and E. R. Boose. *Scholastic Sanskrit: A Handbook For Students.* New York: American Institute of Buddhist Studies: Distributed by Columbia University Press, 2007.

Welwood, J. 'Embodying Your Realization: Psychological Work in the Service of Spiritual Development.' Unpublished manuscript, no date, https://www.johnwelwood.com/articles/Embodying.pdf.

Whicher, I. *The Integrity of the Yoga Darśana: A Reconsideration of Classical Yoga*. New York: State Unversity of New York Press, 1998.

White, D. G. *The Yoga Sutra of Patañjali: A Biography*. Princeton, NJ: Princeton University Press, 2014.

William, J. *The Varieties of Religious Experience: A Study in Human Nature*, translated by Y. Kopilevitch. Jerusalem: Bialik Institute, 1902.

Williams, M. *A Sanskrit-English Dictionary Etymologically and Philologically Arranged with Special Reference to Cognate Indo-European Languages.* Varanasi: Indica, 1996.

Zimmerman, F. *Jungle and the Aroma of Meats: An Ecological Theme in Hindu Medicine (Comparative Studies of Health Systems and Medical Care).* Delhi: Motilal Banarsidass, 2011.

Index

abhimāna (self-importance) 34, 39–40, 50
abhiniveśa (fear of death) 44, 56–57
abhyāsa (repetitive yoga practice) 14, 146
action (*karma*) 1–2, 57
adhyāsa (mutual superimposition) 116
Advaita Vedānta 115, 116, 117
afflictions (*kleśa*) 7–8, 18, 43–44, 58, 119, 146
āgama (testimony) 56
ahaṃkāra (ego) 34, 37, 39–41, 60
ahiṃsā (non-violence) 53–54, 139
aiśvaryam (sovereignty) 38–39
ālambana (object of meditation) 85
ānanda (joy) 97–99, 102
ānanda samādhi 21–22, 97, 102, 144–145
antaḥkaraṇa (internal organ) 41–42
anumāna (inference) 56
anuśāsana (instructions) 7
aparigraha (non-possessiveness) 12, 53, 139
Āraṇya
  on *para vairāgya* (ultimate dispassion) 15
  on *viveka-khyāti* (discerning insight) 106
asaṃprajñāta samādhi 21, 23, 90, 105
asceticism 1–3, 29n4
asmitā (I-am-ness) 9, 26, 28–29, 42–43, 44, 45–55, 57
asmitā samādhi 21–22, 25, 103–104, 144–145
asteya (non-stealing) 139
ātman (true Self) 94–95, 115, 117
attachment 139
attraction (*rāga*) 44, 55–56
aum (*oṃ*) 78
authorship 149–154
aversion (*dveṣa*) 44, 55–56
avidyā (ignorance) 44–45, 104
avikṛta prakṛti (potential mode of phenomena) 33
awareness *see puruṣa*; *rigpa* (awareness); Self, true

Bhagavad Gītā 53, 81
Bhattacharya, Krishna Chandra 38–39, 61n12
bhāvanā (practice) 79–80
Birch, Jason 152
bodhisattva 77
brahmacarya (celibacy) 139
brahman 77, 102
Brahmasūtra 4
Brahmins 1, 2, 29n4
breath control (*prāṇāyāma*) 78, 99–100
Bṛhadāraṇyaka Upaniṣad 2, 2–3, 57
Bronkhorst, Johannes 152
Bryant, Edwin F.
  on *puruṣa* 75
  on *vairāgya* (dispassion) 15
Bryant, Edwin F.: on *samādhi* 145

Buddha 10
buddhi (intellect)
and *asmitā* (I-am-ness) 57
characteristics of 38–39
and *guṇas* (qualities of nature) 16, 46
and *manas* (cognition) 42, 46
and *prakṛti* (phenomenal world) 34, 36–38
and *puruṣa* 67
and *ṛtam bharā* (truth bearing) 23, 25
and self, phenomenal 40–41
and śuddhi (purity) 54
Buddhism
no-self doctrine 10, 115, 152
see also Dzogchen; Kornfield, Jack; Longchenpa; *rigpa* (awareness); Trungpa, Chögyam
Burley, Mikel
on *puruṣa* 76
on *Yogasūtra* 151

cakra (meta-physiological intersections) 90, 99
central channel (*suṣumṇa*) 90, 99
centralisation 37, 54
citi-śakti (power of pure consciousness) 82n7
citta (consciousness) 42
cittasantāna (mindstream) 130, 141n18
cleansing (*śauca*) 12, 139
cognition (*manas*) 41–42, 86
cognitive *samādhi* 19–22, 85–92, 96–98, 101, 105–106, 143–145
see also nirvicāra samādhi; *nirvitarka samādhi*; *savicāra samādhi*; *savitarka samādhi*
Cohen, Signe, *Text and Authority in the Older Upaniṣads* 149
compassion (*karuṇā*) 12, 14
contemplation (*samāpatti*) 19
consciousness (*citta*) 42
contentment (*saṃtoṣa*) 12, 139
craving (*tṛṣṇā*) 10
cycle of birth and death (*saṃsāra*) 73

darśana (vision) 67
dharma (virtues) 38–39
dhyāna (meditation) 19
see also samādhi (yogic meditation)
Dickens, Charles, *A Christmas Carol* 8, 11
discerning gaze *see* phenomenal gaze; uninvolved gaze; vision; *viveka-khyāti* (discerning insight)
discerning insight (*viveka-khyāti*) *see viveka-khyāti* (discerning insight)
discerning wisdom (*jñānam*) 38–39
dispassion *see para vairāgya* (ultimate dispassion); *vairāgya* (dispassion)
dissolution of mind 94
distracting thoughts 87
double reflection (*pratibimba*) 70
draṣṭṛ (seer) 66, 83n12
dreaming 45
dṛk-śakti (power of the seer) 66
dṛśi (gaze) 66
dṛśi-mātra (pure gaze) 66, 83n12
duḥkha (suffering) 7, 9–10, 93
in Buddhism 10
see also vairāgya (dispassion)
dveṣa (aversion) 44, 55–56
Dzogchen 115

Early, Jay: ego characters 122–124
ego
contemporary yoga 51–55
and spiritual materialism 13, 48–49, 119
Western views 27, 49–51
see also ahaṃkāra (ego); *asmitā* (I-am-ness); Buddhism: no-self doctrine; self, phenomenal
ego characters 112–113, 119–120, 126–128
ego identification 139, 147

egocentrism *see abhimāna* (self-importance)
Eliade, Mircea: on *Īśvara* (god, deity) 81
equanimity (*upekṣā*) *12, 14*
evolution (*pariṇāma*) 11, 33, 36, 38

fear of death (*abhiniveśa*) 44, 56–57
Feuerstein, Georg
on cognitive *samādhi* (meditation) 98
on *Ī*śvara (god, deity) 81
on Self, true 65
forgetfulness 94
Foucault, Michel: technologies of the self 12
Freud, Sigmund: on ego 27, 50
friendliness (*maitrī*) *12, 14*

gaze *see* phenomenal gaze; uninvolved gaze; vision; *viveka-khyāti* (discerning insight)
god *see Īśvara* (god, deity)
Godrej, Farah 52
greed 11
*guṇ*as (qualities of nature) 15, 16, 35
and *buddhi* (intellect) 46
and self, phenomenal 41
and *śuddhi* (purity) 74

Haṭhayogapradīpikā 93–94, 100
Horney, Karen 59, 63n43

I-am-ness (*asmitā*) 9, 26, 28–29, 42–43, 44, 45–55, 57
ignorance (*avidyā*) 44–45, 104
inner sounds meditation 93–94
intellect (*buddhi*) *see buddhi* (intellect)
internal organ (*antaḥkaraṇa*) 41–42
involution (*pratiprasava*) 11–12, 14, 65, 143
Īśvara (god, deity) 28, 75, 77
and *prakṛti* (phenomenal world) 80–82
visualisation 79
Īśvara praṇidhāna (mantra recitation) 78–79, 139
Īśvarakṛṣṇa 4, 27

jñānam (discerning wisdom) 38–39
joy *see ānanda* (joy); *muditā* (joy)

Kāmasūtra 4
Kapila 4, 27
kārikā (verses): defined 30n10
karma (action) 1–2, 57
karuṇā (compassion) 12, 14
Kiss, Csaba: on *bhāvanā* (practice) 80
kleśa (afflictions) 7–8, 18, 43–44, 58, 119, 146
knowledge 38, 56
Kornfield, Jack 128
krama (sequence of time) 106–108
Krishna, Gopi 100–101
kṣaṇa (moment of time) 106–108
kuṇḍalinī 79, 99, 100–101

Larson, Gerald
on *Īśvara* (god, deity) 77, 81
on Self, true 76, 77
Levinas, Emmanuel: on ego 49
liberation 36, 48, 74, 81
Longchenpa 116, 132

Maas, Phillip A.
on *Patañjalayogaśāstra* 150
on *Yogasūtra* 5
Mahābhārata 65, 151
maitrī (friendliness) 12, 14
manas (cognition) 41–42, 86
mantras 78–79, 139
Matsyendrasaṃhitā 80
meditation *see dhyāna* (meditation); *samādhi* (yogic meditation)
meditation on the sense of I-am-ness 112, 119, 124–126, 129–140
memory 89
mental imprints (*saṃskāra*) *see saṃskāra* (mental imprints)
mental patterns (*vāsanā*) 7–8, 18, 58, 119, 146
mental processes (*vṛtti*) 58, 130

merchants 2
metaphors 28
dancer 67–71
dreaming 45
mirror 47, 66–67, 69–70, 72–73, 93, 103, 148
rope and snake 62n24, 116–117
vision for Self, true 6
Mīmāṃsāsūtra 4
mind 9–10, 34, 43, 65
mindstream (*cittasantāna*) 130, 141n18
Miśra, Vācaspati
on *ānanda* (joy) 97
on *Īśvara* (god, deity) 80
on *pratibimba* (double reflection) 70
on *śuddhi* (purity) 73
moral rules *see yamas* and *niyamas*
muditā (joy) 12, 14

nāḍī (meta-physiological channels) 99
New Age movement 50
nirodha saṃskāra 18–19, 96, 106
nirvicāra samādhi 21, 93, 95–96, 144
nirvitarka samādhi 20, 89, 143–144
niścaya (certainty) 38–39
non-violence (*ahiṃsā*) *53–54, 139*
Nyāyasūtra 4

object meditation (*samādhi*) *see saṃprajñāta samādhi*
object of meditation (*ālambana*) 85
objectless meditation (*samādhi*) *see asaṃprajñāta samādhi*
one-pointed meditation *see saṃprajñāta samādhi*

para vairāgya (ultimate dispassion) 15, 23, 105
pariṇāma (evolution) 11, 33, 36, 38
Patañjalayogaśāstra 150
Patañjalayogaśāstra sāṃkhyapravacana 150
Patañjali 3, 60, 149
on *saṃskāra* (mental imprints) 18–19
on *vairāgya* (dispassion) 15
phenomenal gaze 3, 6–7
inward turning 10–11
outward turning 12
phenomenal self *see* self, phenomena
phenomenal world (*prakṛti*) 9, 17, 33–35, 76
practicing the opposite (*pratipakṣa bhāvanā*) *26, 59, 120, 135*
prakṛti (phenomenal world) 9, 17, 33–35, 76
prāṇa (vital force) 90, 98–99
prāṇāyāma (breath control) 78, 99–100
pratibimba (double reflection) 70
pratipakṣa bhāvanā (practicing the opposite) 26, 59, 120, 135
pratiprasava (involution) 11–12, 14, 65, 143
pratyāhāra (sense withdrawal) 53
pratyakṣa (direct perception) 56
pure awareness *see puruṣa*; *rigpa* (awareness); Self, true
purity (*śuddhi*) 73, 89, 96
puruṣa
and *guṇa*s (qualities of nature) 73–74
multiplicity of 75–82
in *Sāṃkhyakārikā 67–70*
in *Yogasūtra* 64–67, 69–70
see also ātman (true Self); *Īśvara* (god, deity); metaphors; Self, true

qualities of nature (*guṇa*s) *see guṇa*s (qualities of nature)

rāga (attraction) 44, 55–56
rajas 15, 35
Raveh, Daniel
on Indian literature authorship 149
on *puruṣa* 75
on Self, true 8

on Upaniṣadic period 3
on *vairāgya* (dispassion) 16
on *viveka-khyāti* (discerning insight) 106
regressive meditative process 125, 132, 134, 140, 145–147
restraint 19
rigpa (awareness) 115, 116, 118
Rose, Kenneth: on *samādhi* 21, 145
ṛtam bharā (truth bearing) 23, 25, 95
Rudrauf, David: on mind 34

sacrificial rituals 1, 29n1
samādhi (yogic meditation) *see asaṃprajñāta samādhi*; cognitive *samādhi*; *saṃprajñāta samādhi*
samāpatti (contemplation) 19
Sāṃkhya 4–5, 17–18, 24
on *ahaṃkāra* (ego) 34
on *buddhi* (intellect) 34
on liberation 36–37, 74
on *śuddhi* (purity) 74
Sāṃkhyakārikā 4, 27
kārikā 18
kārikā 19 73, 75
kārikā 20 73
kārikā 23 37–38
kārikā 24 39
kārikā 27 41
kārikā 59 67–70
kārikā 64 67–70
kārikā 66 70
saṃprajñāta samādhi 14, 21, 85–86, 88
saṃsāra (cycle of birth and death) 73
saṃskāra (mental imprints) 57–61, 85, 90–91, 119–120, 146
nirodha saṃskāra 18–19, 96, 106
and phenomenal gaze 7–8
and *ṛtam bharā* (truth bearing) 25
vyutthāna saṃskāra 18–19
saṃtoṣa (contentment) 12, 139
Śaṅkara 116–117, 149
Śaṅkaradigvijaya 149
Sarvadarśanasaṅgraha 152
sattva 15, 16, 35, 57, 70, 108
sattvification 96, 104
satya (truth) 53, 139
śauca (cleansing) 12, 139
Saundarya Laharī 79
savicāra samādhi 20, 89, 91–92, 97, 143, 144
savitarka samādhi 19–20, 91, 97
Schulman, David: on *Īśvara praṇidhāna* (mantra recitation) 79
Schwartz, Richard
on *asmitā* (I-am-ness) 26–27
ego characters 121–122
therapeutic method 112–113, 115, 124
on true self 114–115, 116–119
Scrooge, Ebenezer (fictitious character) 8, 11
self, phenomenal 42, 60–61
and *buddhi* (intellect) 40–41
and *guṇa*s (qualities of nature) 41
Self, true
and *asmitā* (I-am-ness) 10
and *prakṛti* (phenomenal world) 17, 28–29, 36
as pure awareness (*puruṣa*) 9
as seer 6, 46–47, 57
see also ātman (true Self); *puruṣa*
self-deception 128–129
self-importance (*abhimāna*) 34, 39–40, 50
shame 137
Śiva 79
spiritual materialism 13, 48–49, 119
śramaṇa (ascetics) 29n4
śrauta ritual 1, 29n4
śuddhi (purity) 73, 89, 96
suffering (*duḥkha*) *see duḥkha* (suffering)
suṣumṇa (central channel) 90, 99
sūtra (thread): defined 3–4, 30n10
svādhyāya (self-study) 12, 139

tamas 15, 35
Tamil poetry 79
Tantra 102
time (*krama*; *kṣaṇa*) 106–108

Trivedi, Hemal Pradid: on ego 54
tṛṣṇā (craving, thirst) *10*
Trungpa, Chögyam 13, 48–49, 119, 128
truth (*satya*) 53, 139
truth bearing (*ṛtam bharā*) *23, 25, 95*

uninvolved gaze 131
  see also vairāgya (dispassion)
Upaniṣadic period 3
Upaniṣads 2, 150
upekṣā (equanimity) 12, 14
Usharbudh, Arya: on *vitarka samādhi* 87

vairāgya (dispassion) 14–16, 38–39, 53, 146
  see also para vairāgya (ultimate dispassion)
Vaiśeṣikasūtra 4
vāsanā (mental patterns) 7–8, 18, 58, 119, 146
Vedic society 1–3
Vijñānabhikṣu
  on cognitive *samādhi* (meditation) 97
  on *pratibimba* (double reflection) 70
Vijñānavāda 151
vikṛta prakṛti (concrete mode of phenomena) 33
vision 6–7, 66–67
  see also darśana (vision)
visualisation 79
vital force (*prāṇa*) 90, 98–99
vitarka samādhi 86–87
viveka-khyāti (discerning insight)
  and ātman (true Self) 94–95
  and *avidyā* (wrong cognition) 44, 48
  and forgetfulness 94
  and meditation on the sense of I-am-ness 120
  and *prāṇa* (vital force) 98–101
  and *puruṣa* 69
  and *samādhi* (yogic meditation) 85–98, 101–106, 133
  and *saṃskāra* (mental imprints) 85
  and Self, true 105
  and time 106–109
vṛtti (mental processes) 58, 130
Vyāsa 66, 151
  on *ahaṃkāra* (ego) 60
  on cognitive *samādhi* (meditation) 89
  on *Īśvara* (god, deity) 80–81
  on *krama* (sequence of time) 106–107
  on *pratipakṣa bhāvanā* (practicing the opposite) 135
  on *puruṣa* 75
  on *śuddhi* (purity) 73
  on *vairāgya* (dispassion) 15
  on *viveka-khyāti* (discerning insight) 105
Vyāsabhāṣya 150, 152
  bhāṣya 1.21 151
  bhāṣya 3.44 152
vyutthāna saṃskāra 18–19

Welwood, John 58–59, 63n39
Whicher, Ian
  on *Īśvara* (god, deity) 81
  sattvification 96
  on *vitarka samādhi* 87
White, David Gordon: on *Yogasūtra* 5, 151
wisdom 92

yamas and *niyamas* 12, 14, 53, 105, 138–139, 147
yoga
  aims of 39, 109, 120
  as unification 48, 147–148
  in the West 12–13, 24, 51–53
Yogabhāṣya see Vyāsabhāṣya
Yogasūtra 3, 5, 7, 25, 150
  sūtra 1.3 105
  sūtra 1.5 43
  sūtra 1.7 56
  sūtra 1.9-22 152
  sūtra 1.17 19, 21, 85–90, 95, 144
  sūtra 1.21 151
  sūtra 1.22-23 152

sūtra 1.24 84n30
sūtra 1.33 134
sūtra 1.42-47 19, 21, 143
sūtra 1.42-51 96–97
sūtra 1.43 110n5
sūtra 1.47 94
sūtra 2.3 44
sūtra 2.5 44
sūtra 2.6 57
sūtra 2.7 55
sūtra 2.8 55
sūtra 2.9 56
sūtra 2.17 66
sūtra 2.20 70
sūtra 2.22 75
sūtra 2.26 31n20
sūtra 2.34 26, 135
sūtra 3.2 31n36, 82n7
sūtra 3.44 153
sūtra 3.53 106, 109
sūtra 4.14-22 151
sūtra 4.34 82n7
yogins: classification 151–152
Yuktabhavadeva 152

www.ingramcontent.com/pod-product-compliance
Ingram Content Group UK Ltd.
Pitfield, Milton Keynes, MK11 3LW, UK
UKHW020702050125
452872UK00018B/38

9 781800 504844